GOLFER'S GUIDE

ENGLAND AND WALES

150 COURSES AND FACILITIES

MARK ROWLINSON

NEW
HOLLAND

First published in the United Kingdom in 2001 by
New Holland Publishers (UK) Ltd
London • Cape Town • Sydney • Auckland

Garfield House	80 McKenzie Street	Unit 4, 14 Aquatic Drive	Unit 1A, 218 Lake Road
86 Edgware Road	Cape Town 8001	Frenchs Forest, NSW 2086	Northcote, Auckland
London W2 2EA	South Africa	Australia	New Zealand
UK			

1 3 5 7 9 10 8 6 4 2

ISBN 1 85974 671 3

Commissioned, edited and designed by Tim Jollands
on behalf of New Holland Publishers (UK) Ltd
Design concept: Alan Marshall
Cartographer: William Smuts
Production controller: Joan Woodroffe

Reproduction by Pica Colour Separation Overseas (Pte) Ltd, Singapore
Printed and bound in Singapore by Kyodo Printing Co (Singapore) Pte Ltd

Photographic Acknowledgements
All photographs taken by Mark Rowlinson except the following:
All-Sport/David Cannon front cover, pages 6, 21, 37, 39, 131; All-Sport/Stephen Munday page
37; Bowood Golf & Country Club page 57; BBC Philharmonic page 137; Castletown Golf Links
Hotel page 133; Chart Hills Golf Club page 42; English Golf Union page 101; Hallamshire Golf
Club/Steve Doherty page 153; Hadrian's Wall Tourism Partnership/National Trust Library
(Keith Paisley) page 139; Isle of Purbeck Golf Club page 56; Lavinia Johnston page 71; R.C.
Johnston back cover, bottom left; Tim Jollands page 46; King's College, Cambridge page 97;
Lanhydrock Golf Club page 65; Dr Arthur Lindley pages 27, 28; The London Golf Club page 35;
Newscast page 15; Prince's Golf Club page 38; Royal Jersey Golf Club/Steve Wellum page 69;
Royal St David's Golf Club page 165; St Mellion Hotel Golf and Country Club page 64; Saunton
Golf Club page 61; Seacroft Golf Club page 99; Silloth on Solway Golf Club/Peter Cusack page
135; Swinley Forest Golf Club page 26; Trevose Golf & Country Club page 66; Wales Tourist
Board Photo Library page 159; West Sussex Golf Club/Daisy Kane page 45; David J.
Whyte/Scottish Golf Photo Library pages 50, 59, 62, 63.

Front cover: *Wentworth West Course, 8th hole*
Spine: *Lining up a putt at Wilmslow*
Back cover (anti-clockwise from top left): *Wallasey, 3rd hole; Breedon-on-the-Hill, Leicestershire;
Wilmslow, 17th green; Nefyn, 14th green and 15th tee; Barnsley House, Gloucestershire*
Title page: *18th green and clubhouse of Royal Birkdale*

Publisher's Note
While every care has been taken to ensure that the information in this book
was as accurate as possible at the time of going to press, the publisher and author
accept no responsibility for any loss, injury or inconvenience sustained by
anyone using this book

Contents

HOW TO USE THIS BOOK

Finding Your Course

The 150 courses in this book have been chosen to provide a selection of the best golf to be found in England and Wales. Perhaps the top 100 or so select themselves; the rest are chosen to ensure a good geographical spread, variety of style, and courses within every price range. They are grouped in seven regional chapters. To find a course, use the contents list or index, or consult the map located in the relevant chapter then go to the appropriate number within the chapter for a full course description. The courses have been arranged in a loosely geographical sequence to help you to plan an itinerary.

Golf Courses

The date quoted after the course address is that of the foundation of the club, which may differ from the date of construction of the current course. Courses in England and Wales are normally measured in yards, though many now also quote distances in metres. As a rough guide for club selection, golfers used to metres should subtract 10%. Overall yardages are for the maximum length of the course from the white (medal) tees or from the very back tees of those courses which regularly host championships or professional tour events. Male visitors are usually required to play from yellow (forward) tees, ladies from red tees.

Club Facilities

There is considerable variation in the facilities offered at British courses. Generally, the modern country club provides a full service of restaurants and bars, superior practice facilities, and a whole range of creature comforts. At the other end of the scale are those inexpensive clubs with a very basic practice ground (possibly just a warm-up net), a restaurant or bar offering plain, inexpensive food (probably not every day of the week), and changing facilities which are purely functional. Some private clubs do not accept credit cards for bar or restaurant payment.

At most British courses golfers prefer to walk, though many clubs offer buggies for hire (book in advance, as there may only be one or two). On long, modern courses a buggy may be essential as distances from one green to the next tee are often considerable. It is usually possible to hire clubs but there may not be much choice (or even a matched set) available, so ring first. Most club professionals have well stocked shops offering equipment, balls and accessories for purchase at very competitive prices, and PGA professionals offer excellent tuition at remarkably inexpensive rates.

Visitors' Restrictions

All British courses are growing busier. The majority of private clubs restrict visitors at weekends, and some permit no weekend visiting at all. There may be midweek restrictions too. It is essential to ring the club first. One or two clubs within this book accept visitors only as guests of members, but these courses are of such distinction that they could hardly be omitted.

At every club there is a dress code. On the course jeans, trainers, T-shirts, and collar-less shirts are unacceptable; shorts must be tailored (and, at many clubs, only knee socks are permitted); proper golf shoes must be worn, soft-spikes being required at a number of courses. Bag-sharing is not allowed. At private clubs the use of mobile phones is generally banned on the course and, probably, in the clubhouse. Club-house dress rules are gradually being relaxed at some clubs, but visitors are advised to ensure they have a smart dress or jacket and tie just in case.

Visitors are generally required to have a handicap certificate, though at the less formal clubs the visitor may not be asked to produce it.

Key to Green Fees

For each course we have provided a rough guide to the cost of a single round of 18 holes played on a weekday:

£	=	*Below £20 ($30)*
££	=	*£20–£29 ($30–$44)*
£££	=	*£30–£39 ($45–$59)*
££££	=	*£40–£49 ($60–$74)*
£££££	=	*£50 ($75) and above*

It is unlikely that credit cards can be used for payment of green fees (though they may be acceptable for the purchase of equipment or tuition). If weekend visiting is possible it is likely to be much more expensive. A day ticket may be a little dearer but allows unlimited play, and may include lunch. Some clubs in the traditional holiday areas offer weekly or longer tickets.

Introduction

Golf in England and Wales

Golf (or something very like it) is known to have existed in both Scotland and the Netherlands since medieval times. However it is Royal Blackheath in England which can reasonably claim to be the oldest golf club in the world, apparently begun in 1608 by Scottish golfers who came south when King James VI of Scotland acceded to the English throne as James I. The game continued to flourish on Blackheath for the next three hundred years.

Early English Clubs
There are no surviving records of golf being played elsewhere in England (though doubtless it was) until the Old Manchester Club was founded in 1818, described today pitifully as a 'club without a course'. No more followed until 1864 when the Royal North Devon came into being, the earliest English seaside links, and the oldest club still playing over the same piece of ground. The London Scottish at

Left: Royal North Devon, where golfers have shared this common land with sheep, horses and walkers since 1864. Above: Parkland golf at its charming best, the short par-4 17th at Sandiway in Cheshire.

Wimbledon came next, and then, in 1869, the Liverpool Golf Club at Hoylake (the Royal prefix followed later). With this course, English golf moved into the top flight, hosting the first Amateur Championship in 1885. Nine years later the Open Championship left Scotland for the first time, being played at Royal St George's, Sandwich.

Welsh Beginnings
It is known that a group of Royal Liverpool players brought their professional, Jack Morris (Tom Morris's brother), to the Morfa at Conwy where he laid out a nine-hole links in 1876, but it did not last long. Instead, the honour of being the first Welsh club to be officially and permanently established falls to Tenby at the other end of the Principality. Tenby was formed in 1888, the same year as the foundation of the first golf club in the USA, the St Andrew's Golf Club at Yonkers.

The 20th Century
From the 1890s golf clubs sprang up at a remarkable rate throughout the whole of Britain. These early courses were entirely

WHEN TO PLAY GOLF

Golf in England and Wales is at its best from April to October. Most courses are open for play all year round, closed only under snow, severe frost, or during flooding. In the winter months many clubs move onto temporary tees and greens. Some inland courses can be very wet underfoot during a rainy winter. That said, on a crisp, sunny winter day golf on a traditional seaside links or a well-drained heathland course can be every bit as good as it is in high summer. One or two clubs reduce their visitors' green fees in winter.

In summer, in theory, there is light enough to play from 05:00 to 21:00 or even later. In practice, many clubs will not open for visitors before 09:00 or 09:30 in order to let their early-bird members get away before the visitors, green staff having prepared the course from first light. On summer evenings many clubs hold competitions and other matches which may also prevent visitors teeing off after a certain time.

Professionals' shops are usually open from 08:00 or 08:30, closing in the late afternoon or early evening. Green fees are normally paid there, but in a few clubs green fees are paid at the bar. There is wide variation in bar and restaurant opening hours depending on the nature and locality of the club. Enquire first.

others, most influentially Sunningdale. Willie Park, Tom Morris and James Braid came south from Scotland to lay out new courses. The wisdom of the great English players of the day, J.H. Taylor and Harold Hilton, and the Jerseymen, Harry Vardon and Ted Ray, was similarly sought. But also emerging in the early years of the century was a novel creature, the professional course architect, notably Harry Colt, J.F. Abercromby, Alister Mackenzie and W.H. Fowler.

The Present Day

Two world wars and the Depression slowed the rate of expansion during the middle part of the century, and it was not really until the 1980s that a new boom began. The population had become wealthier, leisure time had increased, and farming was entering an era of desperate crises. In 1987 The Royal and Ancient Golf Club decreed that 700 new courses would be needed throughout the UK to cope with the increased demand for golf.

Farmers clearly had to diversify and, thus encouraged, many turned their meadows into fairways and greens. Some got their fingers burned. The big international architects, such as the Trent Jones family and Jack Nicklaus, and the best native designers (Martin Hawtree, Donald Steel, John Jacobs, Nick Faldo) created many spectacular new layouts. Sadly, a frightening number of the big-money establishments went bankrupt, particularly when corporate golf declined with a shrinking manufacturing economy. Municipal or similar public provision in England has been lamentable in recent years. Consequently many of the most successful courses in terms of survival have been the simpler layouts, usually pay-and-play, which have provided an entry into golf for many of those neither fortunate enough nor sufficiently wealthy to be able to join an old-established club.

natural, earthmoving being limited to the capabilities of a few men with wheelbarrows and, perhaps, a horse and scraper. The ground had to be well drained, the indigenous grasses fine and easily mown – cut by hand scythe before the advent of the horse-drawn mower.

As golf increased in popularity sites for new courses were sought close to the main conurbations. In the sand and gravel to the south and west of London those with a far-seeing eye spotted the potential of heathland. The immediate success of Tom Dunn's course at Woking prompted the construction of

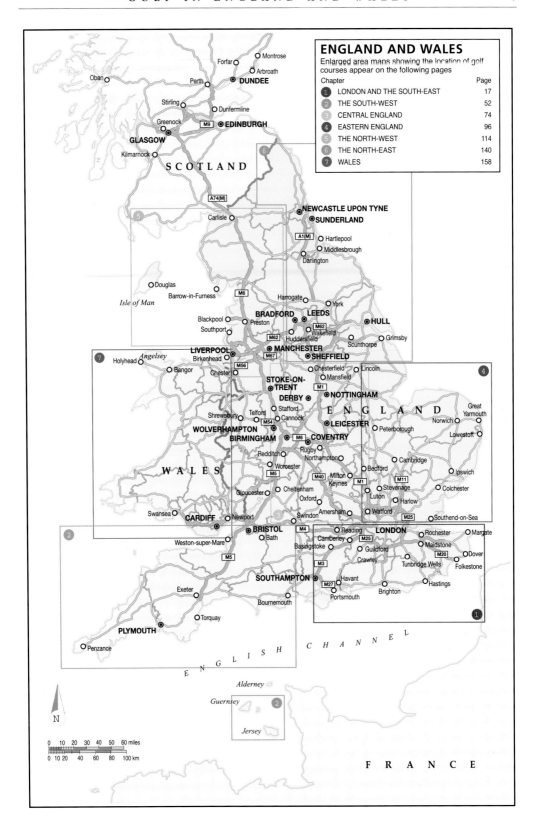

ENGLAND AND WALES

Enlarged area maps showing the location of golf courses appear on the following pages

TRAVELLING TO AND IN ENGLAND AND WALES

Entry Requirements

A passport is required for entrants to the UK. European visitors do not need visas, except those from Poland, Albania and Bulgaria. Citizens of the USA, Canada, Australia and New Zealand do not need visas for short stays. There are no vaccination requirements.

Getting to England and Wales
By air

The majority of visitors to these shores fly into one of the London airports, principally Heathrow and Gatwick. There are connecting flights to many regional airports, such as Newcastle, Tees-side, Leeds-Bradford, the Isle of Man, Cardiff, Birmingham, Liverpool and Manchester. However, if your destination is north of London there is much sense in flying direct to Manchester which has intercontinental services to and from the USA and Canada, Australasia and the Far East. Those on a limited budget should check airport to city centre fares before using taxis, especially from Heathrow or Gatwick, particularly as there are frequent, fast and cost-effective public transport alternatives at many airports.

By rail

The only direct rail-link from overseas is through the Channel Tunnel into Waterloo Station in London.

By sea

With the advent of the Channel Tunnel there is keen competition amongst the ferry and hovercraft companies operating across the English Channel to France and Belgium. Other ferries operate from Spain, other parts of France and Belgium, The Netherlands, Scandinavia and Ireland.

Getting around England and Wales
By rail

The railways did much to help the development of golf in England and Wales, and there is something romantic about taking the train to Royal Birkdale, Aberdovey or Sunningdale. Given the congestion on roads around British cities, especially at peak times, the train is a very practical way to travel between major centres. Inter-city trains are becoming increasingly crowded, and ticket pricing is complex, fares varying with the time and day of travel. If possible, buy tickets in advance. Cross-country trains are relatively slow, minor lines particularly so, but they are rarely crowded.

By road

Cars As most golf courses are situated in the country some distance from rail or bus routes, a car is the most practical way to visit them. Cars can be hired at all airports, principal railway stations, and through most hotels. However, you may find it cheaper to arrange this through your regular hire company or travel agent at home.

Remember to bring your driving licence and to drive on the left. Petrol stations are plentiful and many are open 24 hours a day, except in the remoter parts of the country. The motorway network and principal main routes are well signposted, though heavily congested. Avoid the M25 around London from about 07:30 to 10:00 and again from 16:30 to 19:30, similarly the M6 and M5 around Birmingham. Do not leave your golf clubs or other valuables visible if you leave the car parked – opportunist theft can happen even in the most unlikely spots.

Buses and taxis Inter-city bus services are generally cheaper than the railway, and their vehicles can accommodate plenty of

luggage and golf clubs. While taxis are the sensible way to travel in town, they are a very expensive means of getting to a country golf club.

Southerndown, glorious upland golf overlooking the sea, as good in winter as it is in summer, and typical of the excellent value of many courses in Wales.

HOTELS AND RESTAURANTS

British hotels were once the subject of jokes. Some are now amongst the best in the world. In general, city-centre hotels are big, efficient, orientated towards the business traveller, somewhat anonymous and frequently expensive. The hotels listed in the regional directories have been chosen for their distinctive qualities, for the most part encapsulating the very best in country living. A comprehensive selection of similarly distinguished hotels is published annually in *The Which Hotel Guide.*

English food used to have a dreadful reputation, with some justification. That has all changed, the British as a nation taking a great deal more interest in what they eat and drink. The best chefs and restaurateurs pride themselves on the quality of their raw

ACCOMMODATION AGENCIES

For a reliable selection of comfortable small hotels, guest houses, farms and country homes covering the whole of the UK the following can be recommended:

Bed and Breakfast Nationwide
PO Box 2100, Clacton on Sea, Essex CO16 9BW
Tel: (+44) 1255 831235 Fax: (+44) 1255 831437
Website: http://www.bbnationwide.co.uk

GuestAccom Ltd
Maytrees, Downend, Chieveley, Newbury, Berkshire RG20 8TF
Tel: (+44) 1635 247444 Fax: (+44) 1635 248287
Website http://www.guestaccom.co.uk/

Wolsey Lodges Ltd
9 Market Place, Hadleigh, Ipswich, Suffolk IP7 5DL
Tel: (+44) 1473 822058 Fax: (+44) 1473 827444
Website: www.wolsey-lodges.co.uk

ingredients, often drawing on the cuisines of many nationalities in their search for originality. As with the hotels, the listed restaurants are amongst the very best in the country, in gastronomic terms the equivalent of an Open Championship golf course. Serious eaters and drinkers should also consult *The Good Food Guide* and *The Good Pub Guide*.

TRAVEL FACTS AND TIPS

Climate
The effect of the seas around Britain's shores is to moderate the temperature, being warmer in winter and cooler in summer than continental Europe at a similar latitude. Unfortunately it tends to be rather wetter, too, especially in the west. In winter, snow rarely lingers, except in the mountains, and prolonged icy spells are infrequent.

Currency
The unit of currency is the pound sterling, in which there are 100 pence in £1. Coins are 1p, 2p, 5p, 10p, 20p, 50p, £1 and £2. Notes are £5, £10, £20 and £50.

Travellers' Cheques and Credit Cards
Travellers' cheques are accepted in most hotels and those shops which are geared to international tourism. Banks are generally open 09:30–16:30 on weekdays, sometimes longer and at weekends in larger towns and cities. Bureaux de Change can be found in most towns, often in the offices of travel agents, at main railway stations and all principal airports.

Mastercard and Visa are widely accepted credit cards, American Express and Diner's Club less so. Credit cards can rarely be used to pay green fees. Some small guest houses may not accept credit cards. Supermarkets, filling stations, railway booking offices and most big stores accept credit and direct debit cards. External cash dispensers are available at most banks and at many supermarkets, and credit and direct debit cards may be used for obtaining cash.

Health Care
Health insurance is often part of a general travel insurance – check yours. Most EEC nationals are treated free of charge under a National Health Service scheme. Residents of other countries will be treated as private patients. In an emergency a patient is sent to hospital first, the financial implications being worked out afterwards!

Telephones
Public telephone boxes accept coins (usually 10p, 20p, 50p and £1) and, in some cases, telephone cards purchased from newsagents or hotels. There are also public telephones which accept credit and debit cards. It is usually much cheaper to make international calls using a coded phone card from your country of origin. The cheaper rate for making international calls is 20:00 to 08:00 on weekdays, and all day Saturday and Sunday. For credit card and international reverse-charge calls dial 155.

FESTIVALS AND PUBLIC HOLIDAYS

Public or Bank Holidays are observed on 1 January, Good Friday (the Friday before Easter), Easter Monday, 1 May (or the Monday nearest), the last Monday in May, the last Monday in August, 25 and 26 December. Banks and businesses are closed on these days, though many supermarkets and tourist shops open. Some small hotels close for Christmas, though larger ones usually make it a special celebration.

Useful Operator Numbers

100 for the UK operator
153 for international directory enquiries
155 for the international operator
192 for UK directory enquiries

Emergency Phone Number: 999

This is connected free of charge on any phone but only to be used for genuine emergencies.

Maps and Brochures

An up-to-date national road map can be purchased inexpensively at most filling stations and bookshops. It will be essential to find the more remote golf courses, though many are now adequately signposted.

What's On Guides

The various tourist boards' websites (right) are strongly recommended, giving links to attractions in every possible field. Tourist Information Offices can be found at most motorway services and in most towns. All have plentiful brochures and information, and staff are knowledgeable. What's On guides are available free in hotels in most big cities and are thoroughly comprehensive.

Newspapers

The broadsheets (*Daily Telegraph*, *Guardian*, *Independent*, and *Times*) give good coverage of world events from a British perspective. International editions of American and principal European newspapers are available in the bigger cities. International versions of American golf magazines are often available in city newsagents.

Shopping and Souvenirs

For one person it is a Welsh gold ring, for another a piece of Farmhouse Wensleydale cheese. From smoke houses to cricket bat makers, the traditional crafts and produce of

---

TOURIST INFORMATION

The user-friendly websites of each of the main tourist boards offer comprehensive information on tourist attractions, what's on, hotel, guest house and other accommodation from camp sites to exclusive castles for rent, and links to more specialist sites. The many excellent photographs reproduced in the sites give a good cross-section of the huge variety of attractions on offer, from glorious landscapes to theme parks, medieval buildings to contemporary art.

www.4tourism.com/uk/index.html

The English, Welsh and Scottish Tourist Board
4 Royal Crescent, Cheltenham GL50 3DA
Tel: +44 (0)1242 529509 Fax: +44 (0)1242 228401

www.visitbritain.com

Gives a useful link to all UK public transport information:
www.visitbritain.com/uk/links/external/pti.htm

www.travelengland.org.com

Specifically English tourist information, including details of its own publications listing accommodation of all kinds and in all price ranges

www.tourism.wales.gov.uk

Wales Tourist Board, Brunel House, 2 Fitzalan Road, Cardiff CF24 OUY, Wales, UK
Tel: + 44 29 2049 9909 Fax: + 44 29 2048 5031
For specifically Welsh tourist information

England and Wales thrive. What is more, you can usually buy these things at source. Consult the Tourist Board web sites, tourist offices, and What's On magazines.

Shop Opening Hours

Assume 09:00 to 17:30 for traditional shops such as clothes shops and book shops. In big cities and at many out-of-town sites certain shops may be open until 22:00 and a number of supermarkets are now open 24 hours a day.

Chapter 1

London and the South-East

'One is affected, then infected, by London as by some insidious drug that can act now as stimulant now as sedative, but ruthlessly becomes addiction,' declared art historian, Sir David Piper. London is one of the great cities of the world. Its treasures from Buckingham Palace to the Tower of London, the National Gallery to Westminster Abbey, draw visitors from all over the world at all times of the year. Compared with Madrid or Rome it is a sprawling city, two cities even, for London and Westminster could not be more different. One of the capitals of world commerce, the City of London bustles by day and is deserted by night and at the weekend. Westminster, however, never goes to sleep. The visitor could stay for several years and only begin to scratch the surface of its remarkable heritage: an

extraordinary number of historic buildings stretching back to London's Roman origins; some of the noblest ecclesiastical buildings in Europe; great museums; distinguished art galleries; vibrant theatres and concert halls; Royal and State palaces; famous sporting venues; and the River Thames, 'liquid history'.

Sadly, London is also one of the most expensive cities in the world. Stay in a central London hotel, if you must, for business, shopping or tourism, but for golf you will need a car, for London's golf courses stretch from the outer suburbs down to the Kent and Sussex coasts. The best of them are found on a broad band of sandy heathland which gives a characteristic quality shared by dozens of great courses from Sunningdale to West Sussex. 'Heath-and-heather' is the somewhat tautological term commonly applied to them. A similar north-west/south-east alignment is shared by the ridges of chalk hills, the Downs, which run through Surrey, Sussex, and Kent.

Left: The 7th hole on Sunningdale's Old Course, a classic 'heath-and-heather' course. Above: Visitors can see London from a completely new angle since the opening of the London Eye, which gives breathtaking views over the city.

Surrey

Surrey is an unusual county in that in the middle ages it was so remote from London, cut off by dense forests, that there is hardly a medieval building of any consequence. Its towns are mostly undistinguished, but its charm is found in its villages such as Hascombe, Coldharbour, Chiddingfold, and Thursley. Traditional village greens survive at Ockley, Tilford and Dunsfold, and in the London suburbs at Kew and Ham. The big formal green at Richmond leads on to what little survives of King Henry VIII's royal palace there. Of the larger towns Farnham stands out for its elegant streets. Guildford Cathedral, completed in 1961, dominates a town which has managed to retain many of its older buildings within a busy modern shopping and university environment. At Runnymede, near Egham, King John signed the Magna Carta in 1215, the first charter enshrining the rights of man.

Kent

Kent, the Garden of England, is traditionally divided. Either you are a Kentishman, or you are a Man of Kent. The River Medway serves as the border, Men of Kent coming from east of its banks. The Kent coast around Sandwich provides the only true links golf in this corner of England, and in Royal St George's the only course in the south currently on the Open Championship rota. Maidstone, with Anglo-Saxon if not Roman roots, is the county town. Older still is Canterbury which was a Belgic settlement even before the Romans came, calling their town Durovernum. It retained its importance after the Romans had been replaced by Anglo-Saxon invaders. Then in 597 St Augustine arrived at Canterbury, building his first cathedral, and in due

KEY TO MAP	
1. Royal Mid-Surrey	19. Royal Blackheath
2. Coombe Hill	20. The London Club
3. New Zealand	21. North Foreland
4. St George's Hill	22. Royal St George's
5. Wentworth	23. Prince's
6. Sunningdale	24. Royal Cinque Ports
7. The Berkshire	25. Littlestone
8. Swinley Forest	26. Rye
9. Camberley Heath	27. Chart Hills
10. North Hants	28. Crowborough
11. Hankley Common	Beacon
12. Liphook	29. Royal Ashdown
13. West Hill	Forest
14. Worplesdon	30. East Sussex
15. Woking	National
16. The Wisley	31. West Sussex
17. Walton Heath	32. Hayling
18. The Addington	33. Stoneham

course spreading Christianity throughout England. The present cathedral is a comparative youngster, its oldest part, the crypt, dating from 1100, yet a fitting building for its role as Mother Church to the Anglican Communion.

Dover is the English town nearest to continental Europe and, therefore, the most likely place for invasion from pre-Roman times onwards. Consequently its castle is a mighty citadel, begun by the Ancient Britons, developed by the Romans, and turned by the Normans into the strongest fortress in England. Underground tunnels were excavated deep into the chalk cliffs during the 13th century, providing hiding places in case of French invasion. They were still of immense value during the Second World War when military command posts were established there, within sight of the German-occupied French coast.

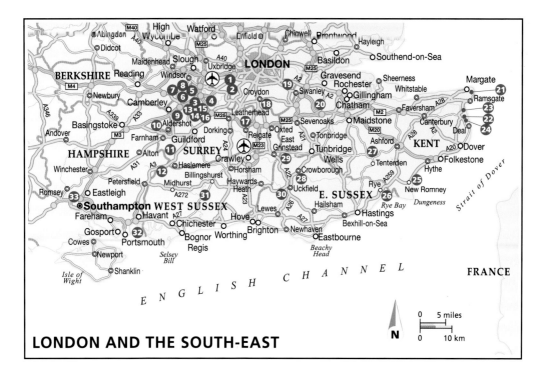

LONDON AND THE SOUTH-EAST

Sussex

Administratively, Sussex has been divided, East and West, for centuries, though it is geology which imparts the greatest character, on the whole a gloriously leafy county but full of bold outbursts such as the wild moorland of Ashdown Forest and the grassy uplands of the South Downs. Unlike Surrey it does have ancient buildings and large towns of distinction. Chichester Cathedral dates from the late-11th century, though its 277ft/84m spire is a Victorian replica of the 14th-century original, which blew down in a storm in 1861. The Sussex coastline varies in character from the wilderness of Romney Marsh in the east, past white cliffs and shingle beaches to the yachting anchorages of the Selsey peninsula in the west. It has one of the best sunshine records in England, and Eastbourne, Brighton, Hove, Worthing and Bognor Regis are popular holiday and retirement towns.

Hampshire

Hampshire falls into two geographical areas, the New Forest south-western in feel, but parts of the county more closely allied to neighbouring Surrey or Sussex. Capital of England under the Anglo-Saxons and William the Conqueror, Winchester is full of interesting buildings, not least those of Winchester College. What is sometimes said to be King Arthur's Round Table hangs in Castle Hall, a 13th-century building in which Sir Walter Raleigh was condemned to death, and the dreaded Judge Jeffreys held court. But none of these can compete for magnificence with Winchester Cathedral.

Portsmouth has been a principal naval port for centuries. In the 18th century the cricket club in the village of Hambledon gave the game its first proper rules. The Bat and Ball Inn at Broadhalfpenny Down where they refreshed themselves is still there to refresh today's cricket pilgrims.

1 Royal Mid-Surrey

Royal Mid-Surrey Golf Club, Old Deer Park,
Twickenham Road, Richmond, Surrey TW9 2SB (1892)
TEL: *(020) 8940 1894* **FAX:** *(020) 8332 2957*
LOCATION: *North of Richmond off A316*
COURSES: *Outer: 18 holes, 6385yd/5838m, par 69,*
SSS 70; Inner: 18 holes, 5544yd/5069m, par 68,
SSS 67
TYPE OF COURSE: *Parkland*
DESIGNER: *J.H. Taylor*
GREEN FEES: *£££££*
FACILITIES: *Pro shop, trolley and club hire, clubhouse*
VISITORS: *Welcome weekdays with handicap certificate*

This is historic ground. The Plantagenet and Tudor Kings used to hunt in the Deer Park when staying at the Palace at Sheen (as Richmond was then called). A Carthusian Monastery once occupied what is now the 14th fairway. King George III built the Royal Observatory which stands beside the 12th and 13th. The Botanical Gardens at Kew adjoin the course, and a loop of the river gives the club remarkable seclusion.

The Outer Course is the championship one. This is flat ground, but many of the greens are raised and there is plenty of length in the par 4s, especially on the back nine. J.H. Taylor's earthworks provide unusual and punishing hazards. A par 3 of 230yd/210m with five bunkers attending the narrow, angled green makes a difficult opening hole. The 9th, 10th and 12th begin to stretch the player, the 10th heavily bunkered around the green.

2 Coombe Hill

Coombe Hill Golf Club, Golf Club Drive, Coombe Lane
West, Kingston-upon-Thames, Surrey KT2 7DF (1911)
TEL: *(020) 8336 7600* **FAX:** *(020) 8336 7601*
LOCATION: *On A238 Kingston to New Malden road*
COURSE: *18 holes, 6293yd/5754m, par 71, SSS 71*
TYPE OF COURSE: *Parkland/heathland*
DESIGNER: *J.F. Abercromby*
GREEN FEES: *£££££*
FACILITIES: *Pro shop, clubhouse*
VISITORS: *Welcome weekdays with handicap certificate*

Only 9 miles/14km from Hyde Park Corner, Coombe Hill has long been a favourite of royalty and distinguished golfing visitors. Bing Crosby said that it was 'perfect for those without the physical strength of yesteryear', and R.T. 'Bobby' Jones described the 14th as one of the finest holes of that length he had ever played. Coombe Hill's remarkable list of past professionals includes four Open champions, Sandy Herd, Arthur Havers, Henry Cotton and Dick Burton.

One of J.F. Abercromby's small corpus of distinguished creations, Coombe Hill is more parkland than heath, its short holes particularly pretty, especially when the rhododendrons are in flower. The toughest holes for the average player are undoubtedly a number of par 4s which climb steeply to their greens, especially the 5th, 8th, 11th and 16th.

3 New Zealand

New Zealand Golf Club, Woodham Lane, Addlestone,
Surrey KT15 3QD (1895)
TEL *and* **FAX:** *(01932) 345049*
LOCATION: *West Byfleet. From Woking Road turn*
right into Sheerwater Road, club straight ahead at
Woodham Lane T-junction
COURSE: *18 holes, 6012yd/5497m, par 68, SSS 69*
TYPE OF COURSE: *Wooded heathland*
DESIGNER: *Tom Simpson*
GREEN FEES: *££££*
FACILITIES: *Pro shop, clubhouse*
VISITORS: *Welcome weekdays with handicap certificate*

Laid out on remarkably level ground, yet full of subtlety, this is a connoisseur's course. Nothing is overstated: bunkers are few but ingeniously positioned; greens are relatively flat – until you putt on them, that is; and the trees which make New Zealand so handsome are well back from the fairway. The one commodity in abundance is heather, nowhere more than on the short 16th where the green and its attendant bunkers are the only safe havens in an ocean of the stuff.

There is plenty of length on the par 4s, the longest of them the fine 2nd with incursions of heather from the right and a bunker reminiscent of the Principal's Nose at St Andrews on the direct line just short of the green. The 15th fairway is split by heather and bunkers, and a pot bunker in front of the green is menacing. Effectively a double dog-leg, the 17th snakes past trees and in through bunkers.

4 St George's Hill

St George's Hill Golf Club, Golf Club Road, St George's Hill, Weybridge, Surrey KT13 0NL (1913)
TEL: (01932) 847758 **FAX:** (01932) 821564
LOCATION: Weybridge 1 mile/1.6km, close to Brooklands, on B374
COURSES: Red and Blue: 18 holes, 6496yd/5940m, par 70, SSS 71; Green: 9 holes, 2897yd/2649m, par 35
TYPE OF COURSE: Wooded heathland
DESIGNER: Harry Colt
GREEN FEES: £££££
FACILITIES: Pro shop, caddies, club hire, clubhouse
VISITORS: Welcome weekdays with handicap certificate

An enormous tract of hilly land close to Weybridge was acquired by a local builder in 1911. He had the remarkable prescience to build a private estate of very opulent residences, weaving through it a golf course, probably the earliest such development

The 9th at St George's Hill, sweeping uphill to a tricky green set below the battlemented clubhouse, rebuilt in this form after a fire destroyed the thatched original.

in Britain. The imposing clubhouse gives glorious views over the course and most of Surrey, too.

There are many who rate St George's Hill as Harry Colt's finest. The opening drive is thrilling, out over banks of heather and a road to the bottom of a wooded valley. The par 3s are first-rate, the 3rd complicated by a spine running the length of the green, while the 8th is unforgiving, though gorgeous to behold. The green is an isolated table top on the far side of a deep gully. Fall short and there are five wicked bunkers set in the heathery upslopes. The 11th, though only 110yd/100m, is again spectacular, all carry across a ravine to a tiny pinnacle green. It is the variety of the par 4s which makes them so interesting, the 12th a short one with a lovely approach through bunkers to a ledge green. The 13th is stern, demanding big-hitting if the second shot is not to die in a broad cross-bunker. Longest of all at 468yd/428m is the 6th, albeit downhill.

The Green Course is shorter but equally full of character. Many members say that its 2nd even outshines the par 3s on the big course.

5 *Wentworth*

The Wentworth Club, Wentworth Drive, Virginia Water, Surrey GU25 4LS (1924)
TEL: *(01344) 842201* **FAX:** *(01344) 842804*
LOCATION: *Virginia Water A30 at junction with A329*
COURSES: *West: 18 holes, 7006yd/6406m, par 72, SSS 74; East: 18 holes, 6176yd/5647m, par 68, SSS 70; Edinburgh: 18 holes, 6979yd/6382m, par 72, SSS 73*
TYPE OF COURSE: *Parkland/heathland*
DESIGNERS: *Harry Colt (West and East); John Jacobs, Gary Player, Bernard Gallagher (Edinburgh)*
GREEN FEES: *££££*
FACILITIES: *Pro shop, range, caddies, buggy and club hire, clubhouse*
VISITORS: *Welcome weekdays only with handicap certificate*

WENTWORTH WEST COURSE

HOLE	YD	M	PAR	HOLE	YD	M	PAR
1	471	431	4	10	186	170	3
2	155	142	3	11	398	364	4
3	452	413	4	12	510	466	5
4	501	458	5	13	441	403	4
5	191	175	3	14	179	164	3
6	356	325	4	15	466	426	4
7	399	365	4	16	380	348	4
8	398	364	4	17	571	522	5
9	450	411	4	18	502	459	5
OUT	3373	3084	35	IN	3633	3322	37

7006YD • 6406M • PAR 72

Wentworth plays host annually to two of the most important events in the European calendar, the PGA Championship in the spring and the World Matchplay in the autumn. Back in the 1920s, Harry Colt was commissioned to lay out two courses in the grounds of the estate. The East saw earliest fame when a team of British professionals

itself the nickname, Burma Road. In 1953 it hosted the Ryder Cup, in 1956 the Canada Cup (now the World Cup), which saw Ben Hogan make his only competitive appearance in England when the Americans won easily – he took the individual prize with 277.

And then came the World Matchplay, Arnold Palmer in 1964 setting the aristocratic tone of events to come. Gary Player almost held a monopoly on the title with his five wins in the 1960s and 1970s but

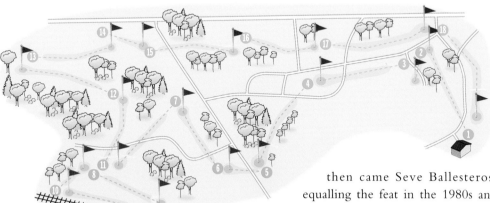

overwhelmed an American team in 1926 – leading to the Ryder Cup contests soon after. Then in 1932 the American ladies saw off the British ladies in the inaugural Curtis Cup match. The West Course, however, was always reckoned to be the tougher, earning

then came Seve Ballesteros, equalling the feat in the 1980s and 1990s. Jack Nicklaus and Bob Charles, Greg Norman and Hale Irwin, Mark O'Meara and Colin Montgomerie, the list of winners continues to reflect the best players of the day, for this is a superb matchplay course, rewarding those whose risk-taking comes off. Gary Player returned more recently, joining Bernard Gallagher and John Jacobs in

the design of a third full-length course, the Edinburgh.

The West begins seriously with a par 4 involving a big carry to the green over a valley. The 2nd is only a short par 3, but the bunker on the right is brilliantly placed. Over the years the 3rd green has been altered to make it fairer, yet putting downhill remains frightening Though less than 400yd/366m long, the 7th is the very devil with a testing uphill pitch over a big bunker. With a pond in front of the green the 8th is pretty, while the 9th is demanding even for the professionals.

A new elevated 11th tee has lengthened the hole, making the pitch to the angled green harder. Driving from the 12th, both height and distance are required to clear trees in front and open up the green. The 13th is

The West Course's substantial par-3 14th is deceptive, for the bottom of the flag cannot be seen from the tee, and the putting surface is sloping and terraced.

also a splendid driving hole, uphill and curving, and the hill on the par-3 14th adds several clubs' length for many golfers.

The last of the long par 4s, the 15th, is tough, calling for a strong drive and an unwavering approach over a stream. But thoughts are already on the 17th, one of the great bunkerless holes of golf. The key is the angle from the tee: with trees eating in from the left, it is all too easy to let the drive slip too far to the right into the rough with the probable loss of a stroke. Professionals expect to reach the 18th in two, the exact line of the drive again being critical.

6 Sunningdale

Sunningdale Golf Club, Ridgemount Road,
Sunningdale, Berkshire SL5 9RR
TEL: *(01344) 621681* **FAX:** *(01344) 624154*
WEBSITE: *www.golfagent.com/clubsites/Sunningdale*
LOCATION: *From M25 Jct 13, take A30 to
Sunningdale, first left after level crossing*
COURSES: *Old: 18 holes, 6619yd/6052m, par 72,
SSS 72; New: 18 holes, 6617yd/6051m, par 71,
SSS 73*
TYPE OF COURSE: *Wooded heathland (1900)*
DESIGNERS: *Willie Park, Harry Colt*
GREEN FEES: *£££££*
FACILITIES: *Pro shop, caddies, trolley and club hire, bar
and restaurant (sandwiches only on Monday, jacket and
tie required)*
VISITORS: *Welcome Monday to Thursday with letter of
introduction and handicap certificate (maximum 18 men,
20 ladies)*

HOLE	YD	M	PAR	HOLE	YD	M	PAR
1	494	452	5	10	478	437	5
2	489	447	5	11	325	297	4
3	319	292	4	12	451	412	4
4	161	147	3	13	185	169	3
5	419	383	4	14	509	465	5
6	415	379	4	15	226	207	3
7	402	368	4	16	438	401	4
8	182	166	3	17	421	385	4
9	273	250	4	18	432	395	4
OUT	3154	2884	36	IN	3465	3168	36

SUNNINGDALE
OLD COURSE

6619YD • 6052M • PAR 72

Sunningdale is the *locus classicus* of English
heathland golf. It was not the first of its
kind, for golf had been played on Blackheath
for centuries, and, more
recently, Woking had
revealed the golfing
potential of Surrey.
But in 1900,

New course
Old course

when the first seeds were sown,
it was already anticipated that this was the
beginning of something special. That
Sunningdale succeeded was largely due to the
skills of Willie Park, former Open Champion,

who laid it out. It opened for play in 1901 and
was immediately acclaimed, the coming of the
PGA Matchplay in 1903 confirming its status.
The appointment of Harry Colt as
Sunningdale's first secretary was also
immensely fortuitous. He went on to become
one of the greatest and most prolific golf
architects of all time, redesigning the course in
the 1920s to equip it to withstand modern
technology, and designing the complementary
New Course. He also instigated the planting
of the thousands of trees which are now such a
feature of the Old
Course.

The two
courses are these
days of similar
length and both are
groomed to perfection.
The New is slightly more
exposed to the winds and it
runs to longer carries and broader
views. Some say its par 3s are even
better than those on the Old. The 5th, an
oasis in a sea of heather, and the 10th, a long
and tightly bunkered hole, stand out. There
are many advocates for the merits of the 3rd,
9th and 12th among the par 4s.

The Old Course starts gently before the
charm is turned on in full. The 5th is a
glorious downhill par 4 with the approach

played over a pond, one of the earliest artificial water hazards. Heather interrupts the fairway on the 6th, and the 7th is even more attractive, with its green in a private glade. Bunkers either side enliven the pretty 8th, a par 3, and many will expect to drive the 9th.

Coming back there is greater length, though not at first, the 10th being a much loved short par 5, with an inviting drive to the fairway far below. A great short par 4, the 11th needs a dab hand with the pitch to an unreceptive crowned green. Into the wind, the par-3 15th can be brutal, and three excellent two-shotters close the round. The final green, in front of the famous oak tree, lies on the far side of a string of bunkers, not all of Colt's making, a German bomb in 1940 having found the ideal spot for an addition to the architecture.

THE PERFECT ROUND OF GOLF

In 1926 Bobby Jones ensured the worldwide fame of Sunningdale when, qualifying for that year's Open Championship, he played what has often been described as the perfect round of golf, a 66 in the days when such scores were quite unknown. His round was made up entirely of 3s and 4s and he hit every green except one in regulation, many of them with long irons or woods. Later he said, 'I wish I could take this golf course home with me.'

The 5th hole on the Old Course. The incomparable character of Sunningdale did not come naturally. It was once open, barren and windswept but, in 75 years' growing, Sunningdale's trees have become, in themselves, things of beauty.

7 The Berkshire

The Berkshire Golf Club, Swinley Road, Ascot, Berks
SL5 8AY (1928)
TEL: (01344) 621495 **FAX:** (01344) 623328
LOCATION: A30 Windlesham, take A322 towards
Bracknell, right towards Ascot, courses on left
COURSES: Red: 6379yd/5833m, par 72, SSS 71;
Blue: 6260yd/5724m, par 71, SSS 71
TYPE OF COURSE: Heathland/forest
DESIGNER: Herbert Fowler
GREEN FEES: £££££
FACILITIES: Pro shop, caddies, buggy and club hire,
clubhouse
VISITORS: Welcome weekdays with letter of introduction
from home club

		THE BERKSHIRE RED COURSE					
HOLE	YD	M	PAR	HOLE	YD	M	PAR
1	517	473	5	10	188	172	3
2	147	135	3	11	350	320	4
3	480	439	5	12	328	300	4
4	395	361	4	13	486	444	5
5	178	163	3	14	434	397	4
6	360	329	4	15	477	436	5
7	195	178	3	16	221	202	3
8	428	391	4	17	532	487	5
9	488	446	5	18	175	160	3
OUT	3188	2915	36	IN	3191	2918	36

6379YD • 5833M • PAR 72

A near neighbour of Wentworth, Sunningdale and Swinley Forest, the Berkshire is an equal partner in this golfing wonderland. Both courses – there is little to choose between them in difficulty or charm – enjoy wooded seclusion, delightful turf, heather aplenty and the architectural genius of Herbert Fowler, whose guile with bunkers and greens still impresses 75 years on. The Red is made up, unusually, of six each of pars 3, 4, and 5. The Blue's card is more conventional. Given their complementary challenges the pair make as agreeable before and after lunch rounds as you could hope to find.

The Berkshire is synonymous with amateur golf at the highest level. Its own Berkshire Trophy is one of the principal events of the amateur calendar, with the youthful Nick Faldo and Sandy Lyle among past winners. The club's ladies have also scaled the international heights, notably Linda Bayman and Angela Uzieli. Neither course has quite the length to challenge the modern professional, but that means they are a more realistic proposition for the rest of us.

Because it is slightly shorter the Blue is sometimes overlooked, but its

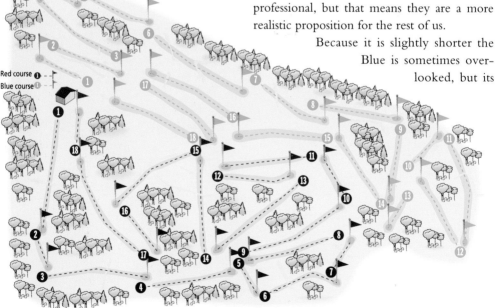

Red course
Blue course

difficulty is apparent on the 1st tee where a big carry over a heather-filled valley is required to find the green on this long par 3. The par-4 7th charms with its drive for position to open up a gap in the trees through which lies the green. A lovely stretch of rolling fairways begins with the pitch to the 9th, the drive at the 14th being blind over a marker post – a short but far from easy par 4. The close is glorious. First, the 15th plays to a hilltop green, then the 16th is a very strong par 4 with a long uphill approach over a stream, and the 17th curves through the trees beguilingly. Driving downhill before another uphill approach, the 18th makes a fine finish.

With none of the par 3s easy, strokes readily slip away on the Red course in a manner the card might not suggest. True, most of the par 5s are short enough to offer chances of saving birdies, but Fowler's cunning often thwarts us. The 4th is only a medium-length par 4 yet its green is narrow and cleverly protected by

At 452yd/413m, the Blue 16th is the longest par 4 on either course, and most probably the hardest, for not only must the approach clear a stream, it must also avoid two prominent bunkers.

bunkers and slopes. The 8th may be the stiffest outward hole, a lengthy par 4 with a steep climb through bunkers to the green.

Stout hearts have been known to quake on the 10th tee, a muscular par 3 across an abyss reminiscent of Calamity Corner at Royal Portrush. It is not simply enough to make the distance. Miss on either side and the ball tumbles to disaster. A ditch crosses the 14th, but it is the approach to the sloping green which calls for considerable skill. From the back it takes a mighty blow to carry all the trouble on the way to the 16th green, and the 17th is the favourite par 5 of many. Unusually, the round ends with a par 3, deceptively uphill and all too frequently causing one to fall short.

8 *Swinley Forest*

Swinley Forest Golf Club, Coronation Road, Ascot, Berks SL9 5LE (1909)
TEL: *(01344) 620197* **FAX:** *(01344) 874733*
LOCATION: *A30 south-west from Sunningdale, take B3020 towards Ascot. Turn left into Coronation Road, and left again to golf club*
COURSE: *18 holes, 6045yd/5527m, par 69, SSS 70*
TYPE OF COURSE: *Heathland/forest*
DESIGNER: *Harry Colt*
GREEN FEES: *£££££*
FACILITIES: *Pro shop, clubhouse*
VISITORS: *Welcome only as members' guests or as part of a small number of visiting societies*

Back in 1964, the distinguished golf writer, Pat Ward-Thomas, wrote, 'The appeal of Swinley is that of a haven, far removed from urgency and conflict, where golfers can enjoy the quieter pleasures of their game in seclusion and peace.' Nothing has changed. Set in part of an old royal hunting forest, its pines and birches engender this tranquillity without interfering unduly with play.

This masterly Harry Colt design begins gently, with no great trouble over the first five holes. The 6th moves up a gear with a bank of heather eating into the fairway and a very narrow entrance to the green. The obligatory drive over heather at the 7th is to a rising fairway with heathery mounds interrupting it. There remains a substantial shot uphill, over a giant bunker, to a domed, hilltop green only 20yd/18m deep. No green at Swinley is overgenerous!

Fall short or right on the 8th and you will be lucky not to drop a shot, and the 9th is both beautiful and demanding as it curves left, climbing the hill. A splendid long par 3, the 10th needs a strong shot over a heather-lined valley to find the tiny green. But the sternest hole for the average player must be the 12th, a double dog-leg with a tight drive close to trees and a severe long second, over a bunker and heather, finally running in through a series of ridges. It is not difficult to understand why the members are so proud of their course and visitors so enthralled.

Swinley Forest's final hole is a short par 4 of only 358yd/327m, but the plateau green in front of the handsome clubhouse is well protected by three bunkers.

The 18th green and clubhouse at North Hants, a course described by that fine player of an earlier generation, Tom Scott, as 'having everything an inland course should have'.

9 Camberley Heath

Camberley Heath Golf Club, Golf Drive, Camberley, Surrey GU15 1JG (1913)
TEL: *(01276) 23258* **FAX:** *(01276) 692505*
LOCATION: *M4 Jct 4, take A325 (Portsmouth Road), Golf Drive on right*
COURSE: *18 holes, 6326yd/5784m, par 72, SSS 71*
TYPE OF COURSE: *Heathland/parkland*
DESIGNER: *Harry Colt*
GREEN FEES: *££££*
FACILITIES: *Pro shop, caddies, buggy and club hire, clubhouse*
VISITORS: *Welcome weekdays with handicap certificate*

At the time of its opening in 1913 Camberley Heath was said to have been one of the most expensively constructed courses in the world. These days it is a frequent host to Open Championship qualifying rounds.

Its many hills make yardages irrelevant on holes such as the 10th, a 430yd/393m par 4, on which the drive over a marker post will run away to the right. A heathery ridge interrupts the fairway. From low down it will take a mighty blow to climb the next hill on

which the green is situated. Similarly, on the 17th a drive which fails to hold the narrow high ground on the left all too easily tumbles into a great depression from which escape is no certainty. Several of the shorter par 4s are engaging, though a pond has been added recently to the 16th to prevent anyone driving the green.

10 North Hants

North Hants Golf Club, Minley Road, Fleet, Hampshire GU13 8RE
TEL: *(01252) 616443* **FAX:** *(01252) 811627*
LOCATION: *Just north of Fleet main street, B3013, first left after railway bridge*
COURSE: *18 holes, 6504yd/5947m, par 71, SSS 71*
TYPE OF COURSE: *Heathland (1904)*
DESIGNERS: *James Braid, Donald Steel*
GREEN FEES: *£££*
FACILITIES: *Pro shop, club hire, clubhouse*
VISITORS: *Welcome with handicap certificate*

North Hants has an enviable reputation for being both beautiful and seriously testing. Justin Rose started his golf here. Then, as a 17 year-old, he so nearly won the 1998 Open, finishing in 4th place two shots behind winner Mark O'Meara. Rose is clearly impressed with the challenge of Donald Steel's new 3rd, a par 5 curving round a pond, with a fir tree complicating the approach considerably, inviting a pitch-and-run approach.

With a good number of long par 4s there are many earnest challenges, few stiffer than the 16th, a big uphill hole alongside the railway, its hilltop green cleverly angled behind bunkers. The 11th is not so long but, again, the bunkered green is hard to find. Only 124yd/113m long, the par-3 8th is, nevertheless, a siren, one of several intriguing short holes. The Hampshire Hog and Hampshire Rose open amateur tournaments are played here annually.

11 *Hankley Common*

*Hankley Common Golf Club, Tilford, Farnham,
Surrey GU10 2DD (1896)*
TEL: *(01252) 792493* **FAX:** *(01252) 795699*
LOCATION: *South-east of Farnham at Tilford*
COURSE: *18 holes, 6438yd/5887m, par 71, SSS 71*
TYPE OF COURSE: *Heathland*
DESIGNERS: *James Braid, Harry Colt*
GREEN FEES: *££££*
FACILITIES: *Pro shop, clubhouse*
VISITORS: *Welcome with handicap certificate, restricted
at weekends*

Of all the great Surrey heath-and-heather
courses only Walton Heath begins to
rival Hankley Common for the extent and
ferocity of its heather, in this case hundreds of
acres of it, habitat of many rare birds and
animals. On the whole, trees have not been
allowed to invade, so the effect is one of
immense spaciousness, much as Sunningdale
must have looked before its planting of
thousands of trees.

The first four holes – including the fine
opener – are slightly untypical, being more
woodland in character. From the 5th, a strong

*Each of the short holes at Hankley Common displays
individual character, the 11th, at 215yd/197m relying
mainly on length for its defences.*

mid-length par 4, play moves to the heath
proper. The 7th is a glorious short hole across
a heathery valley to an exposed hilltop green,
higher at the back than the front. At the 10th
the drive across gorse to an angled fairway is
testing, the gradual climb towards the green
adding to the effective length of this
demanding hole. Another choice par 3 is the
215yd/197m 11th, whose green is sufficiently
raised to ensure that only a full shot will make
the putting surface. On the 14th the drive is
downhill but the approach, uphill over
bunkers to an angled, pear-shaped green, is far
from simple. The 15th charms as it curves past
trees to a tightly bunkered green. Hankley's
finishing hole is renowned, with a do-or-die
second shot across a grassy gully to a shallow
green. Recently *Golf World* magazine ranked
Hankley Common 54th in the British Isles,
and it is a regular qualifying venue for the
Open Championship.

12 Liphook

Liphook Golf Club, Wheatsheaf Enclosure, Liphook, Hampshire GU30 7EH (1922)
TEL: *(01428) 732785* FAX: *(01428) 724853*
LOCATION: *South of Liphook on B2070 (old A3)*
COURSE: *18 holes, 6250yd/5715m, par 70, SSS 70*
TYPE OF COURSE: *Heathland*
DESIGNER: *Arthur Croome*
GREEN FEES: *£££*
FACILITIES: *Pro shop, clubhouse*
VISITORS: *Welcome with handicap certificate*

The only course known to have been designed by Arthur Croome, Liphook could be described as having all the best characteristics of Sunningdale and Wentworth without the latter's length and at a fraction of the cost of either.

The par 3s, in particular, have great charm and individuality, and one opens the round. Of the longer holes, the 2nd is a fine two-shotter over a leaning fairway to a sunken green. Heather encloses the 4th fairway, a noble par 4 on which the eye is drawn to the

The 7th, one of five excellent short holes at Liphook. Its green is protected by heather and sand and intricately contoured. Beyond it, the 8th fairway runs along a valley beside the main London–Portsmouth railway line.

distant billows of the Downs. The 12th is another first-rate driving hole over a sea of heather and a wiggling stream. That stream contributes significantly to the excellent par-5 13th, this time affecting the second shot. The green astride the top of a ridge makes a tricky target from any range. When you get there, having driven off in Hampshire, you hole out in Sussex.

13 West Hill

West Hill Golf Club, Bagshot Road, Brookwood, Woking, Surrey GU24 0BH (1909)
TEL: *(01483) 474365* FAX: *(01483) 474252*
LOCATION: *A322 Bracknell–Guildford road, immediately south of Brookwood railway bridge*
COURSE: *18 holes, 6368yd/5823m, par 69, SSS 70*
TYPE OF COURSE: *Wooded heathland*
DESIGNERS: *Willie Park, Jack White, Cuthbert Butchart*
GREEN FEES: *££££*
FACILITIES: *Pro shop, caddies, club hire, clubhouse*
VISITORS: *Welcome with handicap certificate weekdays only*

There is a five-year waiting list to enter the famous Father and Son matchplay tournament held annually at West Hill. While primarily a relaxed social event its matches are still reported in the broadsheet newspapers, interest extending well beyond these islands, past participants doubtless recalling the fine spirit in which the matches are played. The course, too, is a major factor, lovely to look at and a well balanced test of golf.

The 1st is a fine introduction, sweeping down towards a stream then gently up to the green, and the long par 4s are first class. On the approach to the 3rd a full carry over a brook is required, while the uphill drive at the 6th is followed by a downhill approach over cross-bunkers and in through a tight entrance to the green. New and refurbished bunkers adorn many holes, not least the muscular 14th.

14. Worplesdon

Worplesdon Golf Club, Heath House Road, Woking, Surrey GU22 0RA (1908)
TEL: (01483) 472277 **FAX:** (01483) 473303
LOCATION: West of Woking, signposted off A322 Bracknell–Guildford road south of West Hill Golf Club
COURSE: 18 holes, 6440yd/5889m, par 71, SSS 72
TYPE OF COURSE: Wooded heathland
DESIGNER: J.F. Abercromby
GREEN FEES: ££££
FACILITIES: Pro shop, club hire, clubhouse
VISITORS: Welcome with handicap certificate weekdays only

It is said that J.F. Abercromby neither measured nor even sketched holes, simply eyeing up the land and laying out a course by instinct. That Worplesdon is hardly changed to this day suggests a rare talent. The club's wide renown has been in no small part due to the Mixed Foursomes tournament held here every autumn. From its earliest days it has attracted the best players, not least Joyce Wethered, who won with Roger (her brother), Cyril Tolley, John Morrison and Bernard Darwin, some of the finest amateurs of their day. Such distinguished partners!

Starting outside the professional's shop the opening drive appeals warmly, downhill to a tree-lined fairway defined by bunkers. The 10th, a short hole across a pond, is most attractive, though not difficult. It is the 18th which is most demanding, a 450yd/411m par 4 with a line of bunkers eating into the fairway and devouring second shots which are neither long enough nor straight enough.

15. Woking

Woking Golf Club, Pond Road, Hook Heath, Woking, Surrey GU22 0JZ (1893)
TEL: (01483) 760053 **FAX:** (01483) 772441
LOCATION: West Woking. From A324 Woking–Aldershot road, turn into St John's village centre, Hollibank Road, then Golf Club Road
COURSE: 18 holes, 6340yd/5797m, par 70, SSS 70
TYPE OF COURSE: Wooded heathland
DESIGNERS: Tom Dunn, Stuart Paton, John Low
GREEN FEES: ££££
FACILITIES: Pro shop, trolley and club hire, clubhouse
VISITORS: Welcome weekdays with handicap certificate

Architecturally, Woking has been one of the most influential clubs in England. As the earliest heath-and-heather course in Surrey it was the benchmark for the dozens which followed. Here, too, Tom Simpson studied design in detail, going on to create such distinguished courses as Chantilly, Cruden Bay, Royal Belgique and Morfontaine. Woking's 4th fairway to this day is split by the 'Principal's Nose' bunkers which brought the concept of strategic driving from St Andrews to Surrey.

Little alteration has been necessary over the years, yet it is still a fine test. The 2nd, for instance, is a stout par 3 across a valley, while the 3rd, too, demands length, the fairway bending round trees before climbing to an elevated green. Sturdy par 4s abound, though perhaps the most memorable may be the gentler 18th, its multi-level green set above a pond, to which green the Oxford player, Hugh Alison, once played from the clubhouse roof during a University match!

Woking's 18th. In the 1930s, architect Guy Campbell said, 'Woking possesses more good strategic holes than any other inland course.'

16. The Wisley

The Wisley Golf Club, Ripley, Woking, Surrey GU23 6QU (1991)
TEL: (01483) 211022 FAX: (01483) 211662
LOCATION: Wisley on A3 1 mile/1.6km from M25 Jct 10
COURSES: Garden: 9 holes, 3385yd/3095m par 36; Church: 9 holes 3356yd/3069m, par 36; Mill: 9 holes, 3473yd/3176m, par 36
TYPE OF COURSE: American style parkland, touches of heathland
DESIGNER: Robert Trent Jones Jnr
GREEN FEES: Not applicable
FACILITIES: Pro shop, clubhouse
VISITORS: Members' guests only

Members of The Wisley are shareholders, expecting something exceptional for their outlay. So there is a grandeur about everything here from the 27 holes designed by Robert Trent Jones Jnr, through the imposing Lutyens-inspired clubhouse, to the seclusion of the site, secreted away behind the Royal Horticultural Society's Wisley Gardens and separated from the outside world by the River Wey. It has only been open since 1991 yet already The Wisley is firmly established in the top 50 courses in the British Isles.

Wisley Garden 7th. The lake which separates the 6th and 7th fairways awaits the slightest pulled shot on either hole.

Jones has created what almost amounts to an inland links, landscaping the ground considerably to give the undulations and traditional hazards of seaside golf. Water features widely, six lakes having been excavated and existing streams utilized for strategic challenge. The lakes provide a valuable source of irrigation, enabling green-keeping staff to achieve the superb condition for which The Wisley is renowned.

The Mill, the Garden, and the Church are three nines of roughly equal beauty and difficulty. Just the shortest is the Church. Here water appears for the first time on the par-5 2nd, running the length of the fairway on the right. Alongside the River Wey, the 4th and 5th on the Garden are excellent driving holes. Lakes to the left of the 6th, 7th and 9th await pulled drives, and those 6th and 9th greens, perched high above the water, are sufficiently raised to be real tests of pitching. The Mill's 9th is a cracker, too, with a tough approach to a long, narrow green hard by the water's edge.

17 Walton Heath

Walton Heath Golf Club, Deans Lane, Walton-on-the-Hill, Tadworth, Surrey KT20 7TP (1903)
TEL: *(01737) 812380* **FAX:** *(01737) 814225*
LOCATION: *From A217 Sutton–Reigate road after Burgh Heath turn right for Tadworth and Walton. Deans Lane on left at entrance to Walton*
COURSES: *Old: 18 holes, 6801yd/6219m, par 72, SSS 73; New: 18 holes, 6659yd/6089m, par 72, SSS 72*
TYPE OF COURSE: *Heathland*
DESIGNER: *Herbert Fowler*
GREEN FEES: *£££££*
FACILITIES: *Pro shop, caddies, club hire, clubhouse*
VISITORS: *Welcome weekdays only with handicap certificate*

WALTON HEATH
OLD COURSE

HOLE	YD	M	PAR	HOLE	YD	M	PAR
1	235	215	3	10	399	365	4
2	442	404	4	11	189	173	3
3	289	264	4	12	371	339	4
4	441	403	4	13	529	484	5
5	391	358	4	14	517	473	5
6	427	390	4	15	408	373	4
7	174	159	3	16	510	466	5
8	494	452	5	17	181	166	3
9	400	366	4	18	404	369	4
OUT	3293	3011	35	IN	3508	3208	37

6801YD • 6219M • PAR 72

What an extraordinary entry into golf course design was made by W.H. Fowler! He took up golf at the relatively late age of 35, but soon became a scratch player. His brother-in-law headed a consortium which was to finance a new golf development at Walton Heath and Herbert Fowler, still in his 40s, undertook the design. What we now

know as the Old Course opened in 1904. Three years later he added a 9-hole course, extending it to a full 18 holes before the First World War. Walton Heath has remained in the top flight of inland courses ever since. It saw many high profile professional matches in the inter-war years and has been good enough to host the Ryder Cup and European Open more recently. Big tournaments such as these are

played over a composite course drawn from the Old and New, mainly for reasons of spectator safety, coincidentally demonstrating the almost equal status of the two courses.

Walton Heath lies not at all far from the centre of London and is 700ft/213m above sea level, yet it is usually described as an inland links: the drainage is excellent, the turf beautifully crisp, the lies tight, the bunkers deep and encrusted

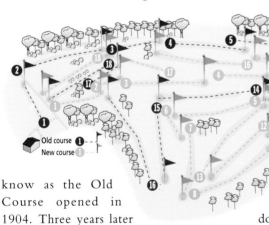

Old course ●
New course ●

with heather, and the greens firm and swift.

The Old Course begins with a long par 3 then moves over the road for the 2nd which sweeps first down and then up to the right. Many will drive the par-4 3rd, but the 4th is a big hole, with a bunker right in the middle of the fairway. The 5th is gorgeous, a downhill drive to an ever-narrowing fairway and a pitch swinging down and left to a cunning green. From here to the turn the golf is, by yardage, less demanding, but how often we lower our guard and drop silly shots! In the golden age of professional challenge matches Henry Cotton, before the Second World War, almost drove the 12th green to set up his partner, Reg Whitcombe, for a stone-dead chip in their match against Sid Brews and Bobby Locke.

Tom Weiskopf reckons the closing sequence is as good as any. The 13th is a strong par 5 climbing and curving to the right, the green running away from the approach shot. Fairway bunkers constricting the drive will be of concern to many on the 14th tee. Playing uphill, the 15th punishes the slice severely. The 16th is a classic, with a superb shot to the green, uphill, the slopes deflecting the weak approach into a horrible bunker low to the right – nor is there a safe shot to the left.

On the New Course the 3rd is mis-chievous, the fairway ending abruptly in a cross-bunker 250yd/229m out, and the 5th and 9th are fine, long par 4s by any reckoning. Coming back the 11th is attract-ive, the 14th a sterling hole with the need to angle the drive precisely, while the 17th is a handsome mid-length par 4 which earned

JAMES BRAID
(1870–1950)

James Braid, a member of the so-called Great Triumvirate, won four of his five Open Championships while serving as the club professional at Walton Heath, a position he held with distinction for some 45 years until his death, aged 80. A Scot, from Fife, he was a powerful player, yet a man with a gentle personality. All his Open Championship victories came on Scottish soil and were compressed into an astonishingly short period, from 1901 to 1910. His golf hardly deteriorated with age, and he would regularly, on his birthday, go round this far from easy course in his age or less!

high praise from that perceptive judge, Bernard Darwin.

For professional tournaments, the Old Course's 16th hole is played as a 475yd/434m par 4, this bunker very much in play on the drive, leaving a mid-iron approach shot.

18 The Addington

The Addington Golf Club, 205 Shirley Church Road,
Croydon, Surrey CR0 5AB (1913)
TEL: *(020) 8777 1055*
LOCATION: *2½ miles/4km south-east of East Croydon.*
Addiscombe Road to Shirley Park, right into Shirley
Church Road, club on right
COURSE: *18 holes, 6242yd/5708m, par 68, SSS 71*
TYPE OF COURSE: *Wooded heathland*
DESIGNER: *J.F. Abercromby*
GREEN FEES: *£££*
FACILITIES: *Clubhouse (no professional)*
VISITORS: *Welcome weekdays with handicap certificate*

The Addington is only 10 miles/16km
from the City of London, a glorious
world of heather, bracken, pines and birches.
It has hardly been altered since the First
World War. Its architect, J.F. Abercromby,
lived at the club during the war years, refining
the contours of the greens and their attendant
bunkers by hand.

Abercromby had great talent for short
holes, and The Addington has two particularly
good examples. Even today the 3rd demands a
full shot uphill to find the green, with awful
perils down the hill to the right. The 13th
remains one of the world's great one-shotters,
all carry over a heather-clad valley to a narrow
green. Henry Longhurst ranked this second
only to the 5th at Pine Valley for difficulty.

But The Addington is much more than great
par 3s. The 9th, for
instance, is an ap-
pealing par 4 that
requires two precise
crossings of deep
gullies, and the 12th
is a monstrously
difficult roller-
coaster two-shotter.
Additionally there
are incomparable
views over the City
of London from the
high ground. Magic!

19 Royal Blackheath

Royal Blackheath Golf Club, Court Road, Eltham,
London SE9 5AF (1608)
TEL: *(020) 8850 1795* **FAX:** *(020) 8859 0150*
LOCATION: *Court Road, Eltham, between A2 and*
Eltham Hill/High Street
COURSE: *18 holes, 6219yd/5687m, par 70, SSS 70*
TYPE OF COURSE: *Parkland*
DESIGNER: *James Braid*
GREEN FEES: *£££*
FACILITIES: *Pro shop, clubhouse, golf museum*
VISITORS: *Welcome weekdays with letter of introduction*
or handicap certificate

Probably 'instituted in 1608', The Golf
Club at the Chocolate House at
Blackheath is almost certainly the oldest golf
club in the world. Today Royal Blackheath
possesses a priceless collection of pictures,
clubs, balls, china, and documents, many
relating to Blackheath's prominence in the
18th century. The 1789 Knuckle Club Medal
is the world's oldest golfing medal.

The coming of the motor car made golf on
the heath impossible, and in 1923 the club
amalgamated with nearby Eltham. Its
clubhouse, a classical mansion of 1664, is an
appropriate home for such a club, though the
course is parkland in nature, very different
from the open heath on which it began.

The course is a good test, the 1st a very
long par 4 of 472yd/432m, while the uphill
17th involves an
approach over an
old-fashioned cross-
bunker set in the
face of a mound.
However, the 18th
is the best-known
hole, a par 4 of only
276yd/252m with a
hedge separating the
fairway from the
green immediately
in front of the noble
clubhouse.

Built originally for Sir John Shaw, banker to Charles II,
Royal Blackheath's clubhouse is no less magnificent inside.

20 The London Club

The London Golf Club, South Ash Manor Estate, Ash, near Sevenoaks, Kent TN15 7EN (1993)
TEL: *(01474) 879899* **FAX:** *(01474) 879912*
WEBSITE: *www.londongolf.co.uk*
LOCATION: *Off A20 near Brands Hatch/M20 Jct 2 signposted Stansted*
COURSES: *Heritage: 18 holes, 7208yd/6591m, par 72, SSS 74; International: 18 holes, 7005yd/6405m, par 72, SSS 74*
TYPE OF COURSE: *Meadowland*
DESIGNERS: *Jack Nicklaus (Heritage), Ron Kirby (International)*
GREEN FEES: *Heritage n/a, International on application*
FACILITIES: *Pro shop, caddies, buggies, club hire, clubhouse with Japanese bath and restaurant*
VISITORS: *Heritage only as members' guests, International only by prior arrangement*

Over 14,000yd/12,800m of Golden Bear golf on one site. The International benefits from a quick-draining chalk base and is rather higher and more exposed to the wind. Lakes play their part, forcing the carry on the short 3rd and 17th, protecting the green on the long 10th, while the 4th is a gambler's hole rewarding those who can guarantee a long straight drive.

The Heritage is more heavily bunkered, the greens harder to hit. The 412yd/377m 2nd is a case in point, with a minefield of bunkers for the drive, and more below the green on both sides. An iron off the tee may be wise on the short par-4 13th as there is plenty of water around the green to catch the overambitious. The 443yd/405m 14th runs sufficiently uphill to play much longer, its green elusive. Water left of the final fairway awaits a pulled shot, the green protected behind a bunker.

21 North Foreland

North Foreland Golf Club, Convent Road, Broadstairs, Thanet, Kent CT10 3PU (1903)
TEL: *(01843) 862140* **FAX:** *(01843) 862663*
LOCATION: *Kingsgate, on B2052 1 mile/1.6km north of Broadstairs*
COURSE: *18 holes, 6430yd/5880m, par 71, SSS 71*
TYPE OF COURSE: *Exposed downland overlooking the sea*
DESIGNERS: *Tom Simpson, Herbert Fowler*
GREEN FEES: *££*
FACILITIES: *Pro shop, buggy, trolley and club hire, clubhouse*
VISITORS: *Welcome with handicap certificate*

North Foreland's many golfing attributes have been recognized by a wider public since the return of the Open to Sandwich, the club hosting final qualifying each year. This is downland, rather than links, enjoying broad seascapes, if always exposed to the wind. The outward half is particularly open, the back nine, over the road, slightly sheltered by trees. There are several very tough par 4s, notably the 8th, 17th and 18th, all running uphill, but the three par 5s are downhill in compensation. Of the short holes, the 14th and 16th both play engagingly towards the sea, though the uphill 9th is easily the hardest.

Many say that Abe Mitchell was the greatest golfer never to win the Open. He was professional here for many years, and the club has produced several outstanding amateurs, notably Douglas Grant, Rex Hartley, and Diana Fishwick who beat the formidable Glenna Collett to win the 1930 Ladies' Amateur Championship. It was on the good par-3 course that 13 year-old Henry Longhurst won his first trophy.

Allowance must be made for the wind at the exposed par-3 3rd on the London Club's International Course.

22 Royal St George's

The Royal St George's Golf Club, Sandwich, Kent
CT13 9PB (1887)
TEL: (01304) 613090 **FAX:** (01304) 611245
LOCATION: Sandwich – follow signs to the Golf Courses
COURSE: 18 holes, 6930yd/6337m, par 70, SSS 74
TYPE OF COURSE: Links
DESIGNER: Dr Laidlaw Purves
GREEN FEES: £££££
FACILITIES: Pro shop, caddies, club hire, clubhouse
VISITORS: Welcome weekdays only with handicap
certificate (limit men 18, ladies 15, permission required
for ladies to play)

ROYAL ST GEORGE'S

HOLE	YD	M	PAR	HOLE	YD	M	PAR
1	441	403	4	10	413	378	4
2	376	344	4	11	216	197	3
3	210	192	3	12	365	334	4
4	468	428	4	13	443	405	4
5	421	385	4	14	551	504	5
6	155	142	3	15	478	437	4
7	530	484	5	16	163	149	3
8	418	382	4	17	425	389	4
9	389	356	4	18	468	428	4
OUT	3408	3116	35	IN	3522	3221	35

6930YD • 6337M • PAR 70

In the 1880s a couple of London golfers, Dr Laidlaw Purves and Mr Henry Lamb, set out to find a patch of land on which to construct something more akin to what they recognized as a proper golf course in their native Scotland. Having begun in Bournemouth they located their grail when looking down from the Norman church tower of the ancient port of Sandwich. Out to the east they spotted as mountainous a collection of sand hills as is to be found on any of the Open Championship links. Indeed, such was the renown of their new course that Sandwich became the first

course outside Scotland to stage the Open – in 1894 when J.H. Taylor won the first of his five championships.

Sandwich hosted many great Opens over the next half century, perhaps the high spot being Cotton's victory in 1934, stemming the tide of American supremacy. But the championship grew in size after the war and, following Bobby Locke's triumph in 1949, it was deemed that neither the roads nor the town of Sandwich could cope with the onslaught. Amateur events of the highest class continued to be held there, the young Jack Nicklaus taking the Grand Challenge Cup in 1959, and it was only a matter of time before the access problems were solved. The building of a new road helped, and in 1981 the Open returned, Bill Rogers seeing off Bernhard Langer by 4 strokes. Langer was in contention again in 1985 when Sandy Lyle won, despite a visit to Duncan's Hollow, the depression just off the 18th green. When Greg Norman won in 1993 there was Langer in third place once again.

Of all the Open Championship courses Royal St George's is probably the most difficult for the moderate player, for no concessions are made. The carries are often distinctly long, sometimes blind, to fairways

Royal St George's 9th, which plays up through a valley to this exposed green. Nick Faldo says it plays harder than its 389yd/356m suggests.

which tumble amidst towering dunes. There is nowhere to bale out.

The 1st is one of the great starting holes, calling for a decent drive to clear The Kitchen and an approach over cross-bunkers. For the ordinary player the 4th is unfathomable, with a monstrous pair of sleepered bunkers set into a giant sand hill on the direct line and a very wobbly fairway low to the left. The wickedly raised green is still far distant, angled round to the left. It is followed by a stirring drive through the dunes on the 5th.

With a par of only 70, the muscle of the course comes from its par 4s. The 8th is as good as you will find with its range of rough-clad hummocks to be avoided on the long approach shot. The next few holes may be less celebrated but they exemplify the variety of challenges at Sandwich, the 10th with its

green on the skyline, the 12th working inland over very bumpy ground. Out-of-bounds and a ditch threaten on the par-5 14th, but the strength of the finish lies in its long two-shotters, the 468yd/428m 18th requiring an utterly unwavering approach.

DR LAIDLAW PURVES

Purves was a distinguished opthalmic surgeon at Guy's Hospital in London, following study in Edinburgh, Berlin, Leipzig, Vienna, Utrecht and Paris. He wrote several medical treatises, but there was another side to his literary talents as he also edited a version of *Robinson Crusoe* and translated *Gil Blas* from the French. Having learned his golf on the historic Bruntsfield links near Edinburgh, Purves became an active member of the Wimbledon Golf Club but conflicts of interest between the military and civilian membership, restricted access, and overcrowding on a public common stifled enthusiasm and led to the Doctor's expedition to the south coast.

23 Prince's

Prince's Golf Club, Sandwich Bay, Sandwich, Kent
CT13 9QB (1904)
TEL: *(01304) 611118* **FAX:** *(01304) 612000*
LOCATION: *Sandwich, follow signs to the Golf Courses,
pass Royal St George's, through toll gate into Sandwich
Estate, follow signs along seafront*
COURSES: *Dunes: 9 holes, 3455yd/3159m par 36;
Himalayas: 9 holes, 3321yd/3037m, par 35; Shore: 9
holes, 3492yd/3193m, par 36*
TYPE OF COURSE: *Links*
DESIGNERS: *Sir Guy Campbell, John Morrison*
GREEN FEES: *££££*
FACILITIES: *Pro shop, buggy and club hire, range,
clubhouse*
VISITORS: *Welcome*

Sadly the course on which Gene Sarazen
won the 1932 Open Championship did not
survive the upheaval of war. Reconstruction
began in 1949, the decision having been taken

*The Shore Course's 9th, showing the dunes so characteristic
of Prince's and the old clubhouse in the distance, where the
courses share a boundary with Royal St George's.*

to create a modern championship course which
would not overwhelm the less proficient. So
three nines of roughly equal challenge radiate
from the clubhouse, sharing an expansiveness
with neighbouring Royal St George's.

On the Shore nine the 4th has a bumpy
fairway and bunkers on the direct approach, and
the 5th takes play out to the 14th tee of Royal
St George's. Dunes interlocks with Shore, the
1st a tough dog-leg, the 4th a tight hole
culminating in a demanding pitch over bunkers.
Himalayas has a slightly different feel, starting
amid trees and ditches, the 2nd quite a tough
proposition. The 6th, along the shore, stretches
to 580yd/530m for championship play.

24 Royal Cinque Ports

Royal Cinque Ports Golf Club, Golf Road, Deal, Kent
CT14 6RF (1892)
TEL: (01304) 374007 **FAX:** (01304) 379530
LOCATION: Deal, north along seafront
COURSE: 18 holes, 6754yd/6176m, par 72, SSS 72
TYPE OF COURSE: Links
DESIGNERS: Tom Dunn, Sir Guy Campbell
GREEN FEES: ££££££
FACILITIES: Pro shop, caddies, buggy and club hire,
clubhouse
VISITORS: Welcome with handicap certificate

J.H. Taylor and George Duncan won the
two Open Championships played at Deal, in
1909 and 1920. But there were occasional
problems with the sea. It invaded at the most
inappropriate moments! Happily championship
golf returned in the 1980s when the Amateur
Championship and Brabazon Trophies were
held here, followed in the 1990s by the St
Andrews Trophy and English Amateur.

Royal Cinque Ports is a classic, and a very
brute in the wind which whistles in off the
sea in winter. The greens have an excellent
reputation. True, there are blind shots, short
par 4s, and uneven fairways, the sort of thing
deplored by some modern players, but they
are appreciated and expected by connoisseurs
of true links golf. No blind shot compares
with the pitch to the 3rd green down in a
hollow beyond a bunkered ridge slightly
reminiscent of the 5th at St Andrews. St
Andrews is recalled on the 1st, too, with its
exacting pitch across a stream. There are only
three short holes, the 4th across a gully, the 8th
well bunkered, and the tough 223yd/204m
14th played to an elevated green. It is part of a
hard finish, especially when played into the
prevailing wind, the 15th a lengthy par 4
climbing past bunkers then running over a
bumpy fairway to a sloping green. The correct
line is essential (and tricky) from the 16th tee,
and from any distance the green is hard to hit
and hold, perched as it is on a minor mountain.

Running along the sea wall, the stretch from the 3rd to
the 7th is typical of the narrow, undulating nature of
much of the golf at Deal.

Harry Colt (1869-1951)

As a schoolboy at Monkton Combe, Harry Shapland Colt thrived on sport, playing cricket and rugby as well as rowing. Although he had enjoyed embryonic golf at home on holiday, it was not until he went up to Cambridge to read law that he took it up seriously. He soon made the University team and was captain in his final year, 1890. Three years later he went to Hastings to join a firm of solicitors, and he soon found himself as the first captain of the new Rye Golf Club. With his friend Douglas Rolland he laid out the course, had it ready for play in a year, and took on the duties of honorary secretary. He was the automatic choice as secretary of the newly completed Sunningdale.

The First World War temporarily halted his burgeoning career as a course designer, but in 1919 he teamed up with Hugh Alison and Alister Mackenzie to form an impressive team which went on to design courses of enduring fame all over the world, John Morrison joining the partnership when Mackenzie emigrated to America for good in the 1920s.

25 Littlestone

Littlestone Golf Club, St Andrews Road, Littlestone, Kent TN28 8RB (1888)
TEL: *(01797) 363355* **FAX:** *(01797) 362740*
WEBSITE: *www.littlestonegolfclub.co.uk*
LOCATION: *Littlestone, turn left at seafront*
COURSE: *18 holes, 6470yd/5916m, par 71, SSS 72*
TYPE OF COURSE: *Links*
DESIGNERS: *W. Laidlaw Purves, Alister Mackenzie*
GREEN FEES: *£££*
FACILITIES: *Pro shop, clubhouse*
VISITORS: *Welcome with handicap certificate*

It is not essential to have mountainous dunes to make a decent links test, and Littlestone proves the point. Its most famous holes, the 16th and 17th, certainly make full use of sandy hillocks, but such par 4s as the 4th, 8th, 10th and 12th demonstrate that in the hands of a master architect gentler undulations can be used to telling effect. The 11th is a delight with a ditch crossing the drive on the diagonal. Take on as much as you dare! The approach to the 2nd, over another ditch and through a gap in the dunes, is fun. Few, however, will reach the exposed hilltop green of the 468yd/428m 16th in two, climbing at full stretch over bumpy ground and bunkers. The angle, elevation, and exposure of the 17th green make recovery difficult for the player who has clubbed wrongly or neglected to take account of the effects of the wind.

Littlestone's condition, even in winter, is always impressive. Each time the Open is played at Royal St George's, Littlestone is an automatic choice for final qualifying.

Littlestone's 1st, a short par 4 of only 297yd/272m, its flat, well-bunkered green overlooked by Littlestone's distinctive water tower.

26 Rye

Rye Golf Club, Camber, Rye, East Sussex TN31
7QS (1894)
TEL: (01797) 225241 **FAX:** (01797) 225460
LOCATION: 3 miles/5km east of Rye on B2075
COURSES: Old: 18 holes, 6308yd/5768m, par 68,
SSS 71; Jubilee: 9 holes, 6141yd/5615m, par 71,
SSS 70
TYPE OF COURSE: Links
DESIGNERS: Harry Colt (Old), Frank Pennink (Jubilee)
GREEN FEES: Not applicable
FACILITIES: Pro shop, clubhouse
VISITORS: Members' guests only

*Rye's 9th green, to the right of the clubhouse, is cleverly
protected by devious mounds and depressions short of the
putting surface.*

Each January Oxford and Cambridge
Blues, past and present, travel from all
over the world to compete in the President's
Putter. It is doubtful they would do it were
it played at any club other than Rye. 'There
is a kind of small fierceness about Rye, as if
one were looking at a wild cat through a
magnifying glass and imagining a tiger,'
wrote the Rye poet and Cambridge Blue,
Patric Dickinson, whose Putter parties were
for many regulars an essential part of the
competition. Rye is the epitome of links
golf, with narrow, undulating fairways and
fast greens which repel all but the most
perfectly struck shots. 'Going from Rye to a

INTERNATIONAL AMBASSADORS

The first international golf tour took place in
1903 when a group of members of the Oxford
and Cambridge Golfing Society set off on a trans-
Atlantic voyage to America. It was very much a
social affair, 10 matches spread over 39 days, but
in this trip were sown the seeds of the many
international contests which are now regular
fixtures in the golfing calendar. The Society,
whose permanent home is in the clubhouse at
Rye, was founded in 1898, membership restricted
to those who had gained their Blue by
representing their university in the Varsity Match.

flatter terrain, you feel like coming ashore
after a voyage.'

There are those who say that Rye's
distinction lies in its collection of superb par 3s,
perhaps the pick of them being the secretive
7th, its green an upturned saucepan amongst
the dunes. On the other hand there is a unique
assembly of longer par 4s: the 4th frighteningly
narrow on top of the sand hills, the 6th
exceptionally long, the 10th through the gorse,
the mighty 13th with a blind approach over a
towering sand dune, the 15th with a crumpled
fairway, the 16th with a diagonal ridge, and the
18th as good (and tough) a finishing hole as
you could wish to find. Here you drive onto a
narrow ridge, with terrible agonies awaiting in
the cavernous hollows either side. The bumpy
downhill approach is played perilously close to
the clubhouse windows.

Frank Pennink's 9-hole Jubilee Course was
constructed at minimal cost in 1977 on land
reclaimed from the sea. It is a flatter course, but
no less engaging.

The 9th at Chart Hills, inspired by the 7th at Augusta, is a short par 4 with 13 bunkers governing strategy. The green is angled to favour an approach from the right.

27 *Chart Hills*

Chart Hills Golf Club, Weeks Lane, Biddenden, Kent TN27 8JX (1993)
TEL: *(01580) 292222* **FAX:** *(01580) 292233*
LOCATION: *East of A274 Maidstone–Biddenden road (turn off at petrol station between Biddenden and Headcorn)*
COURSE: *18 holes, 7119yd/6510m, par 72, SSS 74*
TYPE OF COURSE: *Parkland*
DESIGNER: *Nick Faldo*
GREEN FEES: *££££*
FACILITIES: *Pro shop, buggy and club hire, clubhouse*
VISITORS: *Welcome except Saturdays*

Nick Faldo's entry into golf course design is as impressive as his playing record. Already his course at Sporting Club Berlin has entered the top 20 in Europe. Chart Hills, his British debut, is equally outstanding. The abiding impression is one of bunkers, not only the number of them (around 120) but particularly their size, Anaconda snaking up and across the 5th fairway for some 200yd/183m!

Those bunkers catch the eye prominently from the tee of the immensely long 1st hole. Water, too, plays its part, not least on the island green of the short 17th. Streams are fundamental to the strategy of the 2nd, 4th, 8th, 13th and 14th, though it may be the 6th, only 309yd/283m from the back tee, which causes greatest anguish. It might be driven, but the green is very narrow and raised up above a pond and a pot bunker.

28 *Crowborough Beacon*

Crowborough Beacon Golf Club, Beacon Road, Crowborough, East Sussex TN6 1UJ (1895)
TEL: *(01892) 661511* **FAX:** *(01892) 667339*
LOCATION: *South edge of Crowborough on A26*
COURSE: *18 holes, 6273yd/5736m, par 71, SSS 70*
TYPE OF COURSE: *Downland*
DESIGNER: *Unknown*
GREEN FEES: *££*
FACILITIES: *Pro shop, clubhouse*
VISITORS: *Welcome with handicap certificate*

Golf was not one of the secret vices of Sherlock Holmes, which is slightly surprising given that his creator, Sir Arthur Conan-Doyle, was captain of Crowborough Beacon in 1910. There are few more stirring views than that from the clubhouse terrace, 800ft/244m up overlooking the Weald of Sussex, the South Downs, and, on a good day, the sea.

The golf, on fine downland turf, is at times strenuous and the 448yd/410m 2nd was described by golf writer Peter Allen as 'as fierce a par-four as ever I saw'. It leans insistently as it curves to the right and the green is on the far side of a chasm. The 6th, too, is a brute, a par 3 over a heathery valley with a rocky abyss just below the green to the left. But there are charming holes aplenty, such as the 16th back across that valley shared with the 6th.

29 Royal Ashdown Forest

Royal Ashdown Forest Golf Club, Chapel Lane, Forest Row, East Grinstead, East Sussex RH18 5LR (1888)
TEL: *(01342) 822018* **FAX:** *(01342) 825211*
LOCATION: *A22 to Forest Row, then B2110 for ½ mile/1km. Right into Chapel Lane, at top of hill turn left*
COURSE: *18 holes, 6477yd/5923m, par 72, SSS 71*
TYPE OF COURSE: *Downland, part wooded*
DESIGNER: *Archdeacon Scott*
GREEN FEES: *£££*
FACILITIES: *Pro shop, clubhouse*
VISITORS: *Welcome with handicap certificate*

You have to play Royal Ashdown to begin to appreciate it. The books will tell you that it has no bunkers, and that the 6th is one of the best short holes in golf. What the books cannot recreate is the unique atmosphere of a fascinating course roaming one of the great ancient forests, the feel of its turf, the uplifting effect of striking a ball against the skyline on this elevated site. This is rugged golfing terrain, in parts forest but elsewhere open heath with streams, heather, bracken, gorse, grassy pits, steep hills, and humps and hollows galore providing a wide variety of golfing hazards. Frank Pennink's comment that 'the yardage bears no resemblance to the length the course plays' could not be truer, and he was well placed to make the comment, a very fine amateur player, distinguished course architect, and long-standing member of Royal Ashdown.

There are tough holes, such as the wicked 7th and 13th, both climbing. There are long holes, the 12th stretching 568yd/519m, the par-4 17th fully 473yd/432m, though both run downhill. There are exhilarating holes such as the 249yd/228m 11th, played against a backdrop of miles of unbroken country. But it is the 6th which is utterly uncompromising, despite being little over 100yd/91m long with a green almost 40yd/37m deep. On the left the green falls down into a stream, on the right into a series of depressions. There is simply no margin for error.

Ashdown Forest's 3rd, set in an uncharacteristically sylvan spot on a course which breaks out onto windswept heathland from the 7th. A collar of rough and moundwork demand a perfect pitch.

30 *East Sussex National*

*East Sussex National Golf Club, Little Horsted,
Uckfield, East Sussex TN22 5ES (1989)*
TEL: *(01825) 880088* **FAX:** *(01825) 880066*
WEBSITE: *www.eastsussexnational.co.uk*
LOCATION: *2 miles/3km south of Uckfield on A22*
COURSES: *East: 18 holes, 7138yd/6527m, par 72,
SSS 74; West: 18 holes, 7154yd/6542m, par 72,
SSS 74*
TYPE OF COURSE: *Parkland*
DESIGNER: *Robert E. Cupp*
GREEN FEES: *££££*
FACILITIES: *Pro shop, buggy and club hire, clubhouse*
VISITORS: *Welcome on East Course; West Course only
as members' guests*

Having been open for more than 10 years,
the two courses at East Sussex have
already acquired a welcome maturity.
Importantly, its early praises are sung equally
loudly today. These are big courses, the West
reserved for members and their guests, the
East open to visitors, and arguably the better
course. Here visitors are made to feel special,
being given the Rolls-Royce treatment in the
palatial clubhouse, unlike all too many clubs
where visitors are grudgingly tolerated

because of the money they bring in, but
otherwise treated as second-class citizens.

The ground undulates naturally with
plenty of mature trees, relieving the architect
of the need to trick things up. On the East
Course water is used surprisingly little for a
modern course. It comes into play tellingly on
the approaches at the 1st, 5th and 10th. It is
there in greater measure on the all-carry par-3
16th. The 17th is a different matter, however,
with water left and right of the tee. A creek
runs beside the fairway on the left, crossing at
about the length of a good drive, then
opening out into a pond on the right of the
green. Hills make the 15th and 18th play
much longer than the card suggests, the 15th
green well bunkered on the right, the final
green long, narrow, and angled.

The West Course crosses the busy A26 road
and many of its best holes are on the far side,
such as the gorgeous 10th and daunting 14th.

*With everything visible from the tee, the East Course's
17th is a hole to strike fear into the hearts of average
golfers, though the green is broad and receptive.*

31 *West Sussex*

West Sussex Golf Club, Golf Club Lane, Wiggonholt, Pulborough, West Sussex RH20 2EN (1930)
TEL: *(01798) 872563* **FAX:** *(01798) 872033*
LOCATION: *Off A283 between Pulborough and Storrington*
COURSE: *18 holes, 6221yd/5688m, par 68, SSS 70*
TYPE OF COURSE: *Wooded heathland*
DESIGNERS: *Sir Guy Campbell, C.K. Hutchison*
GREEN FEES: *££££*
FACILITIES: *Pro shop, trolley and club hire, clubhouse*
VISITORS: *Welcome with handicap certificate except Fridays*

It is said that the West Sussex course is laid out on the very end of a tract of sandy heathland which begins at Camberley far to the north-west. Certainly it is an oasis surrounded by heavy clay and marshes. 'There is enough of this precious ground to make one admirable course and there is no more,' wrote Bernard Darwin. Henry Longhurst, Peter Allen, Charles Ambrose and other distinguished commentators have written equally affectionately of this wonderful little course overlooked by Chanctonbury Ring high on the South Downs.

West Sussex's best-known hole, the par-3 6th – the problem is not so much clearing the swamp and pond as avoiding the right-hand bunkers and the hill on the left.

The trees have grown since the course was founded in 1930, and they certainly add to the strategy and beauty, yet the expansive heather and plentiful bunkers remain the principal threat, especially on holes such as the 7th where the drive must carry 180yd/165m over an intimidating wall of sand and heather. Darwin defined the 10th as 'the apotheosis of the dog-leg hole', the direct line from tee to green riddled with bunkers, heather and pines in wait for the big hook. The approaches to the 11th, 14th and 17th call for controlled long irons, those shots which separate the better player from the also-ran. Each of the five short holes is good, but the one for which West Sussex is famed above all is the 6th, a beauty of 224yd/205m played from an elevated tee out over a pond. In Longhurst's words, 'If ever there was an all or nothing hole, this is it.'

 ## Hayling

Hayling Golf Club, Links Lane, Hayling Island, Hampshire PO11 0BX (1883)

TEL and **FAX:** (02392) 464446
LOCATION: *West end of Hayling Island, right at seafront*
COURSE: *18 holes, 6531yd/5972m, par 71, SSS 71*
TYPE OF COURSE: *Links*
DESIGNERS: *J.H. Taylor, Tom Simpson*
GREEN FEES: *££*
FACILITIES: *Pro shop, clubhouse*
VISITORS: *Welcome with handicap certificate*

One of the oldest links in the country, older even than Royal St George's, Hayling was said by Bernard Darwin to possess 'some of the finest, natural seaside golfing country to be found anywhere'. Golf was brought to the island by the Sandeman family of the distinguished port house.

Hayling's famous holes come at the far end of the course. The 12th, Desert, is a long par 4 through the dunes, its green raised up behind a bunker on the straight line, while another awaits if you drift to the left. The 13th, Widow, involves a drive up over

The short 11th at Hayling Island is played over bunkers to a green sheltered in the dunes with the waters of the Solent just beyond.

a troublesome ridge to a fairway which falls away on both sides. On the par-5 14th, Farm, the main problem is a great pit which eats into the fairway all the way to the green, which is set behind undulating ground and tricky to hit and hold. The finish, plainer perhaps but far from easy, is beset with gorse, notably the drive at the 15th, Sailor's Grave, while the drive on the 17th, Jacob's Ladder, also involves a potential skirmish with a lake on the left.

But many earlier holes provide equal challenge, such as the 3rd, on which the drive is made over a marker post to an angled fairway. The 6th ends in a tough approach shot, a forced carry over a watery cutting, while the name, Death or Glory, is perfect for the par-5 7th. Then on the 8th, a seaside special, the drive must find the left of a fairway interrupted by dunes and a bunker.

33 Stoneham

Stoneham Golf Club, Monks Wood Close, Bassett, Southampton, Hampshire SO16 3TT (1908)
TEL: *(01703) 769272* **FAX:** *(01703) 766320*
LOCATION: *3 miles/5km north of Southampton. From M27 Jct 5, take Southampton road, turn right at lights (Bassett Green Road), club about 1 mile/1.6km on right*
COURSE: *18 holes, 6387yd/5840m, par 72, SSS 70*
TYPE OF COURSE: *Parkland/heathland*
DESIGNER: *Willie Park*
GREEN FEES: *££*
FACILITIES: *Pro shop, clubhouse*
VISITORS: *Welcome with handicap certificate*

The first Dunlop Masters was played at Stoneham back in 1946, confirmation of Stoneham's enduring qualities coming with its hosting of the 1993 Brabazon Trophy. On paper it looks short. In reality it is anything but, with any number of really testing approach shots to be played. Laid out in a hilly deer park with heather and gorse in addition to trees it is one of a select band of courses of which it can be said that there is not an uninteresting hole in the round.

Some idea of the challenge comes on the 3rd, a short par 4, yet the drive must be long over a valley, and the approach is made steeply uphill. It is strong enough to be rated Stroke 5. Stroke 1 follows, an exhilarating par 4 of 462yd/422m beginning with a drive out over heather, the fairway plunging steeply downhill thereafter. For most of us, the problem will be in deciding whether or not to attempt to carry the stream at the bottom, only 90yd/82m short of the green. The putting surface slopes down from back to front. Cross-bunkers interrupt the fairway of the par-5 6th and the green, on the far side of a valley, is still a long way off. The outward half ends with another drive out over low ground to a sloping fairway and an approach over the brow of a hill to a ledge green.

Coming back, the 11th is one of the best holes, involving a sizeable carry over a cross-bunker from the tee followed by an uncompromising approach over a deep gully to yet another ledge green perched on the far side. Downhill drives invigorate the 14th and 15th, and also the 17th, playing to a green above a sparkling stream amidst the woods.

OTHER COURSES TO VISIT IN THE SOUTH-EAST

Surrey	West Byfleet	Walmer and Kingsdown	Worthing
Burhill	West Surrey	Wildernesse	**Hampshire**
Drift	Wildwood	**Sussex**	Barton-on-Sea
Effingham	**Kent**	Bognor Regis	Blackmoor
Farnham	Broome Park	Cooden Beach	Bramshaw
Foxhills	Canterbury	Copthorne	Brockenhurst Manor
Gatton Manor	Cherry Lodge	Goodwood	Corhampton
Guildford	Faversham	Littlehampton	Freshwater Bay
Hindhead	Hever	Mannings Heath	Hockley
Merrist Wood	Knole Park	Mid Sussex	Meon Valley
Pyrford	Langley Park	Nevill	Old Thorns
Reigate Heath	Mid Kent	Piltdown	Rowlands Castle
Royal Wimbledon	Moatlands	Royal Eastbourne	Royal Winchester
Selsdon Park	Nizels	Seaford	Shanklin and Sandown
Tandridge	Sundridge Park	Tilgate Forest	Waterlooville

REGIONAL DIRECTORY – LONDON

Where to Stay

London hotels are expensive. If you run to your own oil well you may prefer suites at **Claridge's** (020 7629 8860), the **Dorchester** (020 7629 8888), or the **Ritz** (020 7300 2308). Auguste Escoffier ruled the culinary roost at the **Savoy** (020 7836 4343) in the 1890s. On the South Bank, **London Marriott County Hall** (020 7928 5200) offers splendid views of the Houses of Parliament. **Number Five Maddox Street** (020 7647 0200) boasts chic apartments close to the fashionable shops of Bond Street, and service at **The Connaught** (020 7499 7070) is legendary. For Harrods and Knightsbridge, **Searcy's Roof Garden Bedrooms** (020 7584 4921) are exactly what they say, the **Cadogan** (020 7235 7141) is delightfully restrained, and **Knightsbridge Green Hotel** (020 7584 6274) relatively inexpensive. Also in the area are **Cliveden Town House** (020 7730 6466), **Durley House** (020 7235 5537) and **The Capital** (020 7589 5171). One of the great old station hotels has been lavishly refurbished as the **Landmark London** (020 7631 8000). **The Rookery** (020 7336 0931) in the City is an antique collector's paradise.

Where to Eat

London may well have the widest cosmopolitan choice of restaurants in the world. **Rani** (020 8349 4386) (Gujurati vegetarian), **Dakota** (020 7792 9191) (American), **Saigon Thuy** (020 8871 9464) (Vietnamese), **Chutney Mary** (020 7351 3113) (Indian home cooking), **Istanbul Iskembecisi** (020 7254 7291) (Turkish), **New Tayyab** (020 7247 9543) (Pakistani), **Olivo** (020 7730 2505) (Sardinian), **Nobu** (020 7447 4747) (Japanese), and **Tajine** (020 7935 1545) (Moroccan) hint at the variety available. Sausages from an organic farm feature at **R.K. Stanleys** (020 7462 0099), game at **Rules** (020 7836 5314), the freshest fish at **Fish!** (020 7836 3236), traditional English food at **Butlers Wharf Chop House** (020 7403 3403), with distinguished wines at bargain prices at the **Tate Gallery Restaurant** (020 7887 8825).

Glitterati inhabit **Quaglino's** (020 7930 6767) and **Langan's Brasserie** (020 7491 8822), but for the ultimate gastronomic experience **Chez Nico at Ninety Park Lane** (020 7409 1290) is the highest ranked restaurant in the country. Those most likely to knock it off its perch are: **Gordon Ramsay** (020 7352 4441), **La Tante Claire** (020 7823 2003), **Oak Room Marco Pierre White** (020 7437 0202), **Pied-à-Terre** (020 7636 1178), and **The Square** (020 7495 7100). Otherwise simply take pot luck in the streets of Soho or Chelsea, Charlotte Street or Knightsbridge.

What to See

Most hotels provide comprehensive What's On magazines One of the best ways to discover London is to take the excellent-value **river cruise** from Westminster Bridge to Greenwich. Open-topped **bus tours** are also recommended. For those with very limited time the essential sights are the **Tower of London**, **St Paul's Cathedral**, **Westminster Abbey**, **Buckingham Palace**, the **Houses of Parliament**, **Whitehall** and **Trafalgar Square**.

At least half a day is needed to do justice to the **Tower of London** and the **Crown Jewels**. Anglican choral services are sung daily at **St Paul's Cathedral** and **Westminster Abbey,** Roman Catholic services at **Westminster Cathedral**. Be in **Whitehall** at 11:00 (10:00 on Sunday) when the colourful ceremony of Changing the Guard takes place at Horse Guards. Changing of the Guard at **Buckingham Palace** is at 11:30. The Palace State Rooms are open for a limited period each year, as are the Queen's Gallery and Royal Mews, and at **Kensington Palace** the Royal Ceremonial Dress Collection and State Apartments may be viewed. **Hampton Court** is quite magnificent.

Proceedings in the **House of Commons** may be witnessed, tours taking place when the House is not sitting. The **Cabinet War Rooms** in King Charles Street, off Whitehall, give a fascinating insight into the daily life of Sir Winston Churchill and his staff during the war years. The principal art collections are to be seen in the **National Gallery**, **National Portrait Gallery**, **Tate Gallery**, and the new **Tate Modern**. The **Victoria and Albert Museum**, **Natural History Museum**, and **Science Museum** (all at South Kensington), the **British Museum** in Bloomsbury, and the **Imperial War Museum** in Lambeth, house major collections. Amongst dozens of **other museums and galleries** are the Museum of London, the Wallace Collection, MCC Cricket Museum at Lord's, the Geffrye Museum, Dulwich Picture Gallery, Bank of England Museum, Clink Prison, Bramah Tea and Coffee Museum, Dickens House, London Transport Museum, Florence Nightingale Museum, Sir John Soane's Museum, and Wimbledon Lawn Tennis Museum.

Tickets for Wimbledon are like gold dust. County and Test **cricket** is played at Lord's and the Oval. International **football** matches are staged at Wembley, **rugby** at Twickenham, **athletics** at Crystal Palace, **racing** at Ascot, Epsom, Sandown Park, and Kempton Park. London's **theatres** thrive, and there is **opera** at Covent Garden and the Coliseum, plus **concerts** at the South Bank, Barbican and Wigmore Hall, with the Henry Wood Promenade Concerts at the Royal Albert Hall a highlight of the summer musical calendar.

REGIONAL DIRECTORY – SOUTH-EAST

Where to Stay

Surrey At the heart of the best golf country is **Great Fosters** (01784 433822), near Egham, a magnificent Tudor mansion. A fine restaurant at Ockham, **The Chapel at The Hautboy** (01483 225355) offers comfortable rooms. Dine in a 13th-century crypt in the **Angel Posting House & Livery** (01483 564555) in Guildford. Play a Henry Cotton course at **Gatton Manor Hotel Golf and Country Club** (01306 627555).

Kent **Eastwell Manor** (01233 213000) near Ashford and **Kennel Holt Hotel** (01580 712032) at Cranbrook are conveniently situated, and **Wallett's Court** (01304 852424) at St Margaret's at Cliffe near Dover was once owned by Queen Eleanor of Castille. **Romney Bay House** (01797 364747) adjoins the golf links at Littlestone.

Sussex **Alexander House** (01342 714914) near Crawley and **Gravetye Manor** (01342 810567) at East Grinstead are luxurious, the restaurant at Gravetye highly praised. Note also the **Ashdown Forest Golf Hotel** (01342 842866), and **Horsted Place Hotel** (01825 750581), offering reduced green fees at East Sussex National. **South Lodge Hotel** (01403 891711) is connected with the beautiful Mannings Heath courses.

Hampshire **Marriott Meon Valley Hotel** (01329 833455) maintains a good parkland course. For peaceful elegance, **Lainston House** (01962 863588) at Sparsholt and **Esseborne Manor** (01264 736444) near Andover fit the bill. Convenient for many good courses, the **George Hotel** (01256 702081) at Odiham dates from 1540.

Where to Eat

Surrey American and British cooking styles prevail at, respectively, **Canyon** (020 8948 2944) at Richmond and **The Glasshouse** (020 8940 6777) at Kew. **Michels** (01483 224777) at Ripley, the **Dining Room** (01737 226650) in Reigate, **Kinghams** (01483 202168) at Shere, and **Gemini** (01737 812179) at Tadworth are other highlights.

Kent **Thackeray's House** (01892 511921) and **Hotel du Vin & Bistro** (01892 526455) top the list in Tunbridge Wells. There are high marks for **West House** (01580 291341) at Biddenden, **Honours Mill** (01732 866757) at Edenbridge, and the **Sandgate Hotel** (01303 220444), and fine wines at **Read's** (01795 535344) at Faversham, *Sussex* **Black Chapati** (01273 699011), **One Paston Place** (01273 606933) and **Terre à Terre** (01273 729051) are located in Brighton. **Röser's** (01424 712218) in Hastings has a reputation for its wines. Try also **Sundial** (01323 832217) at Herstmonceux, **Landgate Bistro**

(01797 222829) in Rye, **Crossways** (01323 482455) at Wilmington, **Queen's Room** (01798 831992) at Amberley Castle, **Jeremy's** (01444 441102) at Borde Hill, **Cole's** (01403 730456) at Southwater, and **Fleur de Sel** (01903 742331) and the **Old Forge** (01903 743402) at Storrington.

Hampshire **The Winchester Hotel du Vin & Bistro** (01962 841414), **Old Manor House** (01794 517353) at Romsey, and **Marryat Restaurant** (01425 275341) at Chewton Glen are wine treasures. Excellent food beckons at **Le Poussin** (01590 623063) at Brockenhurst, **36 on the Quay** (01243 375592) at Emsworth, **Dew Pond** (01635 278408) at Old Burghclere, and **Old House Hotel** (01329 833049) at Wickham.

What to See

Surrey **Kew Gardens** and the Royal Horticultural Society's **Wisley Gardens** are world class. Walk Surrey's great heaths at Thursley, Frensham and Hankley, climb Box Hill, Leith Hill and the Devil's Punchbowl near Hindhead. Only part of the legendary **Brooklands** banked track survives, but the museum recreates its history.

Kent Of once fashionable **Tunbridge Wells**, its shaded walk, The Pantiles, and many Georgian houses maintain their grace. Amongst the best houses are **Sissinghurst Castle** (Vita Sackville-West), **Penshurst Place**, **Downe House** (Charles Darwin), **Chartwell** (Sir Winston Churchill), **Knole** (with 365 rooms), and **Leeds Castle** (set on a lake). Near the tiny streets of **Sandwich** is **Richborough Roman Castle**. Ride the narrow-gauge **Romney, Hythe and Dymchurch Railway**.

Sussex **Fishbourne Roman Villa** is one of Britain's largest Roman buildings. **Arundel Castle**, home of the Dukes of Norfolk, dates from Norman times. Historically, the most important church is **Battle Abbey**, founded by William the Conqueror. **Bodiam** is the outstanding Sussex castle. Brighton's elegant 18th-century buildings and the extraordinary **Brighton Pavilion** rub shoulders with the tawdriness of candy floss stalls and fruit machines. Medieval, Tudor, Stuart and Georgian houses line **Rye**'s cobbled streets. **Petworth House** and its magnificent park are rewarding. **Glyndebourne**'s new theatre has improved facilities at this world-famous opera house. **'Glorious Goodwood'** is one of England's foremost race courses. The **Bluebell Railway** was one of the earliest preserved lines in Britain.

Hampshire **Portsmouth** has been one of England's principal naval ports for centuries. Its dockyards, Nelson's flagship, *HMS Victory*, and Henry VIII's favourite warship, *The Mary Rose*, are open to the public. **Beaulieu Abbey**, home of the Montagu family, also houses the **National Motor Museum**.

Chapter 2

The
South-West

For our golfing purposes we stole a bit of Hampshire, translating it into the south-east. Otherwise our south-west comprises Alfred the Great's kingdom of Wessex plus the three counties which make up the traditional West Country, Somerset, Devon and Cornwall.

Wessex

Wessex is England at its gentlest, still remarkably rural, its market towns, which in other parts of the country are now reduced to dormitories, continuing to flourish. Bournemouth, its chief town, is often described as the 'Queen of Resorts', its climate and south-facing aspect in no small way contributing to its pre-eminence.

Traditional country pursuits survive, fishing in particular, the fame of the Itchen and Test extending worldwide.

Left: The little church in the middle of the very individual links at St Enodoc, with the Camel Estuary beyond. Above: Bradford-on-Avon, an architectural microcosm in golden stone.

Salisbury Plain is largely occupied by the military, but they have left plenty to be enjoyed, not least Stonehenge, Avebury and Silbury Hill, the great megalithic ceremonial sites. Salisbury itself is a wonderful cathedral city worthy of detailed study. Nowhere is the lasting wealth of the wool trade better understood than in Bradford-on-Avon, a glorious assembly of narrow streets twisting round buildings ranging from one of the most complete Anglo-Saxon churches in the country to fine Georgian houses, all built in that warmest of ochre stones.

Dorset is Hardy Country. The selected golf courses will serve as a perfect introduction to the unique quality of this special countryside and its precious wildlife habitat. Here in the 1830s, in the village of Tolpuddle, six labourers attempted to bargain for an increase in wages. They failed, and were transported to Australia. The public outcry at this was such that the men were pardoned, and the principle of collective bargaining established.

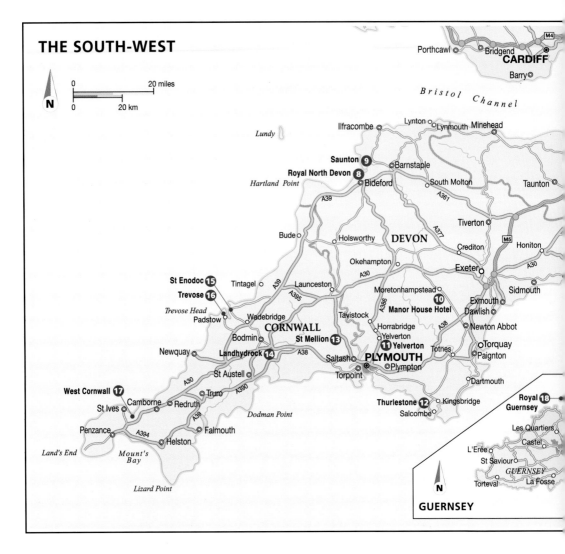

THE SOUTH-WEST

0   20 miles
N
0   20 km

Porthcawl ○   ○ Bridgend ○
CARDIFF
Barry ○

Bristol Channel

Lundy

Ilfracombe ○   Lynton ○ ○ Lynmouth Minehead ○

Saunton 9   ○ Barnstaple
Royal North Devon 8
Hartland Point   ○ Bideford   ○ South Molton   Taunton ○
A39

Bude ○   Holsworthy ○   **DEVON**   Tiverton ○
                                                        Crediton ○   Honiton ○ M5
Okehampton ○   Exeter ○
St Enodoc 15 Tintagel ○   Launceston ○   A30   Sidmouth ○
Trevose 16   Moretonhampstead ○
Trevose Head   Tavistock ○ **Manor House Hotel 10** Exmouth ○
Padstow ○ Wadebridge ○   Dawlish ○
          CORNWALL   Horrabridge ○   Newton Abbot ○
Bodmin ○ **St Mellion 13**   ○ Yelverton
Newquay ○ **Landhydrock 14** A38   **11** Yelverton Totnes ○ Torquay ○
          St Austell ○   Saltash ○ **PLYMOUTH**   Paignton ○
West Cornwall **17**   Torpoint ○ ○ Plympton   Dartmouth ○
          ○ Truro A390   **Royal 18**
St Ives ○ Camborne ○ Redruth ○   **Thurlestone 12** ○ Kingsbridge   **Guernsey**
Penzance ○   Dodman Point   Salcombe ○
          A394 ○ Helston   Les Quartiers ○
Land's End Mount's ○ Falmouth   Castel ○
          Bay   L'Erée ○
          Lizard Point   St Saviour ○
                                        Torteval ○ *GUERNSEY* ○
                                                        La Fosse
N
GUERNSEY

Somerset

Moving on to Somerset, Bath is one of the great cities of Europe, the Aquae Sulis of the Romans, wedded to 18th-century culture, the Royal Crescent hardly less imposing than the Roman baths. Ecclesiastically Bath is linked to Wells, a little town surrounding a great medieval cathedral and its remarkably well preserved precinct. An even greater monastic community once thrived at Glastonbury, of which very little survives. However, its legendary status is assured as it was a place of pilgrimage for the many who believed that there Joseph of Arimathea buried the very cup used at the Last Supper. A later cult grew up around the theory that King Arthur and Queen Guinevere were buried there. In the far west stands the wild upland of Exmoor, through which runs the Somerset–Devon border.

Devon

Devon's other great upland, Dartmoor, occupies a very significant part of the rest of the county. But much of Devon is still

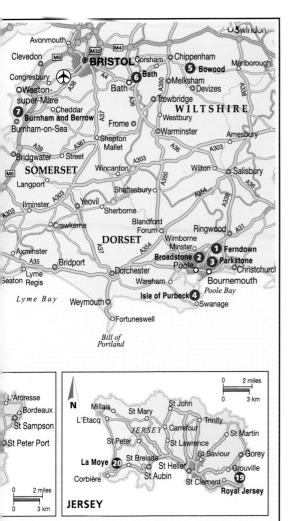

Cornwall

Cornwall is another world, some would say another country. It has its own Celtic culture, its own language, its own place names, even its own saints. A rugged county, its character is formed by its rocky landscape and the winds driving in from the Atlantic. Dolmens, stone-circles, and hill-forts rub shoulders with the vestiges of the industrial revolution. Tin and copper mining and china-clay extraction tested the ingenuity of its engineers, and one of them, Richard Trevithick, is credited by many with the invention of the first practical railway engine. Its main towns are largely unremarkable, the beauty of Cornwall being found in little hamlets or ancient churches sheltering in a valley, the creeks which wriggle their way, sometimes spectacularly, to the sea, the great sea cliffs and pounding waves, the sandy beaches and high-hedged lanes.

St Michael's Mount. A Benedictine monastery was founded on the island in 1044, though from the 12th century its potential as a fortress was recognized and in 1425 the monks were expelled.

that which Poet Laureate John Betjeman summed up: 'The steeply banked lane stuffed with fern and foxglove and honeysuckle, winds down through oaks which interlace their lichened branches to an old stone bridge over a stream which babbles against boulders . . . we will go back to the village for Devonshire tea, with strawberries and cream, where people will call us "my dear" and rustics will be waiting on the cobbles outside the village inn to drink cider at opening time.'

 *Ferndown*

Ferndown Golf Club, 119 Golf Links Road,
Ferndown, Dorset BH22 8BU (1923)
TEL: *(01202) 874602* **FAX:** *(01202) 873926*
LOCATION: *6 miles/10km north of Bournemouth, ½*
mile/0.8km south-east of Ferndown on West Parley road
COURSES: *Old: 18 holes, 6490yd/5934m, par 71,*
SSS 71; President's: 9 holes, 5604yd/5124m, par 70,
SSS 68
TYPE OF COURSE: *Wooded heathland*
DESIGNER: *Harold Hilton*
GREEN FEES: *££££*
FACILITIES: *Pro shop, buggy and club hire, clubhouse*
VISITORS: *Welcome with handicap certificate*

The 1989 Women's British Open Championship won by Jane Geddes reminded many of the golfing and scenic delights of this pine and heather course. The Alliss family are closely linked with its past, though it was the great Hoylake amateur, Harold Hilton, who laid it out.

For the visitor, Ferndown's great merit is that it gives all the challenges of heathland golf

The 6th at Ferndown, one of the strongest holes on the
course, the approach having to be made uphill over deep
bunkers to a sloping green.

without overfacing the shorter hitter. At all times of the year it is attractive and well presented. From the inviting downhill opening drive with its plentiful bunkers it is clear that accuracy will be more important than outright length. The 11th is a possible exception, a hole on which strong players might cut the corner to take out of play a cross-bunker short of the green. For guile there are few short par 4s to compete with the 16th, only 305yd/279m long, with a severely contoured green hidden behind bunkers and trees.

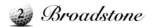 *Broadstone*

Broadstone Golf Club, Wentworth Drive, Broadstone,
BH18 8DQ (1898)
TEL *and* **FAX:** *(01202) 692595*
LOCATION: *4 miles/6.5km north of Poole, B3074 off*
A349
COURSE: *18 holes, 6315yd/5774m, par 70, SSS 70*
TYPE OF COURSE: *Hilly heathland*
DESIGNERS: *Tom Dunn, Harry Colt*
GREEN FEES: *££*
FACILITIES: *Pro shop, trolley and club hire, clubhouse*
VISITORS: *Welcome with handicap certificate*

When Tom Dunn was commissioned to construct Broadstone he was 'not stinted for men, money, or materials'. We have Lord Wimborne to thank for thus enabling us to enjoy the privilege of golfing in such a magnificent, if hilly, situation. Here, on this Site of Special Scientific Interest, all manner of rare flora and fauna surround us as we strive to get the better of an exacting course.

A ditch running the length of the 1st must be crossed twice, posing a challenge and threat for the big-hitter seeking an early birdie. The most demanding hole for the majority is likely to be the 7th, driving out over heather to a leaning fairway interrupted by heather. Depending on where the drive finishes there is still a full carry of about 200yd/183m across a vast gully to a green standing high above a

cross-bunker on the far side. There are superb views over Wimborne Minster and much of Dorset from the high ground of the 9th, but every hole is a picture. Henry Cotton chose Broadstone's 13th as his top 13th in the country. You can understand why as you try to carry your second shot from the plateau fairway to the green. Failure means disaster in the bunkers below. At the 355yd/325m 14th you can see all its problems from the elevated tee, especially a bunker at exactly the right length in the middle of the fairway, and cross-bunkers protecting the green.

 *Parkstone*

Parkstone Golf Club, 49a Links Road, Poole, Dorset BH14 9QS (1910)
TEL: *(01202) 707138* **FAX:** *(01202) 706027*
WEBSITE: *www.parkstongolfclub.co.uk*
LOCATION: *3 miles/5km west of Bournemouth, off A35 (St Osmund's Road)*
COURSE: *18 holes, 6263yd/5727m, par 72, SSS 70*
TYPE OF COURSE: *Heathland*
DESIGNERS: *Willie Park, James Braid*
GREEN FEES: *£££*
FACILITIES: *Pro shop, trolley and club hire, clubhouse*
VISITORS: *Welcome with handicap certificate*

No two holes are alike at Parkstone, giving admirable change of pace and character. The 3rd is a 490yd/448m par 5, beginning with this water carry.

The name 'R. Whitcombe, Parkstone' is inscribed below the claret jug which is the trophy for the Open Championship. Peter Alliss was professional from 1957 to 1970, the years of his finest playing achievements. Club members, male and female, also have a distinguished record in amateur golf. It is obvious why for, though Parkstone is not long, it demands that you shape every shot, there is great variety, and the condition of the course is a matter of pride.

Tony Lema, newly crowned Open Champion, eagled the short par-4 4th twice in one day! With a rolling fairway and a well-bunkered green overlooking a lake, the 5th is handsome and demanding. The sea views from the high ground of the 8th and 13th tees are notable. Strong players are rewarded on the 15th, a long par 4 driving past the Seven Sisters trees, and the par-5 17th, snaking round a heather-clad hillock, both holes requiring uphill approaches to small, naturally-defended greens.

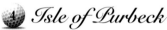 Isle of Purbeck

*Isle of Purbeck Golf Club, Studland, Swanage, Dorset
BH19 3AB (1892)*
TEL: *(01929) 450361* **FAX:** *(01929) 450501*
LOCATION: *Between Studland (ferry from Poole
Sandbanks) and Corfe Castle (road from Wareham)*
COURSES: *Purbeck: 18 holes, 6295yd/5756m, par
70, SSS 71; Dene: 9 holes, 2007yd/1835m, par 30,
SSS 30*
TYPE OF COURSE: *Heathland*
DESIGNER: *Harry Colt*
GREEN FEES: *££*
FACILITIES: *Pro shop, buggy and club hire, clubhouse*
VISITORS: *Welcome with handicap certificate*

Amongst the treasures of Isle of Purbeck is
a photograph of children's author Enid
Blyton and her surgeon husband, Mr Darrell-
Waters, putting outside the clubhouse. They
owned the club during the 1950s and 1960s,
and she was Ladies' Captain in 1952. It is still
family owned, and the Robinsons ensure that
it remains one of the happiest clubs for
members and visitors alike.

Even if it were not a golf course this would
be a place of great interest. The views from
this high ground north over Dorset and east

*The breathtaking view from Isle of Purbeck's 5th tee which
emphasises the challenge of finding the angled fairway beyond
a sea of gorse. Bunkers test the resolve and deter the greedy.*

over Poole Harbour and Bournemouth are
stunning. All around is an area of outstanding
heathland fascinating to the natural historian,
the rocks below crammed with fossilized
dinosaur remains. A Bronze Age burial site
4000 years old forms part of the 7th hole. In
the 12th century the Hundred, a local court,
met on what is now the 14th.

After the famous 5th, Agglestone, the par-5
6th is a tough hole with a leaning fairway
climbing a narrow path through thick gorse.
The other par 5, Thorny Barrow, the 8th, is
almost 600yd/550m long, providing ample
opportunity to take in the glorious scenery.
On the back nine the 11th, The Island, is a
fine short hole across heather with a monster
bunker below the green. It is followed by
Tumuli, an energetic par 4, which requires a
big drive to clear gorse and climb towards a
marker post on a hilly fairway if the distant
green is to be visible.

Bowood

*Bowood Golf and Country Club, Derry Hill, Calne,
Wiltshire SN11 9PQ (1992)*
TEL: *(01249) 822228* **FAX:** *(01249) 822218*
LOCATION: *3 miles/5km south-east of Chippenham on
A342, entry in Derry Hill village*
COURSE: *18 holes, 7317yd/6691m, par 72, SSS 74*
TYPE OF COURSE: *Parkland*
DESIGNER: *Dave Thomas*
GREEN FEES: *£££*
FACILITIES: *Pro shop, range, academy course, clubhouse,
conference facilities, luxury Queenwood Golf Lodge*
VISITORS: *Welcome*

Perhaps the most unaffected of England's newer courses, Bowood exhibits a grace and breeding entirely appropriate to the nobility of the Capability Brown landscape in which it is laid out. Its challenge, however, is anything but genteel, a demanding test, particularly from the back tees. Plentiful bunkers call for thought and accuracy, and the greens are cleverly protected.

Among many outstanding holes, the par-5 4th and 15th make considerable demands on shot placement. Of the par 4s, the 7th and 8th both start with wickedly tight drives, and the narrow approach to the 8th is not for the timid. The 12th, at 187yd/171m, is mischievous. It needs plenty of club to climb the hill and clear the stream in front of the green, but it is the last place you would want to face a downhill putt. In such fashion you are always made to think, but it is the privilege of playing in one of England's great country parks that makes Bowood incomparable.

Teeing off at Bowood's 15th, a short but far from easy par 5 swinging right, defended by a big tree in the middle of the fairway. The 11th fairway is visible in the background.

Bath

*Bath Golf Club, Sham Castle, North Road, Bath,
Somerset BA2 6JG (1880)*
TEL: *(01225) 463834* **FAX:** *(01225) 331027*
LOCATION: *1½ miles/2.5km east of Bath. Turn right
off A36 Warminster Road into North Road, then left
into Golf Course Road towards top of hill*
COURSE: *18 holes, 6442yd/5891m, par 71, SSS 71*
TYPE OF COURSE: *Downland*
DESIGNER: *Harry Colt*
GREEN FEES: *££*
FACILITIES: *Pro shop, trolley and club hire, clubhouse*
VISITORS: *Welcome with handicap certificate*

Bath Golf Club is doubly blessed, not only with its many golfing merits but also with entrancing views over the beautiful city of Bath, the Avon Valley, and the delightful surrounding countryside. Its downland turf gives a good playing surface all year round, and, despite its elevation, it is not tiring to walk.

A couple of short par 4s get the round under way agreeably, the downhill 300yd/274m 2nd potentially driveable if well placed cross-bunkers are avoided. Out-of-bounds constantly threatens on the strong 3rd and 5th, both having narrow, raised greens, the terraced fairway of the 3rd a legacy of a much older civilization. The back nine, on high ground, skirts ancient earthworks, and the pitch to the 16th is made over historic Wansdyke. A downhill approach is difficult to judge on the 469yd/429m par-4 13th, and the memorable short 14th is played across a quarry which once supplied stone for the city's buildings.

Burnham and Berrow

Burnham and Berrow Golf Club, St Christopher's
Way, Burnham-on-Sea, Somerset TA8 2PE (1890)
TEL: (01278) 785760 **FAX:** (01278)795440
WEBSITE: www.BurnhamandBerrowGC.2-golf.com
LOCATION: 1 mile/1.6km north of Burnham (M5 Jct
22), follow signs to golf
COURSES: 18 holes, 6759yd/6180m, par 71, SSS
73; 9 holes, 6120yd/5596m, par 70, SSS 69
TYPE OF COURSE: Links
DESIGNER: Unknown
GREEN FEES: £££
FACILITIES: Pro shop, caddies, trolley and club hire,
clubhouse, Dormy House
VISITORS: Welcome with handicap certificate or letter of
introduction

One of the most natural courses in the land, Burnham has played host to almost every significant championship in the amateur game, confirmation of its superb golfing qualities. No specific architect is credited with the original layout, and Burnham has evolved considerably since five-times Open Champion, J. H. Taylor, was professional and greenkeeper here. He readily acknowledged that the skills acquired playing to Burnham's diminutive greens contributed significantly to his achievements.

There is a sense of anticipation on the 1st tee, with an uphill drive into a narrow gap in the dunes. Like many holes at Burnham it needs no bunkers: fairway undulations, sandy hillocks, and many a deep hollow provide very adequate defence. A tight drive on the 2nd seeks the heaving fairway some distance away, the green long, but narrow, up on a plateau. After the fine short 5th, with any amount of trouble if you miss the table-top green, Burnham's character changes first with a drive over a pond on the 6th, and then with a ditch and marshes as company until the turn.

Driving blind over a hillock at the 10th the golf moves to the leeward of the dunes, the 11th very flat, and all the harder for it, distance and line notably tricky to gauge. Then it is back into the sandhills on the 12th with its fine approach across a gully to yet another bunkerless green. The finish from here is simply glorious, entirely appropriate for such a distinguished championship course.

The 12th green at Burnham and Berrow set engagingly beside Berrow Church. Like many greens here it is raised up significantly and angled, no easy target.

8 · *Royal North Devon*

*Royal North Devon Golf Club, Golf Links Road,
Westward Ho!, Bideford, Devon EX39 1HD (1864)*
TEL: *(01237) 473817* **FAX:** *(01237) 423456*
LOCATION: *2 miles/3km north of Bideford, through
Northam, signposted*
COURSE: *18 holes, 6653yd/6084m, par 72, SSS 72*
TYPE OF COURSE: *Links*
DESIGNERS: *Tom Morris, Herbert Fowler*
GREEN FEES: *££*
FACILITIES: *Pro shop, club hire, clubhouse, golf museum*
VISITORS: *Welcome with handicap certificate*

The pioneering spirit of early golf is easily recaptured at Westward Ho! where golf is played on common land shared with sheep and ponies, and many a dog and its owner. 'North Devon and West of England' was founded in 1864, making it the oldest links club in England. Here on this extraordinary wilderness the games of Horace Hutchinson and Michael Scott, two of the great amateur golfers, were nurtured, but even their achievements pale beside those of J. H. Taylor, once a caddie for Hutchinson, later five-times Open Champion. A visit to the club's excellent golf museum is recommended.

Royal North Devon's 4th hole features the Cape Bunker, one of the best known bunkers in golf. At 170yd/155m, it is still a significant carry for the average player.

Visitors might at first be bewildered by the flatness of the opening holes, though the 1st is bedevilled with ditches. A glance at the photograph of the 4th (above) is enough to illustrate how alarming this tee shot must have been with the clubs and balls of 1908. That was when Herbert Fowler 'modernized' old Tom Morris's original course. The 5th is a nice par 3 up over humps to a ledge-green, and the next few holes enjoy good undulating ground beside the sea.

Westward Ho! is famed for its sea rushes – tall, spiky clumps affecting play, particularly after the turn. You must carry them from the 10th tee, while the 11th fairway is totally surrounded by them. The 15th is a testing long par 4, especially in the wind, while the diminutive 16th is a rogue, its unreceptive green throwing weak shots into surrounding bunkers and depressions. Then it is home on the flat, but ditches must be carried to find these last two greens.

Saunton

*Saunton Golf Club, Saunton, nr Braunton, Devon
EX33 1LG (1897)*
TEL: *(01271) 812436* **FAX:** *(01271) 814241*
LOCATION: *6 miles/10km west of Barnstaple, on
B323 from Braunton*
COURSES: *East: 18 holes, 6729yd/6153m, par 71,
SSS 73; West: 18 holes, 6403yd/5855m, par 71,
SSS 72*
TYPE OF COURSE: *Links*
DESIGNERS: *Herbert Fowler (East), Frank Pennink
(West)*
GREEN FEES: *£££*
FACILITIES: *Pro shop, trolley, buggy and club hire,
clubhouse*
VISITORS: *Welcome with handicap certificate*

SAUNTON
EAST COURSE

HOLE	YD	M	PAR	HOLE	YD	M	PAR
1	478	437	4	10	337	308	4
2	476	435	5	11	362	331	4
3	402	368	4	12	414	379	4
4	441	403	4	13	145	133	3
5	122	112	3	14	455	416	4
6	370	338	4	15	478	437	5
7	428	391	4	16	434	397	4
8	380	348	4	17	207	189	3
9	392	358	4	18	408	373	4
OUT	3489	3190	36	IN	3240	2963	35

6729YD • 6153M • PAR 71

If ever it were decided to increase the number of courses on the Open Championship rota the East Course at Saunton would be one of those most seriously considered. In its West Course the club has a further 18 holes reckoned by many to be equally fine. Both run through the majestic sand hills of Braunton Burrows, a nature lover's paradise – over 300 varieties of wild flowers have been identified – owned by the Christie family, founders of Glyndebourne Opera.

the 3rd, the fairway again running down a valley before the approach is made over a bump to a green raised just sufficiently to repel all but the truest of shots. On the 4th only a well placed drive gives a sight of the flag through a gap in the dunes.

After four big holes the 5th comes as a surprise, a brilliant par 3 of negligible length and considerable mischief! The very sloping green is raised up, difficult to hold in a strong wind, and requires the most delicate of chipping touches if you miss. The next short hole does not appear until the 13th. Its name, Saddle, describes it perfectly, 'rejecting all imperfect

Saunton was founded in 1897, its original course redesigned by Herbert Fowler in 1919. Since then there have been remarkably few revisions to what is now the East Course. It begins with an inspiring shot from a high tee to a valley fairway bunkered at driving length where it bears right. Behind bunkers, the putting surface narrows between mounds towards the back. No bunker is necessary on

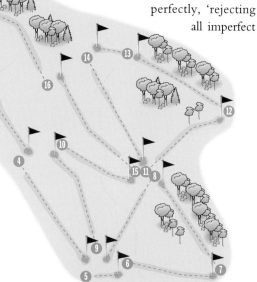

attempts to mount it like an angry horse' (Donald Steel). From here the finish is relentless, the 14th a lengthy two-shotter bunkered on the right of the drive, and the 15th involving a drive over the dunes to an angled fairway.

When Bernard Darwin selected his best 18 holes he chose Saunton's for his 16th. Its fairway curves all the time to the left, hugging the side of the sand hills. A ridge and mounds plus a bunker complicate the approach. The 17th plays into the prevailing wind, a substantial par 3. A handsome hole ends the round, curving right up a valley in the dunes, climbing to a green in an amphitheatre below the clubhouse.

In the 1930s a second course was built, but it did not survive the Second World War. Frank Pennink was commissioned to revive it in the 1970s and since then this West Course has been revised and upgraded until it now rivals the East Course. Its dunes are equally

Saunton's clubhouse and the 18th green of the East Course. J.H. Taylor described Saunton as 'the one golf links that has not been spoilt,' words which hold true to this day.

HERBERT FOWLER
(1856–1941)

William Herbert Fowler's earliest course design was stunning – Walton Heath (q.v.). Before the First World War he joined with Tom Simpson in a partnership which later included J.F. Abercromby and Arthur Croome as consultants. His courses are few but strikingly individual – no fewer than eight in this book alone – and it would be hard to define a Fowler trademark. Of his surviving American designs mention should be made of Del Monte, Lake Merced and Los Angeles CC in California, and the beautiful Eastward Ho! in Massachusetts.

imposing and, as with the East, there are holes in flatter country giving contrast. The 1st takes us straight into the sand hills, while the 7th is one of the best holes on either course, a sharp dog-leg governed by a ditch. A short hole finishes the round, played through a gap in the dunes from a high tee to a green protected by bunkers and the humps and bumps which are such a feature of Saunton.

Manor House Hotel's 1st, a very individual opening to a charming course, and an immediate introduction to the golfing threat posed by the River Bovey.

10   Manor House Hotel

The Manor House Hotel and Golf Course,
Moretonhampstead, Devon TQ13 8RE (1929)
TEL: (01647) 440998 **FAX:** (01647) 440961
E-MAIL: *manortee@aol.com*
LOCATION: *1 mile/1.6km west of Moretonhampstead on B2312 to Yelverton*
COURSE: *18 holes, 6016yd/5501m, par 69, SSS 69*
TYPE OF COURSE: *Parkland/moorland*
DESIGNER: *J. F. Abercromby*
GREEN FEES: *££*
FACILITIES: *Pro shop, full hotel facilities*
VISITORS: *Welcome with handicap certificate*

At the north-east gateway to wildest Dartmoor, the Manor House Hotel enjoys wonderful views onto the moors, though its golf course is far from wild. In fact it is pretty and gentle as it winds through the woods beside the River Bovey. Its crystal-clear waters come into play over the first eight holes. It complicates several drives, and you must pitch over it to find the 1st, 2nd,

and 5th greens. Many will try to play safe on the 293yd/268m 1st only to find their lay-up tee shot bounding down the hill to the left and into the stream. The 7th is demonic, with the river on the right, a ditch and wooded hillside on the left, and a devious little green almost an island in the river. On higher ground, the back nine is more open, the 11th a fine par 4 with a long carry over a gully to the green.

11   Yelverton

Yelverton Golf Club, Golf Links Road, Yelverton,
Devon PL20 6BN (1904)
TEL and **FAX:** *(01822) 852824*
LOCATION: *South of Yelverton on A386*
COURSE: *18 holes, 6351yd/5807m, par 71 SSS 72*
TYPE OF COURSE: *Moorland*
DESIGNER: *Herbert Fowler*
GREEN FEES: *£££*
FACILITIES: *Pro shop, clubhouse*
VISITORS: *Welcome with handicap certificate*

Moorland golf at its best is invigorating, and it does not come much better than at Yelverton. Close to Plymouth, the course is shared with Dartmoor ponies on one of those upland sites which makes you glad to be alive. It is one of the less constructed of Fowler's courses, but when every fairway is bordered by impenetrable gorse, who needs artificial hazards? However, man-made obstacles from earlier generations are utilized tellingly. The Devonport Leat of the 1790s forms a mostly waterless ditch crossing several fairways, and 19th-century tin workings have left many mischievous mounds and depressions around greens.

The 13th is the strongest hole, a long par 4 with a gully short of the green. Many of the shorter par 4s are full of character, such as the 15th with its drive over abundant gorse and pitch over yet more. The par 3s are engaging and individual.

12 *Thurlestone*

Thurlestone Golf Club, Thurlestone, Kingsbridge, Devon TQ7 3NZ (1897)
TEL *and* **FAX:** *(01548) 560405*
LOCATION: *At Thurlestone, 5 miles/8km west of Kingsbridge*
COURSE: *18 holes, 6340yd/5797m, par 71, SSS 70*
TYPE OF COURSE: *Downland/clifftop*
DESIGNER: *Harry Colt*
GREEN FEES: *££*
FACILITIES: *Pro shop, trolley and club hire, clubhouse*
VISITORS: *Welcome with handicap certificate*

Thurlestone's chief delights are the glorious seascapes from its clifftop holes. The 2nd climbs beside the beach to a hilltop green and the views remain utterly magnificent all the way from here to the 18th. But sights alone do not make a good golf course, so Thurlestone provides plenty of strategic challenges for players of all abilities.

The early holes occupy a headland with three excellent short holes in the first six. Of these, the 5th is tough, particularly into the wind, a 226yd/207 par 3 out towards the sea with bunkers and plunging cliffs should you slice. The contours of the land add to the natural defences of the shortish two-shot 4th and 7th, both instantly appealing. Then three long par 4s make considerable demands, the 8th, 9th and 10th all over 400yd/366m in length, before the 11th takes us to the far end of the course, and the end of the clifftop sequence. Big-hitters may be tempted to try to cut off the dog-leg on the right-angle 16th, and they will have an advantage over the close with four par 5s in the last seven holes. The 503yd/460m 18th is a fine finisher with out-of-bounds and bunkers threatening the drive and a well-protected green.

But Thurlestone also boasts one of the most remarkable opening holes in golf, an extraordinary downhill par 4 of only 268yd/245m. That you must drive out over a road and ditch, avoid out-of-bounds on either side, and could easily clatter into the clubhouse or car park is sufficient cause of anxiety for most of us. Deep seaside bunkers and a green angled across the line complete the defences.

Thurlestone 11th, a 365yd/334m par 4 played to a green guarded by three bunkers and, more significantly, the natural slopes of this clifftop site.

St Mellion

St Mellion Hotel Golf and Country Club, St Mellion, Saltash, Cornwall PL12 6SD (1976)
TEL: *(01579) 351351* **FAX:** *(01579)350116*
WEBSITE: *www.st-mellion.co.uk*
LOCATION: *10 miles/16km north-west of Plymouth on A388 Saltash–Launceston road*
COURSES: *Nicklaus: 18 holes, 7019yd/6418m, par 72, SSS 74; Old: 18 holes, 5782yd/5287m, par 68, SSS 68*
TYPE OF COURSE: *Wooded parkland*
DESIGNERS: *Jack Nicklaus (Nicklaus Course), J. Hamilton Stutt (Old Course)*
GREEN FEES: *£££*
FACILITIES: *Pro shop, caddies, buggy and club hire, range, full hotel and conference facilities*
VISITORS: *Welcome*

Opened in 1988, St Mellion has had time to mature into what Jack Nicklaus acknowledges to be one of his finest designs. Its playing qualities were not found wanting when examined by star-studded fields in the six Benson and Hedges Internationals held here in the 1990s, with José Maria Olazabal, Bernhard Langer and Seve Ballesteros among the winners.

A stringent test of driving, many of St Mellion's fairways are particularly narrow, the

The 11th at St Mellion – 'I knew it was going to be good, but not this good,' said architect Jack Nicklaus.

2nd typical with a stream down the left and a hillside out-of-bounds on the right, the persistent curve of the fairway adding to the pressures on accuracy. With a big drop into ruin on the right, the 3rd seems even tighter, the fairway a mere shelf on the hillside. A precision pitch must follow a 200yd/185m carry over a lake to a pocket-handkerchief fairway on the 5th. There is no let up on the 6th with a stream forming the right margin of the fairway, an out-of-bounds hill the left. With the green perilously close to the stream this is a very strong hole.

The back nine descends a different valley, though the problems are similar – the narrowest of fairways, wooded hillsides and another stream. It broadens into a pool on the 11th, a gorgeous downhill par 3 to a green on the far side. On the 12th, a handsome but treacherous par 5, the stream is a slicer's nightmare, eventually crossing just in front of the rolling green. In such dramatic country Nicklaus had little need of bunkers, employing refreshingly few.

OTHER COURSES TO VISIT IN THE SOUTH-WEST

Cornwall	St Austell	Woodbury Park	Weston-super-Mare
Bowood	Tehidy Park	**Dorset**	Yeovil
Bude & North	**Devon**	Bridport & West Dorset	**Wiltshire**
Cornwall	Bigbury	Came Down	Cumberwell Park
Cape Cornwall	Churston	East Dorset	High Post
Carlyon Bay	Dartmouth	Sherborne	Manor House (Castle
China Fleet	East Devon	**Somerset**	Coombe)
Falmouth	Ilfracombe	Clevedon	Marlborough
Looe	Staddon Heights	Minehead & West	North Wilts
Mullion	Tavistock	Somerset	Salisbury & South Wilts
Newquay	Teignmouth	Oake Manor	Tidworth Garrison
Perranporth	Warren	Orchardleigh	West Wilts

14 *Lanhydrock*

Lanhydrock Golf Club, Lostwithiel Road, Bodmin, Cornwall PL30 5AQ (1991)
TEL: *(01208) 73600* **FAX:** *(01208) 77325*
WEBSITE: *www.lanhydrock-golf.co.uk*
LOCATION: *1 mile/1.6km south of Bodmin off B3286*
COURSE: *18 holes, 6100yd/5578m, par 70, SSS 70*
TYPE OF COURSE: *Parkland*
DESIGNER: *J. Hamilton Stutt*
GREEN FEES: *££*
FACILITIES: *Pro shop, buggy and club hire, range, 19th Island Hole, clubhouse, conference facilities, lodge accommodation*
VISITORS: *Welcome with handicap certificate*

One of the most charming of Cornish courses, Lanhydrock is a mere infant, opened as recently as 1991, but such is the benevolence of the climate that it has already matured impressively. It is not long, nor does it dishearten the occasional golfer, yet it satisfies the good player with its calls on the brain. You have to think on every tee shot, the mark of a good design.

There are several short par 4s which might be driven by strong players, but they are appropriately tight. However, the longer par 4s, especially the 10th, do reward the big-hitter. A tree in the middle of the 12th must be negotiated as the fairway rises and curves to the left. Then it is uphill to a green amidst the gorse. It may only measure 392yd/358m, but it is quite a handful! The par 3s are all intriguing, the 6th a 187yd/171m 'signature hole' across a pond.

By making full use of the mature trees and gentle slopes, J. Hamilton Stutt has produced, in Lanhydrock, a course which is both pretty and rewarding.

15 St Enodoc

St Enodoc Golf Club, Rock, Wadebridge, Cornwall
PL27 6LB (1890)
TEL: *(01208) 863216* **FAX:** *(01208) 862976*
LOCATION: *Rock, 6 miles/10km north-west of*
Wadebridge, signposted
COURSES: *Church: 18 holes, 6243yd/5709m, par*
69, SSS 70; Holywell: 4103yd/3752m, par 63,
SSS 61
TYPE OF COURSE: *Links*
DESIGNER: *James Braid*
GREEN FEES: *£££*
FACILITIES: *Pro shop, trolley and club hire, clubhouse*
VISITORS: *Welcome with handicap certificate*

St Enodoc is like a religion, asking some awkward questions and demanding total commitment. But once you have discovered it you are a convert for life, and you accept willingly its paradoxes: romantic yet stern, a links yet highland, a short course yet long.

The romance is there in the little church of St Enodoc (see page 50), the resting place of Sir John Betjeman. You play round it in a loop from the 10th to 15th. Romance is there also in the delightful views over the Camel Estuary to the Atlantic beyond. It is stern on holes such as the 10th, its fairway narrow between a high grassy bank and treacherous marsh. You are advised to aim your second shot at the church door – divine guidance?

Before you on the 1st tee is spread that uniquely crumpled ground that is true linksland. It is a fine hole, the second shot blind over a ridge, the green elusive on its plateau. But there is mountaineering, too, the 14th climbing the narrowest of fairways above a steep drop.

At 6243yd/5709m St Enodoc is not long, yet so often we are at full stretch to reach the green in regulation, not only on the long par 4s such as the 2nd, 10th and 18th, but also when approaching greens such as the 3rd, beyond a stone wall with out-of-bounds dreadfully close. And then there is the pitch at the 6th, blind over the highest sandhill in English golf.

16 Trevose

Trevose Golf and Country Club, Constantine Bay,
Cornwall PL28 8JB (1924)
TEL: *(01841) 520208* **FAX:** *(01841) 521057*
LOCATION: *4 miles/6.5km west of Padstow (via*
B3276, follow signs)
COURSES: *Championship: 18 holes, 6608yd/6042m,*
par 71, SSS 72; New: 9 holes, 3031yd/2772m, par
35; Short: 9 holes, 1360yd/1244m, par 29
TYPE OF COURSE: *Links*
DESIGNER: *Harry Colt*
GREEN FEES: *££ to £££*
FACILITIES: *Pro shop, buggy and trolley hire, boutique,*
clubhouse, accommodation
VISITORS: *Welcome with handicap certificate*

Trevose is a country club in the nicest sense. It can accommodate 120 visitors in chalets, apartments and so on, without the affectation of some country clubs. The course is maintained to encourage the visitor, with broad fairways and mown rough, yet without

The celebrated 4th at Trevose. On a calm summer day it
offers a definite birdie chance, but when the wind is up
and the waves pound the shore it can be a brute.

discouraging the good player who will find it a solid test.

The 1st is a case in point, driving off invitingly downhill towards the Atlantic, but the better player must place the drive to open up the green through a gap in the sandhills. Typically, the short holes do not intimidate, yet they are far from easy, the 3rd across a valley to a ledge green in the dunes being particularly attractive. It is followed by the star hole, a short par 5 curving left past big sand hills to a green on the Ocean's edge, only a few feet above the breakers. In favourable conditions many will expect to reach the green in two, but the second shot is blind over a ridge and difficult to judge for distance.

Colt used few bunkers at Trevose. There are none on the 5th, a demanding two-shotter, slightly uphill, with a ridge cutting in from the left and an exposed, elevated green. The 7th is another fine par 4, needing a full second shot to carry uphill between bunkers to a stepped green. The finish is excellent, the 16th a tough par 3 over a deceptive ridge, the 17th with a pitch over a stream, and a long, uphill home hole.

17 West Cornwall

West Cornwall Golf Club, Church Lane, Lelant, St Ives, Cornwall TR26 3DZ (1889)
TEL *and* **FAX:** *(01736) 753401*
LOCATION: *2 miles/3km east of St Ives. A30 towards Penzance, A3074 towards St Ives, golf signposted*
COURSE: *18 holes, 5884yd/5380m, par 69, SSS 69*
TYPE OF COURSE: *Links*
DESIGNER: *Rev. F.F. Tyack*
GREEN FEES: *££*
FACILITIES: *Pro shop, club hire, clubhouse*
VISITORS: *Welcome with handicap certificate*

In Jim Barnes, winner of the US Open, USPGA, and Open Championship between 1916 and 1925, West Cornwall has a son of whom to be proud. The links he knew

Each hole at West Cornwall has great beauty, not least the 1st, a long par 3 aimed at the church with out-of-bounds awaiting the slice.

differed little from those of today, one of the most individual of our seaside courses. Its situation is superb, overlooking St Ives Bay, presided over by the church of St Uny. Fine links turf calls for crisp striking, and with heavily undulating fairways you must be prepared to adapt your game on every shot. The undulations also mean that you will have to play blind shots, the very essence of links golf but anathema to the golfing couch potato.

What the early holes may lack in length is more than made up in character, the 2nd, through the dunes, an absolute beauty, while on the 4th a faded drive will perish amongst the gravestones of St Uny's churchyard. Alongside the railway the 9th climbs to a hilltop green, its bunkers and steep slopes punishing the slice unmercifully. One of the most interesting holes is the 11th, involving an approach which must be made through mountainous sand hills. The par-5 16th may prove even harder.

The Jersey School

Golfers from Jersey, an island with a population well short of six figures, dominated the European game in the late 19th and early 20th centuries. In the field for the 1899 Open Championship, for instance, there were no fewer than seven Jersey players, three Vardons, Ted Ray, two Gaudins and a Renouf. Harry Vardon won that year, the third of his still unequalled six Open victories. Later he and Ray became the only British players until Tony Jacklin to win the US and British Opens. Tom Vardon never quite equalled Harry's achievements, but he represented England in an international match against Scotland alongside his brother in 1909.

Ray captained the England team which played (and thrashed) the Americans at Wentworth in 1926, the forerunner of the Ryder Cup. Ray was a member of that first Ryder Cup side the following year at Worcester, Massachusetts, along with four-times French Open champion, Aubrey Boomer, whose father had taught Vardon at Grouville School. For good measure, Herbert Jolly, another golfer from the Channel Islands, joined the team as a late replacement.

Between them, Phillippe Gaudin and T.G. Renouf represented England 11 times in international matches. Renouf, who spoke little or no English, left Jersey to become professional at the Manchester Golf Club, where he stayed for twenty years, during which time he built a reputation as an outstanding teacher, attracting Fred Astaire and his sister, Adele, to the club for tuition.

A Royal Jersey Golf Club history of 1930 summed up this remarkable situation: 'It is still among the marvels of the history of the game that one little village in the Channel Islands should have produced a group of players who have figured more prominently in championship golf than the professionals of the whole of England put together.'

18 Royal Guernsey

The Royal Guernsey Golf Club, L'Ancresse, Guernsey, Channel Islands GY3 5BY (1890)
TEL: *(01481) 47022* **FAX:** *(01481) 43960*
LOCATION: *North-east coast of Guernsey*
COURSE: *18 holes, 6215yd/5683m, par 70, SSS 70*
TYPE OF COURSE: *Links*
DESIGNERS: *Mackenzie Ross, F.W. Hawtree*
GREEN FEES: *£££*
FACILITIES: *Pro shop, club hire, clubhouse*
VISITORS: *Welcome weekdays with handicap certificate*

You are never very far from the sea here, little sheltered from the wind, and, with the natural undulations of the site supplemented by banks of gorse and heather, the golf is always scenic and entertaining. The original course probably predated the foundation of the club in 1890 – it became Royal a year later – but it was rebuilt several times, a totally new course having to be constructed after the Second World War.

As early as the 2nd hole you have to steer a straight course between the beach and a bank of gorse, a substantial par 4. The 5th gets high marks for its bunkering which gives access to the tricky green only if your drive is on the right line. Coming home your card is easily ruined on the 11th, its difficulties similar to those on the Road Hole at St Andrews. Ending the round, the 17th climbs the hill of Spion Kop before the par-3 18th drops you down to the clubhouse door in a single blow, but not before you have taken in the fine views over the island from the tee.

 ## *Royal Jersey*

*Royal Jersey Golf Club, Grouville, Jersey, Channel
Islands JE3 9BD (1878)*
TEL: *(01534) 854416* **FAX:** *(01534) 854684*
LOCATION: *Grouville Bay, Gorey*
COURSE: *18 holes, 6089yd/5568m, par 70, SSS 70*
TYPE OF COURSE: *Links*
DESIGNER: *Unknown*
GREEN FEES: *£££*
FACILITIES: *Pro shop, trolley and club hire, clubhouse*
VISITORS: *Welcome weekdays with handicap certificate,
restricted weekends*

*Royal Jersey's situation alone would make it worth
visiting, but the golf itself is no less fascinating.*

Founded in 1878, Royal Jersey was laid out
along the shores of Grouville Bay past the
cottage in which Harry Vardon had been
born eight years earlier. It is a magical site
little changed since Vardon's day, the eye
drawn to the commanding castle of Mont
Orgeuil on its rocky promontory. The first
drive is along the bay between the walls of
Fort Henry and the remains of wartime
concrete gun emplacements.

It is said that Vardon was particularly fond
of the short 2nd and many commentators
single out the par-5 3rd with its undulating
fairway and sunken green. None of the par 4s
is long, the 7th at 398yd/364m being the
longest. It is also a tricky hole, with plenty of
gorse and an elevated green. Like many greens
here, that on the 17th is raised up – standing
on what was in darker days a German bunker!

La Moye

*La Moye Golf Club, St Brelade, Jersey, Channel
Islands JE3 8GQ (1902)*
TEL: *(01534) 743401* **FAX:** *(01534) 747289*
LOCATION: *South-west of island*
COURSE: *18 holes, 6664yd/6094m, par 72, SSS 72*
TYPE OF COURSE: *Links*
DESIGNER: *James Braid*
GREEN FEES: *££££*
FACILITIES: *Pro shop, buggy and club hire, range,
clubhouse*
VISITORS: *Welcome with handicap certificate, restricted
weekends*

La Moye was founded in 1902 by George
Boomer who was a local schoolmaster
and father of the distinguished professionals
Percy and Aubrey. His chosen spot was one
of the most striking in British golf, on high
ground overlooking St Ouen's Bay and
Corbière lighthouse. More distant views
extend to Guernsey and some of the smaller
islands. Such splendid views come at a golfing
price, for when the wind is up there is
absolutely no shelter from it on such an
exposed site.

James Braid's layout has seen considerable
change over the years, not least to fit it for
the Jersey Open which was a regular event
in the European Tour calendar until
recently. New holes were constructed in the
heart of the dunes adding contrast to the
back nine. After an unusual 3–5–3 start the
course picks up with a series of holes up and
down to the beach, substantial par 4s and a
short par 5, while the 7th skirts a gorge
dropping to the sea.

REGIONAL DIRECTORY

Where to Stay

The climate in the South-West has ensured that it is well stocked with hotels and guest houses catering to every need, and these can be found in innumerable guide books and on the Internet. However, even in this company, several are notable for their exceptional qualities:

Wessex For the epitome of quiet town hotels, the **Priory Hotel** (01929 551666) at Wareham in Dorset is exemplary, and in Wiltshire why not take the luxurious Georgian manor house, **Queenwood**, situated between the 7th and 8th fairways of Bowood Golf and Country Club (01249 822228), fully staffed?

Somerset Try **Langley House Hotel** (01984 623318) at Wiveliscombe in the Brendon Hills, or **Ston Easton Park** (01761 241631) near Bath for the best in a country house hotel, or **Bindon Country House** (01823 400070) at Wellington to recreate the world of the Iron Duke.

Devon Off the Devon coast at Bigbury is **Burgh Island** (01548 810514) at which Agatha Christie stayed while writing several of her detective stories, now restored meticulously to its pre-war grandeur. Also in Devon, the **Horn of Plenty** (01822 852528) near Tavistock matches sumptuous accommodation with a long-famous kitchen.

Cornwall The **Tregildry Hotel** (01326 231378) near Helston attracts with its stunning views and imaginative cuisine. No less handsomely situated, the **Polurrian Hotel** (01326 240421) at Mullion is renowned for the attention to detail of its staff. On the Atlantic Coast, **Trebrea Lodge** (01840 770410) at Tintagel is a 600-year-old mansion with spectacular views.

Where to Eat

The West Country teems with good food, but one restaurant stands above all others in the ratings charts, **Gidleigh Park** (01647 432367) at Chagford, Devon, simply one of the top restaurants in the country. To enjoy one of the most distinguished wine lists of all, oenophiles should dine at **Harveys** (0117 927 5034) in the mediaeval cellars of this celebrated Bristol wine merchant. Open only in the summer months, the **White House** (01984 632777) at Williton in Somerset has a reputation for brilliant simplicity allied to a connoisseur's wine list, while **Summer Lodge** (01935 83424) at Evershot, Dorset, sets off its superb wines against traditional country house cooking. As for Padstow, it simply means Rick Stein, celebrity television chef and proprietor of several restaurants in the town, his **Seafood Restaurant** perhaps taking the honours (01841 532700).

What to See

Wessex Part of the charm of Wessex is that progress, in general, must be leisurely – often behind a haycart on a country lane. Its country towns, **Marlborough** and **Sherborne**, **Wareham** and **Devizes**, **Romsey** and **Dorchester**, retain their traditional purposes and their family businesses. The prime example is found at the Old Brewery in Mere where one of the best independent wine merchants in the country, **Yapp**, is based. On a sunny summer's day a picnic in the brewery courtyard, washed down with a bottle of the finest Rhône or Loire wine, the specialities of this distinguished firm, is idyllic. Do not attempt to drive afterwards! Book into The Talbot for the night.

Castle Combe is certainly a candidate for the title of England's prettiest village. Standing on an isolated hill, **Corfe Castle** is one of the most spectacular of ruined castles, surrounded by its attractive village. A few miles west are **Lulworth Cove** and **Durdle Door**, where the sea has carved its way into the vertical chalk cliffs dramatically. **Maiden Castle**, near Dorchester, is the finest surviving pre-Roman fortress in Britain.

Somerset **Cheddar Gorge** manages to retain some of its imposing majesty despite the invasions of hordes of tourists. Worthy of a detour are: **Chard**'s main street, possibly Roman in origin; **Cleeve Abbey**; the hamlet of **Cothelstone**; minuscule **Culbone Church**; **Dunster Castle**; cobbled Cheap Street in **Frome**; the interior of **Martock Church**; Elizabethan **Montacute House**; **Oare**, the Exmoor hamlet encapsulated in Lorna Doone; the ceiling of **Shepton Mallet** church; **Taunton**'s beautiful church spire; and the caves of **Wookey Hole**. The **Fleet Air Arm Museum** at Yeovilton presents a very different attraction.

Devon For many Devon starts at **Exeter**. Astonishingly its cathedral, described by Alec Clifton-Taylor as 'the Decorated cathedral par excellence', survived heavy bombing in 1942 when many of the city's other old buildings were destroyed. Devon is certainly a county in which its **parish churches**, great and small, should not be overlooked: **Ottery St Mary**, **Ashton**, **Branscombe**, **Coldridge**, **Crediton**, **Cullompton**, **Harberton**, **Honeychurch**, **Kenton**, **Parracombe**, **Tawstock**, **Torbryan**, **West Ogwell**, and **Widecombe-in-the-Moor** will do for starters.

With two long coasts, Devon ports, harbours, and fishing villages naturally proliferate. **Plymouth** became the principal base of the English navy in the 16th century at the time of the Spanish Armadas. Tradition has it that Drake insisted on finishing his game of bowls on the Hoe before setting out to repel the Spaniards. It is also a tradition that naval men soon acquire a particular enthusiasm for Plymouth gin, whose aromatic qualities differentiate it from the more usual London variety.

Other maritime delights are to be found in: the tiny streets leading down to the quay at **Appledore**; Queen Anne's Walk in **Barnstaple**; the merchants' houses of **Bideford**; the pretty fishing port of **Brixham**; traffic-free **Clovelly**; the Elizabethan house fronts of **Dartmouth** quay; the huge Victorian hotels and boarding houses of **Ilfracombe**; **Lynton** and **Lynmouth**, one by the sea, the other vertically above it; the anchorage at **Newton Ferrers**; the cottages of **Shaldon**; **South Pool**, between the wooded slopes and strands of Kingsbridge Estuary; and, last but not least, 'The Queen of Watering Places', **Torquay**, where the climate is reckoned to be the gentlest in the country.

Buckfast Abbey is one of the small number of Benedictine communities in England. **Dartington Hall**, an estate dating from the 9th century, is today home to the arts, hosting a summer school attracting very distinguished international musicians as soloists and coaches.

Cornwall Cornwall's principal towns are functional rather than attractive, though there is a charm to the sweep of Mount's Bay as it leads into Penzance past **St Michael's Mount** which began in the 11th century as an offshoot of Mont St Michel in Brittany, to which it bears a great similarity. Romantics will also go to **Tintagel**, indissolubly linked with Arthurian legend, a dramatic peninsula even for those with no interest in the legend. Nearby is **Boscastle**, one of those uniquely Cornish beauty-spots where streams from Bodmin Moor suddenly plunge through a wooded glen into the full force of the Atlantic, resulting in sensational spray.

The oldest identifiable English village street is at **Chysauster**, a village thriving from well before Roman times until about the 3rd century AD. **Fowey** was once one of the most important ports in England, in the 14th and 15th centuries its sailors amongst the most feared of all, their many raids on the coastal towns of Normandy and Brittany fabled. **Helford** is one of the few really pretty villages in Cornwall, while **Helston** is a place to visit on 8 May when the famous Furry Dance takes place – all day, if the constitution and liquor intake allow! At either end of Mount's Bay, **Land's End** is the western end of England, while **Lizard Point** is the southern equivalent, both on their cliff tops. Much of the coast boasts fine cliffs, the highest being Hennacliffe at **Morwenstow**. **Mevagissey** has been likened to a Greek fishing

Fishermen at Lulworth Cove, Dorset. Many of the traditional skills and crafts of England are still practised in the South-West.

village, **Port Isaac** less specifically to the Mediterranean in general. The beaches at **Newquay** are amongst the best in the country, and amongst the few off which surfing is possible. **Porthcurno** beach is equally renowned, though visitors here should not miss the amazing Greek theatre constructed out of the rocks 200 feet above the waves. The village of **Mousehole** attracts, as much by its name as its little harbour, while **Padstow** is one of the more attractive fishing ports, its Hobby Horse dance festival on May Day said to be the oldest dance festival in Europe. Overlooking the east coast of the Lizard Peninsula is **St Anthony in Meneage**, very sheltered, in an idyllic spot.

But there are equally beautiful inland spots, such as the **Coombe Valley** (also near Morwenstow) and **Luxulyan Valley** near St Blazey. The ruins of **Restormel Castle** near Lostwithiel date back to about 1100 AD. **St Cleer** is at the centre of a remarkable collection of ancient monuments amidst the ruins of abandoned mining hamlets. At luxuriant St Mawgan in Pydar is **Lanherne**, the Arundel family house in whose chapel hang both a Rubens and a Van Dyck. But you are never far from the sea, **St Endellion**'s little church the venue for a fine music festival, **St Enodoc** surrounded by the famous golf course. At **St Just-in-Roseland** the church is situated at the head of a tiny creek, and at Church Cove near **Gunwalloe** is a 15th-century church so close to the beach that it is frequently showered with ocean spray. **St Ives** attracts artists, **St Mawes** the elegant with its genteel shops and smart houses.

Chapter 3

Central England

We make two golfing excursions from London, first out into the Cotswolds and back, and then north up the M1 to the Midlands proper.

The Thames Valley

Effectively our first journey follows the Thames upstream, the expedition chronicled so amusingly by Jerome K. Jerome in *Three Men in a Boat*. The first major landmark encountered is Windsor Castle, one of the principal royal residences and the largest inhabited castle in the world. Across the river

from it is the most famous school in the world, Eton College, founded by King Henry VI in 1440. Beside the Thames the towns and villages are attractive, including Maidenhead, Cookham, Marlow, Pangbourne, Streatley, Dorchester, and Clifton Hampden. We are heading for

Left: The Belfry's 10th hole, a short par 4 which challenges the conceit of golfers. Above: Sir Christopher Wren's Tom Tower adorns the entrance to Christ Church, Oxford's largest college.

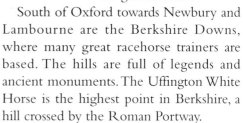

Oxford, the ancient University city, and gateway to the Cotswolds, the gentle uplands with some of the loveliest villages in England. Their houses are built in a golden ochre stone which seems to radiate a warmth even in the depths of winter. At Woodstock is the vast Blenheim Palace, the gift of a grateful nation to John Churchill, 1st Duke of Marlborough, who had halted Louis XIV with his victory at Blenheim in 1704. Sir Winston Churchill was born in a little room on the ground floor.

South of Oxford towards Newbury and Lambourne are the Berkshire Downs, where many great racehorse trainers are based. The hills are full of legends and ancient monuments. The Uffington White Horse is the highest point in Berkshire, a hill crossed by the Roman Portway.

The Midlands

The second leg of our journey takes us past another of the great stately homes of England, Woburn Abbey, residence of the

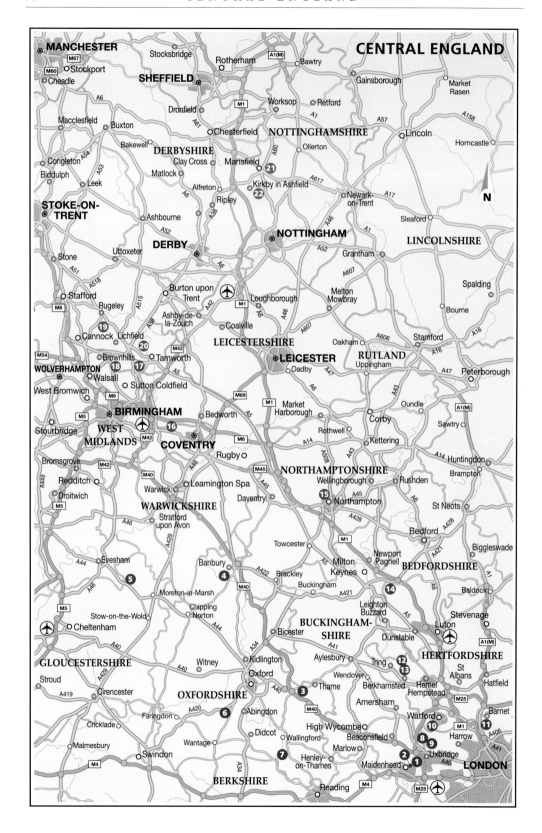

CENTRAL ENGLAND

Duke of Bedford. But in general there is little to detain us in Bedfordshire, nor in Northamptonshire, which once kept its gems quietly hidden away until the death of Princess Diana brought a sombre prominence to Althorp, the family seat of the Spencers. Stratford-upon-Avon and William Shakespeare are synonymous, the surrounding countryside both beautiful and historic.

The West Midlands remain heavily industrialized, retaining many of the traditional crafts which flourished during the Industrial Revolution: Redditch (needles), Bilston (enamels), Stourbridge (glass), Bromsgrove (nails). Birmingham expanded at an enormous rate during the 19th century, thriving on making everything from toys to guns, though its manufacturing base was well-established long before the industrial revolution – in the 1640s it had made over 16,000 swords for Cromwell's army. The decline in fortunes of Britain's car manufacturers in Coventry and Longbridge has seriously affected the economy of the region as a whole.

Unfortunately golf has not taken us west into Shropshire, despite the fact that

Warwick Castle, one of the great fortresses of Europe, stands proudly on the banks of the River Avon in the centre of one of England's finest county towns.

Ryder Cup stars Sandy Lyle, Ian Woosnam and Peter Baker were all born in the county. Quite simply it is one of the most beautiful parts of England.

In neighbouring Staffordshire is the city of Lichfield, the three spires of its red sandstone cathedral known as the Ladies of the Vale. Its most prized treasure is the 7th-century St Chad Gospels, and the glass in the Lady Chapel is some of the finest in England. Lichfield also has links with Dr Johnson and Charles Darwin. Nearby is the attractive upland country of Cannock Chase. It is but a short journey thence to Burton-upon-Trent, the brewing capital of England, where, permanently, the smell of beer hangs appetizingly in the air.

To Nottinghamshire there is a northern feel, partly the consequence of the mining which exploited its rich coal fields, leaving its scars in spoil tips and the back-to-back terraced housing of many of its towns. Its beauty is principally in its woodlands, the oaks and beeches which survive from the once magnificent Sherwood Forest, the legendary home of Robin Hood.

KEY TO MAP

1. Stoke Poges	12. Ashridge
2. Burnham Beeches	13. Berkhamsted
3. The Oxfordshire	14. Woburn
4. Tadmarton Heath	15. Northamptonshire
5. Broadway	16. Forest of Arden
6. Frilford Heath	17. The Belfry
7. Goring and Streatley	18. Little Aston
8. Denham	19. Beau Desert
9. Buckinghamshire	20. Whittington Heath
10. Moor Park	21. Sherwood Forest
11. South Herts	22. Notts

1 *Stoke Poges*

Stoke Poges Golf Club, Park Road, Stoke Poges, Bucks
SL2 4PG (1908)
TEL: *(01753) 717171* **FAX:** *(01753) 717181*
LOCATION: *M4 Jct 6 take A355 towards Beaconsfield,
turning right at Farnham Royal into Park Road*
COURSES: *18 holes, 6744yd/6167m, par 71, SSS
72; 9 holes, 3060yd/2798m, par 36*
TYPE OF COURSE: *Parkland*
DESIGNER: *Harry Colt*
GREEN FEES: *£££££*
FACILITIES: *Pro shop, caddies, buggies, clubs for hire,
clubhouse and hotel on site*
VISITORS: *Welcome*

Stoke Poges is inseparable from Thomas
Gray's much parodied Elegy. Fans of the
Bond film, *Goldfinger*, will recognize the
magnificent mansion, a study in white, built
by the grandson of William Penn. It has
always been a fashionable place to play, now
further enhanced with nine additional holes.

The charming par-3 3rd is played across a
valley, and soberly bunkered. It is said that the
7th was the model for the famous 12th at
Augusta National. Its angled green is broad,
but shallow, fronted by a stream, with

THE TRENT JONES FAMILY

By the time of his death at the age of 93, in June
2000, Robert Trent Jones had built 310 courses
and remodelled another 150, in 30 countries, one
of the most prolific and influential of all golf
course architects. On his courses there have been
played 20 US Opens, 12 USPGAs, and two
Ryder Cups. After collaborating with Bobby
Jones at Peachtree, Atlanta, in 1948 Jones quickly
established an innovative school of design, with
vast, tortuous greens, the abundant and strategic
use of water, and, above all, extensive use of
earth-moving. His two sons, Robert Junior and
Rees, have clearly inherited their father's
originality and talent.

---

bunkers set in the slope behind. The 9th is
stout for a two-shotter, the drive over a
stream and up a steep hill, and the green
threatened by an out-of-bounds on the right.
On the back nine one of the stars is the
superb 12th, a long par 4 played uphill
diagonally over a stream, cleverly bunkered
and alongside very elegant gardens.

2 *Burnham Beeches*

Burnham Beeches Golf Club, Green Lane, Burnham,
Slough, Bucks SL1 8EG (1891)
TEL: *(01628) 661150* **FAX:** *(01628) 668968*
LOCATION: *M4 Jct 7, between Slough West and
Beaconsfield, follow signs to Burnham Beeches*
COURSE: *18 holes. 6449yd/5897m, par 70, SSS 71*
TYPE OF COURSE: *Woodland/parkland*
DESIGNER: *Unknown*
GREEN FEES: *£££*
FACILITIES: *Pro shop, clubhouse*
VISITORS: *Welcome weekdays with letter of introduction
or handicap certificate*

'Welcome to our club. We hope you
enjoy golfing in this area of
outstanding natural beauty.' That description,
quoted from the course guide, encapsulates
the friendliness, challenge, and charm of the
club. Founded in 1891, Burnham Beeches
has welcomed ladies as members since the
start, and, perhaps in deference to them,
there are few severe carries from the tee.
However, there are six par 4s over
400yd/366m and a par 5 of 557yd/509m to
compensate.

As early as the 2nd the gauntlet is laid down
with a stern drive uphill to a sloping fairway.
The 5th introduces a characteristic chasm, full
of rough and trees, putting pressure on the
second shot, the green angled behind an
extensive bunker. The 446yd/408m 12th is
serious, and everyone remembers their first
encounter with the 14th, a fine par 4
demanding a well-positioned drive to open up
the green on the far side of an abyss.

 ## The Oxfordshire

The Oxfordshire Golf Club, Rycote Lane, Milton
Common, Thame, Oxon OX9 2PU (1993)
TEL: (01844) 278300 FAX: (01844) 278505
LOCATION: M40 Jct 7, take A329 towards Thame,
club on right
COURSE: 18 holes, 7187yd/6572m, par 72, SSS 74
TYPE OF COURSE: Meadowland with lakes and links-
like features
DESIGNER: Rees Jones
GREEN FEES: Not applicable
FACILITIES: Pro shop, range, clubhouse with extensive
restaurants, conference suites, Japanese bath etc
VISITORS: Members' guests only

The Benson and Hedges International is
the latest professional event to bring a
distinguished field to this young club, with
Stephen Ames, Bernhard Langer, Darren
Clarke and Colin Montgomerie winning the
first four tournaments. From the palatial
clubhouse there is a panoramic view of the
course, its lakes, and the moundwork which
is such a feature of Rees Jones's creation. The
mounds and pot bunkers hint at Birkdale,
though the 4th suggests one of those famous
American par 5s – such as the 17th at

*The essence of Rees Jones's creation at The Oxfordshire
is captured on the 17th – plentiful, deep pot bunkers,
strategically used water, and extravagant moundwork.*

Baltusrol – with a vast expanse of sand to be
cleared with the second shot. There is an
even larger desert to avoid when driving on
the tough par-4 12th, and something similar
on the 16th.

There are several compulsory water carries
on short holes and heroic ones elsewhere, such
as the 8th, with a lake on the right and the
green jutting out into it. From the back tees of
the 11th a big drive must carry a great deal of
water and it will be a factor all the way to the
green. The 17th is quite brilliant. You are
going to have to cross the water some time,
so, depending on the outcome of the drive,
you might prefer to play your second shot
over the lake to the left leaving a relatively
straightforward pitch to the green. Or,
ducking that particular challenge by playing a
simpler, drier second up the right, you must
then play a much harder approach over the
lake with absolutely no margin for error.

Tadmarton Heath's 13th, a long par 4 favouring those who drive close to an out-of-bounds.

Tadmarton Heath

Tadmarton Heath Golf Club, Wigginton, Banbury, Oxon OX15 5HL (1922)
TEL: (01608) 737278 **FAX:** (01608) 730548
LOCATION: South-west of Banbury, take A361 towards Chipping Norton, signposted to right after village of Bloxham
COURSE: 18 holes, 5917yd/5411m, par 69, SSS 69
TYPE OF COURSE: Heathland
DESIGNER: C.K. Hutchison
GREEN FEES: ££
FACILITIES: Pro shop, clubhouse
VISITORS: Welcome weekdays with handicap

Tadmarton is for connoisseurs of the traditional game. Not a long course, it is, however, high on quality. Excellent drainage gives perfect turf even in mid-winter. The greens are a joy, and vast expanses of gorse and broom penalize the wayward.

The old farmhouse which acts as a clubhouse sets a delightful tone and forms an unusual backdrop to the short 7th, an admirable par 3 across a deep gully containing a holy spring. The finish, through the gorse, is full of personality, only a long and straight drive on the 14th opening up the green,

hiding in the gorse. The 15th, a par 4 of merely 288yd/263m, is appropriately narrow. Gorse must be cleared from the tee on the short 16th, while it is close on both sides of the 17th. The closing hole is, again, typical, demanding a big drive on the correct line to give a sight of the green.

Broadway

Broadway Golf Club, Willersey Hill, Broadway, Worcestershire WR12 7LG (1895)
TEL: (01386) 853683 **FAX:** (01386) 858643
LOCATION: 1 mile/1.6km east of Broadway, take A44 towards Moreton-in-Marsh, golf club signposted on left part way up Fish Hill
COURSE: 18 holes, 6228yd/5695m, par 72, SSS 70
TYPE OF COURSE: Hilltop
DESIGNER: Mr Hobley of Cheltenham, Alister Mackenzie, Tom Simpson, James Braid, members
GREEN FEES: £££
FACILITIES: Pro shop, clubhouse
VISITORS: Welcome with handicap certificate, not Saturdays

On a clear day you can see 78 miles/125km from side to side from this majestically sited course perched at 900ft/274m on the very edge of the Cotswolds. The air is fresh, the turf crisp, and it has been described as the driest course in England. As the course manager was National Greenkeeper of the Year in 1996 the grooming is impeccable all year round.

The wind is seldom absent from such exposed ground and the 177yd/162m 5th may require a full driver one day and a wedge the next. Dropping steeply from tee to green (with superb views), any directional error is magnified. It has been said that the 370yd/338m 6th is the best test of golf in Gloucestershire (sic), with big undulations affecting play considerably. Not all the hazards are natural, however, as demonstrated by the stone wall and quarry awaiting a pulled shot on the 13th.

6 Frilford Heath

Frilford Heath Golf Club, Frilford Heath, Abingdon, Oxon OX13 5NW (1908)
TEL: *(01865) 390864* **FAX:** *(01865) 390823*
E-MAIL: *reservations@frilfordheath.co.uk*
LOCATION: *South-west of Oxford on A338 Oxford–Wantage road*
COURSES: *Red: 18 holes, 6884yd/6295m, par 73, SSS 73; Blue: 18 holes, 6728yd/6152m, par 72, SSS 72; Green: 18 holes, 6006yd/5492m. par 69, SSS 69*
TYPE OF COURSE: *Mostly heathland with water holes on Blue Course*
DESIGNERS: *J.H. Taylor (Red), J.H. Turner and C.K Cotton (Green), Simon Gidman (Blue)*
GREEN FEES: *££££*
FACILITIES: *Pro shop, caddies, trolley, buggy and club hire, clubhouse*
VISITORS: *Welcome with handicap certificate*

Few British clubs offer almost 20,000yd/18,288m of golf, and it is admirable that all three courses begin and end close to the clubhouse. Frilford's quality was recognized when it hosted the 1987 English Amateur and 1999 Seniors' Amateur Championships.

The Green is the shortest course, but there are tough challenges, such as the long par-4 7th and the demanding 14th to 16th,

Frilford Heath's Green Course ends with a short, but subtle, par 4 to this narrow green.

stretching almost 1300yd/1189m between them. The longer Red, similarly heathland in character, includes a fine sequence of strong holes from the 5th to 8th, and the 15th is a tough proposition when played into the wind. On the Blue Course there is much more emphasis on water, the first three holes being typical, the 3rd a classic water hole with a big pond on the left of this dangerous par 3. Unusually, the par 5s rate highly on the Stroke Index, an indication of their challenge.

7 Goring and Streatley

Goring and Streatley Golf Club, Rectory Road, Streatley-on-Thames, Berks RG8 9QA (1895)
TEL: *(01491) 872688* **FAX:** *(01491) 875224*
LOCATION: *Off A417 Reading–Wantage road, follow signs at Streatley*
COURSE: *18 holes, 6320yd/5779m, par 71, SSS 70*
TYPE OF COURSE: *Hilly downland*
DESIGNER: *Tom Dunn*
GREEN FEES: *££*
FACILITIES: *Pro shop, clubhouse*
VISITORS: *Welcome on weekdays*

Given the location in an affluent part of the Thames Valley the green fee is exceptionally good value, giving access to an airy downland course with splendid views and lovely fairway turf. The opening and closing holes are on low ground. Coming down from the heights is fun, the par-5 17th tumbling and twisting down the hillside. Going up is rather harder work, the climb from the 2nd to the 4th not to be rushed!

On top of the downs the golf is glorious, perhaps the pick being the very strong par-4 7th, 455yd/416m, uphill, ending in a green to be neither overshot nor missed on the left. The parallel 8th is handsome, with a big slope to be taken into consideration on the drive. The expansive views from the 10th may distract, another hole on which the drive must be held up against the slope.

After a drive to a steeply sloping fairway, the pitch to Denham's 11th is made downhill to a well-bunkered green.

8   *Denham*

Denham Golf Club, Tilehouse Lane, Denham, Bucks UB9 5DE (1910)
TEL: *(01895) 832022* **FAX:** *(01895) 835340*
LOCATION: *Just off M40 Jct 1, take A412 towards Watford, second turn left*
COURSE: *18 holes, 6456yd/5903m, par 70, SSS 71*
TYPE OF COURSE: *Parkland*
DESIGNER: *Harry Colt*
GREEN FEES: *£££*
FACILITIES: *Pro shop, clubhouse*
VISITORS: *Welcome Monday to Thursday with handicap certificate*

One of a tiny number of clubs having its own railway station, Denham is close enough to London to lie within the M25 yet retain a very rural feel. This Colt design 'teases rather than torments, but it cannot be overrun' (in the words of Donald Steel, distinguished golf architect and course record holder). For visual beauty the plunging 11th and woodland 12th take the honours, along with the clubhouse, a gem. Of the golfing challenges, the 456yd/417m length of the 9th, the bunkering of the 4th and 7th, and the heathland exposure of the par 5s will examine the best. It is on the shorter par 4s that Denham teases, the 2nd with a sunken hollow, the sloping fairway of the 6th, the

15th green protected by a gully, and the 17th curving through trees. And there is also the possibility of slicing onto an airfield at the 3rd.

9   *The Buckinghamshire*

The Buckinghamshire Golf Club, Denham Court, Denham Court Drive, Denham, Bucks UB9 5BG (1992)
TEL: *(01895) 835777* **FAX:** *(01895) 835210*
LOCATION: *M40 Jct 1, on A40 roundabout turn into Denham Court Drive (signposted)*
COURSE: *18 holes, 6880yd/6291m, par 72, SSS 73*
TYPE OF COURSE: *Parkland*
DESIGNER: *John Jacobs*
GREEN FEES: *£££££*
FACILITIES: *Pro shop, range, caddies, trolley and club hire, clubhouse with extensive dining and conference facilities and Japanese bath*
VISITORS: *Welcome with handicap certificate or letter of introduction*

Those who despair of the artificial nature of some contemporary course design should visit The Buckinghamshire to study the sensitive manner in which John Jacobs has used the landscape presented to him. The dignity of his layout complements the nobility of Denham Court, the Grade 1 listed mansion serving as an elegant clubhouse.

The 6th at The Buckinghamshire, a modern course which manages not to feel out of place in venerable surroundings.

The early holes are comparatively benign, the 6th green charmingly set off by the church gates. Good course management is required on the 7th with two water crossings, while the 8th is a jewel, the green beckoning on the far side of a lake. There is greater length on the back nine with several very strong par 4s, the greens of the 10th and 12th both closely guarded by water. The excellent 448yd/410km 13th is in traditional style, a woodside dog-leg on which there are no marks for excessive greed. Water only makes a reappearance beside the final green.

10 *Moor Park*

Moor Park Golf Club, Rickmansworth, Herts WD3 1QN (1923)
TEL: *(01923) 773146* **FAX:** *(01923) 777109*
LOCATION: *1 mile/1.6km south-east of Rickmansworth off Batchworth roundabout (A4145)*
COURSES: *High: 6713yd/6138m, par 72, SSS 72; West: 5823yd/5325m, par 69, SSS 68*
TYPE OF COURSE: *Parkland*
DESIGNER: *Harry Colt*
GREEN FEES: *££££*
FACILITIES: *Pro shop, caddies, buggies, trolleys, clubs for hire, clubhouse*
VISITORS: *Welcome weekdays with handicap certificate*

Moor Park's 8th green (West), overlooking the mansion in which James, Duke of Monmouth, lived only briefly, being executed after leading a rebellion against James II.

This is noble golf, befitting the grandest clubhouse in England, built as a mansion for the Duke of Monmouth in the 17th century. Moor Park has hosted many professional tournaments for men and women, plus top amateur events, though not all played over Colt's High Course, such is the challenge of the West.

From the opening drive, the fairway climbing through bunkers and trees, the nature of the task on the High Course is clear. The 2nd drive is demanding, across low ground and bunkers to find the fairway swinging right, the views expansive. None of the par 3s is easy, all necessitating full carries, the 12th a prime example. Of the longer par 4s the 8th is a beauty, and the 14th demands a big drive over, or around, trees on the left to give a sight of the green up a hill beyond a ditch, on two levels split left and right. Unusually, the round ends with a par 3, an excellent hole to a well defended green.

11 South Herts

South Herts Golf Club, Links Drive, Totteridge,
London N20 8QU (1899)
TEL: *(020) 8445 0117* **FAX:** *(020) 8445 7569*
LOCATION: *Totteridge Lane, right off A1 northbound
at Mill Hill*
COURSE: *18 holes, 6432yd/5881m, par 72, SSS 71*
TYPE OF COURSE: *Parkland*
DESIGNERS: *Willie Park Jnr, Harry Vardon*
GREEN FEES: *££*
FACILITIES: *Pro shop, clubhouse, 9-hole short course*
VISITORS: *Welcome weekdays with letter of introduction
or handicap certificate*

As there are a great many courses worthy
of a day's visit in the London suburbs,
what makes South Herts stand out? It has
imperishable links with Harry Vardon and Dai
Rees who between them served the club as
professionals for over 70 years. Willie Park Jnr
laid out the original course but Vardon made
numerous alterations over the years. The
current course is largely his design, though he
did not live to see it completed.

The ground undulates sufficiently to give no
level holes. Accurate driving is imperative as
the greens are well protected, most having
narrow entrances,
several with cross-
bunkers to clear,
and many sloping
significantly from
back to front. Try
not to leave yourself
a downhill putt!
The strongest holes
are two long par 4s,
the 7th and 11th,
but the hole with
most character is
the 16th, a cunning
dog-leg with big
slopes and a secret-
ive green beside
Dollis Brook.

12 Ashridge

Ashridge Golf Club, Little Gaddesden, Berkhamsted,
Herts HP4 1LY (1932)
TEL: *(01442) 842244* **FAX:** *(01442) 843770*
LOCATION: *North of Berkhamsted, take A41 towards
Aylesbury, turn right onto B4506. Golf club about 1
mile/1.6km on right*
COURSE: *18 holes, 6547yd/5987m, par 72, SSS 71*
TYPE OF COURSE: *Parkland*
DESIGNERS: *C.K. Hutchison, Sir Guy Campbell,
S.V. Hotchkin, Tom Simpson*
GREEN FEES: *£££*
FACILITIES: *Pro shop, trolley and club hire, clubhouse*
VISITORS: *Weekdays only with handicap certificate*

Ashridge is about the art of deception and
subtle understatement. Four distinguished architects have been involved in the
design and each has laid his hand on only
lightly. So, as you play to the green on the
par-5 5th it seems that all you must do is clear
a diagonal line of bunkers. In fact they conceal
much dead ground and an all-gathering
depression. It is much the same on the short
hole which follows. Only as you approach the
green do you become aware of a vast pit front
left, a large bunker on the right, and trouble
through the back should you over-club. The
celebrated 9th was
named after Henry
Cotton who was
professional here
and devised a
method of driving
the green. It looks
straightforward
enough, downhill,
but from close
range the pitch to
this green is far
from simple. The
problems posed by
the 14th are similar
to those of the
Road Hole at St
Andrews.

*The pond on Ashridge's charming, short 16th should not
normally come into play, the main defences being two
perfectly sited bunkers and the prominent tree.*

13 *Berkhamsted*

Berkhamsted Golf Club, The Common, Berkhamsted, Herts HP4 2QB (1890)
TEL: *(01442) 865832* **FAX:** *(01442) 863730*
LOCATION: *North-east of Berkhamsted. From A41 in town centre take road to Nettlesden and Frithsden, turning left towards Little Gaddesden and Ashridge. Clubhouse on left*
COURSE: *18 holes, 6605yd/6040m, par 71, SSS 72*
TYPE OF COURSE: *Bunkerless heathland with abundant natural hazards*
DESIGNERS: *Harry Colt, James Braid*
GREEN FEES: *££*
FACILITIES: *Pro shop, club hire, clubhouse*
VISITORS: *Welcome weekdays with handicap certificate, weekends restricted*

The Berkhamsted Trophy is one of the high spots of the amateur golf year. You might wonder why, looking at the card, full of shortish par 4s. Nor are there sand bunkers. Yet, as the distinguished amateur and Walker Cup Captain, Peter McEvoy, said, 'I can assure you that it is very difficult. I still cannot put my finger on why . . .' That is Berkhamsted's attraction.

This heathland period piece with its Chiltern chalk and excellent turf is utterly unique. One of the recurring hazards is the

Berkhamsted's opening hole. Typical mounds and serious rough provide a good test on this course despite the total absence of sand bunkers.

ancient earthwork, Grim's Dyke, a combination of 6ft/2m bank covered in heather and 3ft/1m trench, often stony, and it enters play as early as the 1st hole, a short par 4 with the green just beyond this uncompromising obstacle. Mounds of this kind constrict many drives and not a few approach shots, not least on the 568yd/519m 11th, the green again lurking behind a rampart

BUNKERLESS GOLF

Berkhamsted, Royal Ashdown Forest and Piltdown are the best known British courses without a single bunker, and there are many great bunkerless holes amongst the courses in this book, such as the Royal Liverpool 1st, Royal St George's 3rd, Rye 4th, Royal Worlington 5th, St Mellion 12th, and Wentworth 17th. Uniquely amongst Open Championship venues, the Old Course at St Andrews opens and closes with bunkerless holes, making up for this elsewhere!

 Woburn

The Woburn Golf and Country Club, Bow Brickhill,
Milton Keynes, Bucks MK17 9LJ (1976)
TEL: (01908) 370756 **FAX:** (01908) 378436
LOCATION: M1 Jct 13 or 14, situated between A5 and
A5130
COURSES: Duke's: 18 holes, 6973yd/6376m, par 72,
SSS 74; Duchess: 18 holes, 6651yd/6082m, par 72, SSS
72; Marquess: 18 holes, 6744yd/6167m, par 72, SSS 74
TYPE OF COURSE: Forest
DESIGNERS: Charles Lawrie; Peter Alliss, Clive Clark,
Ross McMurray, Neil Coles, Alex Hay (Marquess)
GREEN FEES: ££££ (depends on time of year,
number of visitors and availability)
FACILITIES: Pro shop, buggy and club hire, clubhouse
VISITORS: Welcome midweek with handicap certificate
subject to availability

In its first quarter-century Woburn has
established an enviable reputation. As the
home of the British Masters it has a prominent
status in world golf with winners such as Greg
Norman, Lee Trevino, Seve Ballesteros, and
Nick Faldo. The fifth major of women's golf
has also been held here, the Women's British
Open. It is unquestionably one of the
handsomest woodland courses in England,
designed by Charles Lawrie in the Woburn
estate of the Duke of Bedford.

*The pretty 4th on the Duke's Course becomes even
narrower as the green is approached.*

Out-of-bounds is a serious threat throughout
the par-5 1st. The 2nd, curving downhill
through the trees, is very attractive, and the
plunging short 3rd is much photographed. No
less handsome are the dog-leg 4th, climbing
through the trees to a narrow, stepped green,
and the long 5th, with its grassy valley to
chastise the overambitious. The next par 3, the
6th, is the longest, all carry across a ravine.
From the 7th – with its green high above a
Norman church – play swings back and forth
on gentler ground, no two consecutive holes
running in the same direction until the end.

With much greater length, the back nine
applies the pressure, especially the 13th with
its long approach across a gully. There is
considerable length to the par-5 14th, and the
15th, 16th and 17th are all well over
400yd/366m. The 18th is nominally a drive
and pitch, but it is tight for those who insist
on taking a wood from the tee.

The new Marquess Course has already been
assigned future European Tour events.

15 Northamptonshire County

Northamptonshire County Golf Club, Sandy Lane, Church Brampton, Northampton NN6 8AZ (1909)
TEL *and* FAX: *(01604) 843025*
LOCATION: *South side of Church Brampton between A428 and A50 north-west of Northampton*
COURSE: *18 holes, 6461yd/5908m, par 70, SSS 71*
TYPE OF COURSE: *Parkland*
DESIGNER: *Harry Colt*
GREEN FEES: *££££*
FACILITIES: *Pro shop, clubhouse*
VISITORS: *Welcome with handicap certificate*

To represent a traditional British rural golf club for insertion in a time capsule, say, Northamptonshire County would do very well. In the 90 years since Colt's layout at Church Brampton opened very few changes have had to be made, yet it still satisfies the top player without overpowering the less gifted. It is pretty, always in lovely condition, and has a pleasing variety of holes, some quite tough, others more forgiving. There is a touch of nobility, too, having had the Duke of York as captain in 1932 and later – as King George VI – as patron.

A short par 4, the 4th involves a compulsory carry over intimidating bushes from

The 12th at Forest of Arden, a mid-length par 5 to an angled green behind a pond.

an elevated tee. The hardest holes are the lengthy par-4 5th and 16th, but the 378yd/346m 7th is also a beauty, cleverly bunkered and hardly altered from Colt's original. The short 15th is a visual delight.

16 Forest of Arden

Marriott Forest of Arden Hotel and Country Club, Maxstoke Lane, Meriden, Coventry, Warwickshire CV7 7HR (1970)
TEL: *(01676) 522335* FAX: *(01676) 523711*
LOCATION: *M42 Jct 6, A45 towards Coventry, about 1 mile/1.6km turn left (signposted) into Shepherds Lane. Golf Club on left*
COURSES: *Arden: 18 holes, 7173yd/6559m, par 72, SSS 73; Aylesford: 18 holes, 6525yd/5966m, par 72, SSS 71*
TYPE OF COURSE: *Parkland with lakes and bracken*
DESIGNER: *Donald Steel*
GREEN FEES: *£££££*
FACILITIES: *Pro shop, caddies, buggy and club hire, driving range, full hotel and leisure facilities*
VISITORS: *Welcome*

Packington Hall, with historic royal links, is one of the most remarkable Italianate houses in England. Capability Brown laid out the grounds, and it is in this magnificent setting that golf is now played, shared with pheasant, geese, swans, duck and deer. The European Tour came six times during the 1990s, playing over the Arden Course, with Ian Woosnam and Colin Montgomerie (twice) among the winners.

The first nine are on flattish ground beside (sometimes over) the famous Packington trout lakes, the climax being the 9th, with a substantial water carry to a fairway narrowing between trees. The back nine roams the deer park. The 12th and 17th sweep downhill in parallel to greens raised behind a pond, but the perfect foil for greed is the clever 16th, almost a right-angle dog-leg, trees blocking many drives. Drive conservatively and the approach is then much longer and must carry a pond.

17 The Belfry

*The Belfry, Wishaw, North Warwickshire B76 9PR
(1977)*
TEL: *(01675) 470033* **FAX:** *(01675) 470256*
WEBSITE: *www.thebelfry.com*
LOCATION: *2 miles/3km north of M42 Jct 9 on
A446, well signposted*
COURSES: *Brabazon: 18 holes, 7118yd/6509m, par
72, SSS 74; PGA National: 18 holes,
7053yd/6449m, par 72, SSS 74; Derby: 18 holes,
6009yd/5495m, par 69, SSS 69*
TYPE OF COURSE: *Parkland*
DESIGNERS: *Peter Alliss and Dave Thomas (Brabazon
and Derby), Dave Thomas (PGA National)*
GREEN FEES: *£££££*
FACILITIES: *Complete hotel, business, golf and leisure
facilities*
VISITORS: *Welcome with handicap certificate*

This was the place where European golf came of age, the 1985 Ryder Cup matches the touchstone, when European players proved that they could beat the best in the world. The Ryder Cup returned in 1989 and 1993 – a tied match, and an American win. Several very distinguished courses have staged this event twice. Nothing can compare with The Belfry hosting a fourth Ryder Cup in 2001.

Since 1993 over 120 changes have been made, to increase the playing challenge and improve spectator facilities. The first new hole is the par-5 3rd, on which big drivers have to run the gauntlet of fairway bunkers. Then it is a nail-biting second, all carry across a pond and bunker, to find the angled and elevated green. Water affects almost every hole.

The 10th is already a classic, rare in a hole so young. For most it is a drive and pitch to a green in the trees beyond a stream. It took Seve Ballesteros to prove that it could be driven. It is so hazardous that, at first, the Americans were forbidden even to try!

The 18th is so simple in philosophy: cross the first stretch of water as comfortably as you can to leave a reasonable second across a further stretch of the same water, uphill to boot. Under the pressure of Ryder Cup competition golfers from both sides have handed in the towel here. It is that sort of hole, and wonderful for spectators with its natural terrace immediately behind.

The revised 3rd hole on The Belfry's Brabazon Course, once a dull par 4, now an attractive par 5.

18 *Little Aston*

Little Aston Golf Club, Streetly, Sutton Coldfield, Staffs B74 3AN (1908)
TEL: *(0121) 3532066* **FAX:** *(0121) 3532942*
LOCATION: *North of Sutton Coldfield off A454*
COURSE: *18 holes, 6670yd/6099m, par 72, SSS 73*
TYPE OF COURSE: *Parkland*
DESIGNER: *Harry Vardon*
GREEN FEES: *£££££*
FACILITIES: *Pro shop, clubhouse*
VISITORS: *Welcome by prior arrangement weekdays with handicap certificate*

The Brabazon Trophy, English Amateur, many other national championships and a smattering of professional tournaments attest to Little Aston's distinctive challenge and pedigree. Laid out on quick-draining sand and gravel in the grounds of Little Aston Park, the fairway turf, all year round, is fine and close-cut, yet resilient. The bunkers, over 100 in number, encompass just about every shape imaginable. They are serious affairs, some as tall as a man, and an object lesson in design and placing.

Many par 4s here are not overlong, eight being under 400yd/366m. How many other

At Little Aston the parallel 1st and 17th holes are both inviting, downhill, mid-length par 4s ending in neighbouring greens overlooking the lake.

golf courses of the first rank award Stroke Index 1 to a hole little more than 300yd/274m long? The 4th is just this, a scamp of a hole with a great wall of sand to be cleared 190yd/174m out and then a pitch down to a green attended by four further bunkers.

On the 10th, a stern hole, the drive must flirt with trees and scrub, the long approach having to fly three cross-bunkers and curl to the right without fading into further trees. A lake cuts into the fairway over the last 50yd/46m of the par-5 12th. Visitors scarcely believe their eyes on the 14th tee, confronted by an enormous bunker, almost 50yd/46m long, cutting diagonally across the fairway. The narrow green is also encased in sand. Surpassing all for beauty, however, is the 17th, running downhill to a green set above a lake. Aristocratic golf in a noble setting!

Beau Desert's 5th. The need to place the drive precisely is emphasized on this dog-leg, the approach being uphill over a vast bunker to a wicked green.

19 *Beau Desert*

Beau Desert Golf Club, Hazel Slade, Cannock, Staffs WS12 5PJ (1921)
TEL: *(01543) 422626* **FAX:** *(01543) 451137*
LOCATION: *Between Cannock and Rugeley, Hazel Slade is signposted off A460*
COURSE: *18 holes, 6310yd/5770m, par 70, SSS 71*
TYPE OF COURSE: *Heathland/forest*
DESIGNER: *Herbert Fowler*
GREEN FEES: *££££*
FACILITIES: *Pro shop, trolley hire, clubhouse*
VISITORS: *Weekdays only with handicap certificate*

Over this 'beautiful wilderness', haunt of that singular bird the nightjar, Beau Desert's fairways weave a narrow path through heather and bracken, pines and birches, rarely sheltered from the wind on high ground. Their quality is such that hosting of regional qualifying for the Open is almost a permanent fixture.

Every hole has enormous character, with fascinating greens, in which company the 5th excels with its drive over expanses of rough to an angled fairway and a difficult approach to an extraordinary green, on three levels, highest in the middle! The 7th is a beautiful par 3, all slopes in the woods, and the outward half ends with a handsome, gambling, par 4 of only 263yd/240m. The 12th is a brilliant double dog-leg and, returning to the extensive new clubhouse, the short par-5 18th has, possibly, the largest single green in the country.

20 *Whittington Heath*

Whittington Heath Golf Club, Tamworth Road, Lichfield, Staffs WS14 9PW (1886)
TEL and **FAX:** *(01543) 432317*
LOCATION: *2 miles/3km east of Lichfield on A51*
COURSE: *18 holes, 6458yd/5905m, par 70, SSS 71*
TYPE OF COURSE: *Heathland*
DESIGNER: *Harry Colt*
GREEN FEES: *££*
FACILITIES: *Pro shop, clubhouse*
VISITORS: *Welcome weekdays with handicap certificate*

Whittington began as an adjunct of the neighbouring military camp, enjoying springy turf amidst birches, heather, gorse and brambles. It is an advantage if the drive can be placed in the correct part of the fairway, and Whittington has been described, with good reason, as one of those courses it is wise to play several times simply to get to know before tackling it in serious competition.

The layout is well arranged to turn near the clubhouse, and on the back nine the 14th is likely to impress, a long par 4 gradually working its way to the right into a cleverly protected green at the bottom of the hill. The 15th is a par 3 across a gully and open ground on which judgement of distance is difficult. The last three holes, each a strong par 4, demand confident approach work, their greens very adequately protected by slopes and bunkers.

OTHER COURSES TO VISIT IN CENTRAL ENGLAND

Bedfordshire
Aspley Guise
Dunstable Downs
Berkshire
Bearwood Lakes
East Berkshire
Mill Ride
Temple
Buckinghamshire
Beaconsfield
Ellesborough
Gerrards Cross
The Lambourne
Gloucestershire
Long Ashton

Minchinhampton
Herefordshire
Belmont Lodge
Ross-on-Wye
Hertfordshire
Brocket Hall
Sandy Lodge
Verulam
Leicestershire
Kirby Muxloe
Leicestershire
Kilworth Springs
Middlesex
Fulwell
Mill Hill

Stockley Park
Northamptonshire
Collingtree Park
Wellingborough
Nottinghamshire
Coxmoor
Worksop
Oxfordshire
Henley
Huntercombe
Southfield
Shropshire
Hawkestone Park
Hill Valley
Oswestry

Staffordshire
Enville
Leek
South Staffordshire
Warwickshire
Copt Heath
Stratford-upon-Avon
Sutton Coldfield
Welcombe Hotel
The Warwickshire
Worcestershire
Blackwell
Fulford Heath
Kings Norton
The Worcestershire

21 *Sherwood Forest*

Sherwood Forest Golf Club, Eakring Road, Mansfield, Notts NG18 3EW (1895)
TEL: *(01623) 626689* **FAX:** *(01623) 420412*
LOCATION: *To north of A617 Mansfield–Newark road at eastern edge of Mansfield*
COURSE: *18 holes, 6715yd/6140m, par 71, SSS 73*
TYPE OF COURSE: *Heathland/forest*
DESIGNERS: *Harry Colt, James Braid*
GREEN FEES: *££££*
FACILITIES: *Pro shop, clubhouse*
VISITORS: *Welcome weekdays with handicap certificate*

It has been claimed that the back nine at Sherwood Forest is the best consecutive nine holes in English inland golf. In truth the rest are just as searching, as aspirants in many Open Championship qualifying rounds and the 1997 British Seniors Open Amateur will testify. Over the years thousands of trees have grown to add enormously to its beauty. Heather, gorse and broom are serious golfing threats.

With a fairway sweeping through heather and sand, the 2nd hints at things to come, nor is the engaging 3rd easy into the wind with a line of cross-bunkers and a plateau green. At 462yd/422m the 11th is rugged with its run in through bunkers. The shorter 12th is uphill with heather, gorse and trees awaiting the slightest error. The 13th is again long and demands an approach from the correct angle. It goes on just like this to the very end.

Sherwood Forest's 18th – a lovely sweeping hole to close the round at this handsome and challenging course. It was the first UK club to appoint its professional as secretary.

22 Notts

Notts Golf Club, Hollinwell, Kirkby-in-Ashfield,
Nottingham NG17 7QR (1887)
TEL: *(01623) 753225* **FAX:** *(01623) 753655*
LOCATION: *On A611 4 miles/6.5km south of*
Mansfield
COURSE: *18 holes, 7030yd/6428m, par 72, SSS 74*
TYPE OF COURSE: *Parkland/heathland*
DESIGNERS: *Willie Park, J.H. Taylor*
GREEN FEES: *££££*
FACILITIES: *Pro shop, caddy, trolley and club hire,*
driving range, clubhouse
VISITORS: *Welcome with handicap certificate weekdays*
only

NOTTS

HOLE	YD	M	PAR	HOLE	YD	M	PAR
1	376	344	4	10	362	331	4
2	430	393	4	11	365	334	4
3	511	467	5	12	433	396	4
4	455	416	4	13	236	216	3
5	193	177	3	14	403	368	4
6	533	487	5	15	440	402	4
7	403	368	4	16	355	325	4
8	410	375	4	17	490	448	5
9	178	163	3	18	457	418	4
OUT	3489	3190	36	IN	3541	3238	36

7030YD • 6428M • PAR 72

The immediate impression at Notts is one of spaciousness and grandeur, of being cut off from the mundane by the wooded hills surrounding the club. On the course that impression is reinforced as hole succeeds hole, each in its own private cocoon of heather and gorse, birch, oak and chestnut.

There are only around 80 bunkers yet they feel more like 150, so well placed and influential are they. Nature, too, is a major factor. On the par-4 2nd, for instance, you must drive to the right if you hope to see the green round the corner of a hill for your second shot. Drive too far right, however, and there is no hope of reaching it. Go over

of them – and on the front nine only the 1st is under 400yd/366m long. So it is to the par 5s that we look to sneak strokes back. A new tee low to the right in the trees now starts the 6th, the drive on this substantial par 5 being out over a big, central cross-bunker, the green at the end of a roller-coaster fairway. Two huge bunkers eat into the 7th fairway about 100yd/91m short of the green, and further green-side bunkers call for an approach on the correct angle.

From the back tee at the 8th the prospect is daunting. There is a lake to be carried, the gap in the trees beyond them is narrow, and the fairway is angled away to the right. In the trees

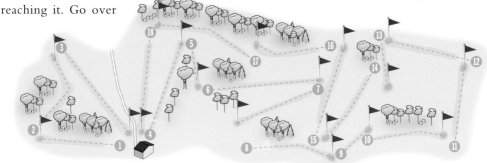

the hill and the slopes may well push your approach into the bunkers attending this shallow green.

The great length of the course (over 7000yd/6400m from the championship tees) comes mainly from the par 4s – there are 12

alongside is the spring, the holy well, which gives its name to Hollinwell.

Climbing in earnest, the 11th is delightful, with a narrow drive between tall banks. The small green is yet further up, protected by gorse-clad hills and bunkers. At the 12th between tee and fairway is a gorse-filled chasm. The fairway is above and, with trees on the right and a big drop into trouble on the left, not one to miss. There remains a substantial shot over a depression to a green perched on the end of the high ground. The descent from it is made in spectacular fashion, a great plunge down a narrow valley to a tightly bunkered green, the famous 13th.

Big hitting is required on the 15th, driving on to a bunkered ridge from which it is a very full second shot over a valley to the narrow green set into the hillside in front. From the last tee there is a fine view down the fairway to the distant clubhouse and 18th green. This has seen many historic golfing moments, not least the young Sandy Lyle taking his first important title, the Brabazon Trophy, in 1975. Five years earlier the ever-competitive Irishman Christy O'Connor won the John Player Classic, earning himself what was then a world record first prize, £25,000.

BRIAN WAITES

In the days before the full-time tours, professional golfers spent most of their working lives attached to a golf club. So James Braid (Walton Heath), Arthur Havers (Coombe Hill), Henry Cotton (Ashridge) and so on were representing their clubs when they won the Open Championship. Probably the last tournament professional to carry his club's name into European Tour events was Brian Waites, who was appointed to the Notts Golf Club in 1969. He combined his club duties with frequent tour appearances to such effect that he was selected for the 1983 European Ryder Cup team which came within a point of the Americans at PGA National in Florida.

The grand sweep of the closing hole at Notts is typical of the sheer scale and imposing nature of this highly rated championship course.

REGIONAL DIRECTORY

Where to Stay

Thames Valley To the west of London the **Inn on the Green** (01628 482638) at Cookham Dean, is a village pub beside a traditional cricket ground, the **Red Lion Hotel** (01491 572161) at Henley overlooks the river, or there is the grandeur of **Stoke Poges Golf Club** (01753 717170). The fabulous **Waterside Inn** (01628 620691) at Bray, presided over by Michel Roux, has a few rooms at a similar price level to the restaurant. Near Oxford, **Le Manoir aux Quat' Saisons** (01844 278881) is legendary, not only for its exceptional cuisine but also for the quality of its rooms and service.

The Cotswolds The **Bull Inn** (01608 810689) is a proper country pub in the attractive Cotswold village of Charlbury. **The Feathers Hotel** (01993 812291) and **Holmwood** (01993 812266) are, respectively, a historic hotel and a charming town house just outside the gates of Blenheim Palace in Woodstock. No visit to the Cotswolds would be complete without a stay at the gorgeous **Lygon Arms** (01386 852255) at Broadway which has accommodated both King Charles I and Oliver Cromwell in their times. Luxurious **Buckland Manor** (01386 852626), near Broadway, is even older, dating back to AD 709!

The Midlands Heading for the Midlands, **The Falcon** (01604 696200) at Castle Ashby near Northampton is both convenient for the M1 and a traditional inn noted for its excellent food. Three golfing hotels stand out, **The Belfry** (01675 470033) and **Marriott Forest of Arden** (01676 522335) hosting important tour events, the **Welcombe Hotel** (01789 295252) at Stratford-upon-Avon offering a good golf course in the heart of Shakesperean England. In the west of the region, the **Old Vicarage** (01746 716497) at Worfield lists no fewer than 600 different wines, while rather deeper into Shropshire **Hawkstone Park Hotel** (01939 200611) runs to two charming 18-hole golf courses. Here Sandy Lyle learned his golf from his father who was the professional. To play the Nottinghamshire courses accommodation might be sought at **Langar Hall** (01949 860559), an exceptionally comfortable country house hotel, or at **Peacock Farm** (01949 842475) at Redmile, both a farm and hotel.

Where to Eat

Thames Valley **The Waterside Inn** (see above) is not the only distinguished restaurant in Bray, the **Fat Duck** (01628 620691) giving it a good run for its money. **La Petite Auberge** (01494 865370) at Great Missenden, **Alfonso's** (01628 525775) at Cookham, the **Water Rat** (01635 582017) at Marsh Benham, **L'Ortolan** (0118-988-3783) at Shinfield, the **Royal Oak** (01635 201325) at Yattenden, and **La Chouette** (01296 747422) at Dinton stand out in Berkshire and Buckinghamshire, with the **Vineyard** at Stockcross (01635 528770) appropriately noted for its cellar.

The Cotswolds Good restaurants abound in the Cotswolds, including, in addition to those hotels mentioned above, **Baker's** (01865 881888) at Eynsham, **Lower Slaughter Manor** (01451 820456), **Marsh Goose** (01608 653500) at Moreton-in-Marsh, **Old Woolhouse** (01451 860366) at Northleach, and the **Churchill Arms** (01386 594000) at Paxford. Near Oxford the **Sir Charles Napier** (01494 483011) at Chinnor, the **Beetle and Wedge** (01491 651381) at Moulsford, and **The Goose** (01491 612304) at Britwell Salome have high reputations, and in Oxford the **Lemon Tree** (01865 311936) and **Cherwell Boathouse** (01865 552746) are favourites amongst the dons.

The M1 corridor is surprisingly well provided with eating houses, top spot going to the **French Partridge** (01604 870033) at Horton, though no one should attempt to drive after sampling their celebrated wines. Also in Northamptonshire there are good reports of **King's Cliffe House** (01780 470172), **Vine House** (01327 811267) at Paulerspury, and **Roade House** (01604 863372).

Nearer to Birmingham are **Grafton Manor** (01527 579007) at Bromsgrove, and **Restaurant Bosquet** (01926 852463) and **Simpson's** (01926 864567) at Kenilworth, but it is surely worth making the extra journey south to Malvern Wells to sample the delicious fare on offer at **Croque-en-Bouche** (01684 565612), one of the finest restaurants in the land.

Shropshire By the same token it would be worth visiting Ludlow in Shropshire simply to dine at **Merchant House** (01584 875438), **Mr Underhill's** (01584 874431), or **Overton Grange** (01584 873500), all of which are in the first culinary division. But there are so many other rewards to be found in this lovely old town, not least the cooking at **Oaks** (01584 872325) and **Courtyard** (01584 878080).

What to See

See life in miniature at **Legoland** or **Bekonscot**, life in the natural state at **Windsor Safari Park** or **Whipsnade**, life on the grand scale at **Woburn Abbey** or **Blenheim Palace**, and life in academia at **Oxford**.

Oxford On a working day it is almost impossible to drive in Oxford, but park-and-ride and tourist buses operate from the outskirts direct to the city centre where town and gown are inextricably bound together, ancient colleges marching with the shops and offices of 21st-century commerce. The open spaces around the **Bodleian Library**, the **Radcliffe Camera** and **Sheldonian Theatre** have an academic air, and the views over the various colleges from the tower of **St Mary's Church** are impressive. Perhaps attend Choral Evensong in the fine chapels of **New College** or **Magdalen**, or at **Christ Church Cathedral** which is both the college chapel and England's smallest cathedral. Then a walk in **Magdalen Deer Park**, **Christ Church Meadow**, or the **Botanical Gardens**, or, in summer, a punt on the **Cherwell**. (Those who have never punted are advised not to make their first attempt on the Isis from Folly Bridge. The river there is deep and flows fast.) Worcester College gardens, Merton Chapel, Library and Mob Quad, Queen's Library and Chapel, the statue of Shelley in University College – each college has much to offer the visitor. The **Ashmolean Museum** and **Christ Church Gallery** house major collections.

The Cotswolds The whistle-stop tour of the essential Cotswolds is **Oxford**, **Woodstock**, **Burford**, **Bibury**, **Cirencester**, **Northleach**, **Bourton-on-the-Water**, **Stow-on-the-Wold**, **Chipping Camden**, **Broadway**, but those with the time to potter might profitably take in **Banbury**, **Bourton-on-the-Hill**, **Broughton Castle**, **Chastleton House**, **Chedworth Roman Villa**, **Chipping Norton** (highest Cotswold town), **Cornwell**, **Fairford**, **Kelmscott** (with its Pre-Raphaelite connections), **Minster Lovell**, **Moreton-in-Marsh**, the **Rollright Stones**, **Stanton Harcourt**, **Swinbrook** (with its amazing Fettiplace stacked tombs), and **Witney**.

Worcester and Gloucester As our golf has taken us to Broadway we should allow ourselves a detour to Worcester, its fine cathedral the burial place of King John. The **Royal Worcester** porcelain factory is world famous, and can be visited. The **Three Choirs Festival** is one of the oldest of all festivals having taken place with very few interruptions each year since 1715. It is held in Worcester one year, Hereford the next, and then Gloucester. Incidentally, a visit to **Gloucester Cathedral** is essential for the golfing historian, for in the Great East Window is a 14th-century stained-glass depicting scenes from the Battle of Crécy in 1346. One of the panels clearly shows a man in the act of hitting a golf ball. More precisely, he is pictured during the take-away and he is in perfect position with the club parallel to the ground, the face exactly square to the line, the weight transferring correctly to the right foot!

Towards Wales Continuing our detour in the west, towards the Welsh border is the wonderful hill country of **Clun Forest**, **Stiperstones**, and the **Long Mynd**. The castles at **Ludlow**, **Stokesay**, and **Acton Burnell** fascinate, while it is impossible to journey along **Wenlock Edge** without reciting the poetry of A.E. Housman. The arcading of **Much Wenlock Priory** is outstanding, and over the hill at **Buildwas** is another haunting monastic ruin. Yet almost immediately we are thrown into one of the cauldrons of the industrial revolution, the **Ironbridge Gorge**. The bridge is the very earliest iron bridge in the world, and you can still cross it on foot. The whole area has been developed into an outstanding series of museums of industrial archaeology.

Shrewsbury has been an important border stronghold for centuries, a strategic river crossing. It is full of interesting buildings, one of the lovely timber-framed buildings in Wyle Cop housing one of the best independent wine merchants in the land, **Tanners**.

West Midlands Returning to the West Midlands for our golf, it is worth taking the route past **Cosford** where the Imperial War Museum keeps one of its fine collections of historic aircraft. Walsall was once the tannery of England. Its Arboretum typifies the vision of its commercial forefathers, a verdant open space created for the lasting benefit of present and future citizens. A kaleidoscope of Birmingham's industrial past is available in its excellent **Museum of Science and Technology**. Music lovers will want to admire the brilliant acoustics of **Symphony Hall**.

To the south of Birmingham, **Stratford-upon-Avon** is synonymous with **Shakespeare**, its theatre overlooking the River Avon. **Charlecote Hall**, **Coughton Court** and **Ragley Hall** are worthy of expeditions, not to mention the beautiful village of **Henley-in-Arden**. **Warwick Castle** is one of the great fortresses of Europe, the town full of interesting buildings, too, and here we meet up with the route we might have taken from London straight up the M40, or M1.

North and East Midlands To see the North and East Midlands at their best search out the little roads, taking in the ancient churches at **Tutbury** (Staffordshire), **Repton** (Derbyshire), and **Breedon-on-the-Hill** (Leicestershire). **Belvoir Castle** dominates much of the Leicestershire skyline, a historic place, though most of the building is 19th century. In Nottinghamshire, **Newstead Abbey** was the ancestral home of the poet Lord Byron, and **Southwell Minster** is possibly the least known, but certainly one of the most charming, of England's great churches.

Chapter 4

Eastern England

There is a flatness shared by all the counties to the east of the Great North Road (A1) as it makes its way north from London to Lincolnshire. The majority of this area constitutes East Anglia, and it used to be said that East Anglia was cut off on three sides by the sea and the fourth by the Great Eastern Railway. No one ever went *through* East Anglia, though many went *to* it, until recently that is, when the development of Harwich and other ports as ferry terminals has resulted in juggernauts from as far afield as Poland and Turkey regularly crossing the region bearing their cargoes to the Midlands and North. Road connections have been improved immeasurably in recent years, though, once you turn off the main roads,

Left: The incomparable setting of the 9th green at Royal West Norfolk, high in the dunes overlooking salt marshes and creeks. Above: Coastal erosion has left the 16th-century Moot Hall at Aldeburgh standing today on the beach.

the country lanes are still for those for whom time is not money, and very pretty a good number of them are.

True East Anglians claim only to come from Suffolk, Norfolk and the Isle of Ely, but it would be churlish to disallow the claims of wider Cambridgeshire and Essex which share many features beyond geographical proximity. The ancient tribe of the Iceni held sway before the Romans made Colchester their capital. When the Romans departed, the region was easy prey for the invading Angles, Saxons and Jutes whose influence has not entirely vanished today. Then most of Norfolk and Suffolk was covered in dense forest, in utter contrast to the near prairie-like landscape of their modern agriculture. What was not forest was wet, the tidal creeks around the coast, the Norfolk Broads, and the Fens, a once impenetrable network of bogs and marshes turned, in the 17th century, into a brilliant system of controllable dykes and sluices by the Dutch engineer Vermuyden.

Lincolnshire

Our golfing journey north from London takes us briefly into Lincolnshire, neither East Anglia nor the north country, an enormous county for the most part sharing with East Anglia its expansive skies. On their 'hill-fort by a pool' the castle and cathedral command the rest of Lincoln and Lincolnshire. Lincoln Cathedral is a magnificent building, rebuilt as we know it today by Hugh of Avalon in 1192.

Norfolk

The barrier presented by the Fens ensured that Norfolk in particular retained its own cultural identity far longer than, say, the Midlands. Its metropolitan centre was, and still is, Norwich, a city retaining much of its medieval layout commanded by Bishop Longa's magnificent Norman cathedral with its elegant spire. Of a similar age the castle keep is one of the finest pieces of military architecture in the land. The ancient streets are littered with old inns and medieval churches.

Suffolk

Suffolk's wealth came from wool, and the magnificent churches at Long Melford and Lavenham owe their splendour to it. The painter Thomas Gainsborough came from Sudbury and he was an inspiration to the Flatford miller's son, John Constable. Through their works many who have never visited Suffolk have, nevertheless, a clear identification with this gentle corner of England. Once the site of one of the most powerful ecclesiastical institutions in England, Bury St Edmunds reflects its importance in its motto, 'Shrine of a King, Cradle of the Law'. The county town is Ipswich, a busy working town and port, with a number of fine buildings.

Essex

Two of England's greatest musicians of the golden age had Essex associations, Thomas Tallis as organist of Waltham Abbey (for which he may well have composed his astonishing 40-part motet

The Choir of King's College, Cambridge, famous for its traditional 'Festival of Nine Lessons and Carols' broadcast throughout the world every Christmas Eve.

Spem in alium), and William Byrd who lived in later life at Stondon Massey, giving him access to the Roman Catholic services held secretly at nearby Ingatestone Hall, Protestant England then persecuting recusants mercilessly. Visually Essex is a less interesting county than its neighbours, the western part very much a dormitory for London, yet all roads lead to Colchester, not London, for, as capital of the Icenic kingdom and Roman Britain, it has a 2000-year history.

Cambridgeshire

Cambridgeshire is dominated by water, though there is a touch of relief from the undeniable flatness in the uplands of the south. Cambridge itself is one of the most beautiful towns in Europe, especially when viewed from the 'backs', the lawns running down to the river from a number of the university colleges. Immortalized by Chaucer, Byron and Brooke, the village of Grantchester is guaranteed its place in the literary memorabilia of the nation.

VINTAGE FLYING

Because of their proximity to continental Europe the eastern counties were, during the Second World War, almost wholly covered in concrete runways. One of the most famous air bases, Duxford (off the M11 south of Cambridge), now houses much of the Imperial War Museum's magnificent collection of aeroplanes. The pretty village of Old Warden in Bedfordshire boasts the Shuttleworth collection of vintage aeroplanes and cars. The home of the Battle of Britain Memorial Flight is at RAF Coningsby in Lincolnshire, close to Woodhall Spa, where its precious Avro Lancaster, Hawker Hurricane and several Supermarine Spitfires are on display when not out flying at an air display. All are open to the public, and have flying days from time to time. Not quite strictly in this golfing region, but no less demanding of a visit, is the fascinating RAF Museum at Hendon in North London, signposted from the M1.

🏌 *Hanbury Manor*

Marriott Hanbury Manor Golf and Country Club,
Ware, Herts SG12 0SD (1990)
TEL: *(01920) 487722* **FAX:** *(01920) 487692*
LOCATION: *On A10 just north of Ware*
COURSE: *18 holes, 7016yd/6415m, par 72, SSS 74*
TYPE OF COURSE: *Parkland*
DESIGNER: *Jack Nicklaus II*
GREEN FEES: *On application*
FACILITIES: *Full hotel, leisure and golf facilities*
VISITORS: *Hotel and members' guests only*

An 1890s mansion in Jacobean style forms the hub of the sumptuous hotel in whose parkland grounds Jack Nicklaus II has laid out an impressive course. Though youthful it has already welcomed the men's and women's European tours. The two nines are very different in character, the first enjoying rolling open country, the second traditional parkland.

A decision must be made on the 1st tee. Either take the easier line to the right, leaving a harder pitch, or take the braver drive involving a much longer carry to the left to find a strip of isolated fairway. Every green is cleverly defended, with sometimes an open entrance on one side for general play, and a really hard tournament position behind bunkers or water on the other side. Water enlivens the approaches to the 2nd, 8th, 13th and 17th.

The 18th green at Hanbury Manor, scene of impressively low-scoring wins by Per-Ulrik Johansson, Lee Westwood and Darren Clarke in the three English Opens played here.

🏌 *John O'Gaunt*

John O'Gaunt Golf Club, Sutton Park, Sandy, Beds
SG19 2LY (1948)
TEL: *(01767) 260360* **FAX:** *(01767) 262834*
LOCATION: *B1040 Biggleswade–Potten road,*
clubhouse on right
COURSES: *John O'Gaunt: 18 holes, 6513yd/5955m,*
par 71, SSS 71; Carthagena: 18 holes, 5869yd/
5367m, par 69, SSS 69
TYPE OF COURSE: *Parkland, with heathland feel to*
Carthagena
DESIGNER: *F.W. Hawtree*
GREEN FEES: *££££*
FACILITIES: *Pro shop, buggy hire, clubhouse*
VISITORS: *Welcome with handicap certificate (maximum*
28 men, 36 women)

Two complementary courses occupy historic ground, John O'Gaunt in gentle parkland, Carthagena across the road in a more heathland setting. Two- and four-ball play is alternated daily between the courses.

On John O'Gaunt a splendidly undulating green on the short 4th prefaces two very demanding par 4s, the 472yd/432m 6th narrowing where the best drives finish. The 327yd/299m 7th charms with its elevated green amongst the trees. On the back nine the 13th is tough with water to be driven and the green in a curve of the stream. The 17th green is set on a hill surrounded by an ancient moat, a unique and fascinating hole.

Carthagena was designed and built by the club and, though shorter, is no less interesting. The greens are bigger and the closing sequence is full of character.

Luffenham Heath

Luffenham Heath Golf Club, Ketton, Stamford, Rutland PE9 3UU (1911)
TEL: *(01780) 720205* **FAX:** *(01780) 722416*
LOCATION: *5 miles/8km west of Stamford on A6121*
COURSE: *18 holes, 6273yd/5736m, par 70, SSS 70*
TYPE OF COURSE: *Heathland*
DESIGNER: *James Braid*
GREEN FEES: *£££*
FACILITIES: *Pro shop, clubhouse*
VISITORS: *Welcome with handicap certificate*

At Luffenham Heath, close to the butterstone village of Ketton, there is a great feeling of space as the course unfolds over high ground. The 2nd is a fine hole if you get your drive away over a chasm towards a fairway which leans to the right. There remains a

Seacroft's 5th, a tough 439yd/401m par 4 on which out-of-bounds threatens on each shot.

substantial second shot across a wide valley to the green. The 4th plunges encouragingly downhill, and the problem may well be in nipping the second shot off a sloping lie to stop the ball on the green. Whether as a short par 5 from the back tees or a long par 4 from the yellow plates, the 6th is demanding, and the 7th is a beauty, with the approach shot having to climb over bunkers to find the hilltop green. The last high-ground hole, the 17th, is great fun, a tumbling par 3 with extensive views over the surrounding countryside.

Seacroft

Seacroft Golf Club, Seacroft, Skegness, Lincolnshire PE25 3AU (1895)
TEL *and* **FAX:** *(01754) 763020*
LOCATION: *On coast 1 mile/1.6km south of Skegness on road to Gibraltar Point nature reserve*
COURSE: *18 holes, 6479yd/5924m, par 71, SSS 71*
TYPE OF COURSE: *Links*
DESIGNERS: *Willie Fernie, Herbert Fowler, C.K. Cotton*
GREEN FEES: *££*
FACILITIES: *Pro shop, clubhouse*
VISITORS: *Welcome, restricted at weekends*

One of the few genuine links courses in the east of England north of the Wash, Seacroft is a traditional out-and-back layout on a narrow site with out-of-bounds on the right of no fewer than 14 holes, no slicer's paradise! Adaptation to the modern game has not spoiled the gloriously old-fashioned feel to the golf, with tight, undulating fairways and a number of blind or semi-blind shots, 75 bunkers and occasional, impenetrable buckthorn.

The par-3 4th is the first stern examination with the green on top of a mound, while on the 7th the long approach is made over or around a substantial hillock to a green very close to the road. If anything, the 8th is even tighter. Pride of place goes to the 13th, not long as par 5s go, but a classic with the green set up beyond a rise in which two bunkers are set.

Woodhall Spa

Woodhall Spa Golf Club, The English Golf Union, The Broadway, Woodhall Spa, Lincolnshire LN10 6PU (1905)

TEL: (01526) 352511 **FAX:** (01526) 351817
WEBSITE: www.englishgolfunion.org
LOCATION: East of Woodhall Spa on B1191 to Horncastle
COURSES: Hotchkin: 18 holes, 7047yd/6443m, par 73, SSS 75; Bracken: 18 holes, 6735yd/6158m, SSS 74
TYPE OF COURSE: Heathland (Hotchkin), parkland (Bracken)
DESIGNERS: S.V. Hotchkin (Hotchkin), Donald Steel (Bracken)
GREEN FEES: ££££ (reduced for EGU members)
FACILITIES: Pro shop, clubhouse, golf academy
VISITORS: Welcome with handicap certificate (maximum men 20, women 30)

HOLE	YD	M	PAR	HOLE	YD	M	PAR
1	361	330	4	10	338	309	4
2	442	404	4	11	437	400	4
3	415	380	4	12	172	157	3
4	414	379	4	13	451	412	4
5	148	135	3	14	521	476	5
6	510	466	5	15	321	294	4
7	470	430	4	16	395	361	4
8	192	175	3	17	336	307	4
9	584	534	5	18	540	494	5
OUT	3536	3233	36	IN	3511	3210	37

WOODHALL SPA HOTCHKIN COURSE

7047YD • 6443M • PAR 72

In the featureless agricultural land that makes up much of Lincolnshire, Woodhall Spa is an oasis, a handsome little town with a world famous golf course. We should now call it the Hotchkin Course because when the English Golf Union bought Woodhall Spa in 1995 they engaged Donald Steel to construct a second course, the complementary Bracken Course.

No English course can rival Woodhall Spa for the depth and extent of its bunkers, huge sandy caverns, many so deep that in

them tall men disappear from sight completely. The Hotchkin Course also has great length, over 7000yd/6400m of it from the championship tees. An abundance of heather lines each fairway and encrusts many bunkers. Trees frame some holes, affecting strategy on others. Narrow entrances to the greens are a recurring challenge. Sandy soil ensures excellent drainage, and the course is maintained in superb condition, even in winter.

In the league tables which are now so fashionable, Woodhall Spa and Ganton regularly vie for the position of highest-ranked inland course in the British Isles, and recently it was rated as the 29th best course in the world by *Golf Magazine* of America. Revisions to the bunkering over the winter of 1999/2000 have removed one or two anachronisms without in any way affecting the seriousness of the challenge.

After the gentle 1st, the course opens out onto the heath and the real trial begins. With the ruined red tower beyond it the 3rd green is memorably sited. Moving now towards the middle of the course, the 4th turns into the wind, its greenside bunkers being exceptionally deep. There are only three short holes at Woodhall Spa, the 5th having a long, narrow green higher at the front than the back and notably difficult bunkers either side.

Woodhall Spa, 3rd hole. Since the demise of the little railway which once ran through the course this ruined tower is the only reminder that there is a world outside on this wonderfully secluded course.

Inevitably there are bunkers which force the drive to the left on the long par-4 7th, effectively adding to its already considerable yardage. Like the 5th, the short 8th usually plays into the wind and is, yet again, plentifully bunkered. On the lengthy par-5 9th cross-bunkers interrupt the fairway on the second shot, while on the 10th a particularly enormous specimen affects the drive.

Trees now begin to enclose the fairways, the 11th most appealing as it sweeps slightly downhill, curving gently to the left. The last short hole, the 12th, features a thin plateau green attended by the customary array of bunkers. A dog-leg to the right with bunkers throughout its length, the 13th is a very strong hole, whereas, remarkably, the 16th has only a single bunker, a little one set into a ridge short of the green. The round finishes with a classic

hole, on which many have suggested that a rifle would be of more use on the back tee than a golf club! There are the familiar bunkers, of course, but what commands the hole is a large oak tree standing alone on the right of the fairway. Finish behind that at your peril!

S. V. HOTCHKIN
(1876–1953)

Born in Woodhall Spa, Stafford Vere Hotchkin served with the Lincolnshire Yeomanry before becoming a Member of Parliament and County Councillor. He totally remodelled Colt's original layout after buying it in 1920. Since then the Hotchkin Course is said to have hosted more amateur championships than any other course in England. So his first essay in golf architecture is no less impressive than Fowler's at Walton Heath. Hotchkin went on to design Ashridge and West Sussex in England, amongst others, and his work in South Africa is celebrated, notably his remodellings of Mowbray and the Durban Country Club.

🏌 *Hunstanton*

Hunstanton Golf Club, Golf Course Road, Old
Hunstanton, Norfolk PE36 6JQ (1891)
TEL: *(01485) 532811* **FAX:** *(01485) 532319*
LOCATION: *Off A149 1 mile/1.6km north of*
Hunstanton, follow signs down lane to left
COURSE: *18 holes, 6735yd/6158m, par 72, SSS 72*
TYPE OF COURSE: *Traditional links*
DESIGNERS: *James Braid, James Sherlock*
GREEN FEES: *££££*
FACILITIES: *Pro shop, clubhouse*
VISITORS: *Welcome with handicap certficate, two-ball*
play only

HUNSTANTON

HOLE	YD	M	PAR	HOLE	YD	M	PAR
1	343	314	4	10	375	343	4
2	532	486	5	11	439	401	4
3	443	405	4	12	358	327	4
4	172	157	3	13	387	354	4
5	436	399	4	14	219	200	3
6	337	308	4	15	478	437	5
7	166	152	3	16	189	173	3
8	505	462	5	17	445	407	4
9	513	469	5	18	398	364	4
OUT	3447	3152	37	IN	3288	3006	35

6735YD • 6158M • PAR 72

Hunstanton features in all the record books, for it was on the 16th here in 1974 that Bob Taylor, a Leicestershire county player, holed in one on three consecutive days. But it would be wrong to think of Hunstanton solely for this remarkable feat for it is a links course of the highest calibre with a great many outstanding holes and some of the best greens in the country day in, day out. Hardly surprisingly, Hunstanton has hosted a goodly number of national and international championships since its foundation in 1891.

Only after the Second World War were the present 17th and 18th created, providing a sterling finish, but robbing us of the notorious opening drive which previous generations faced, a huge carry over a monstrous bunker. That bunker is still there but is now a less intimidating challenge from a

repositioned tee, the greater threat being a series of bunkers low to the right. A spine of dunes runs down the middle of the course and the best holes climb on and off them, so from the 2nd the golf is quieter until the 6th on which they are next encountered, entailing a devilish pitch to a narrow, sloping hilltop green. The 7th is no less exciting, a par 3 which is all carry

over a wild ravine and steep-faced bunker. Not a green to miss!

Into the wind, the carry from the 9th tee is substantial with a lot of rough ground and a track to be cleared, bunkers to either side emphasizing the need for straightness. A bowl of water is to be found beside this green for the refreshment of those dogs who have chosen to accompany their owners during the round. The 11th is demanding, despite the fact that it is the only bunkerless hole on the course. The next three holes run back and forth across the spine of dunes, the 13th a

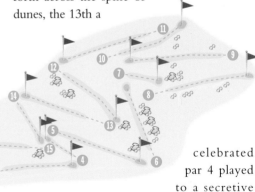

celebrated par 4 played to a secretive green, the only flat spot in a jumble of mounds and hillocks. For good measure, the longish par-3 14th plays blind across the dunes, the sort of hole nobody would be allowed to build today, and the sort of hole championed vigorously by all lovers of traditional golf.

There is no let up from here in, the 15th short as par 5s go but very narrow amidst some rough country. Up on top of the dunes is the 16th tee giving the loveliest view on the course, the Wash sparkling in the distance, the salt marshes closer. Taylor's remarkable feat notwithstanding, it is a fine hole, heavily bunkered around the distinctly undulating putting surface. The post-war 17th is a stern test at this stage of the round, calling for a huge drive up the left and a long approach which must be arrow straight to hold the narrow high ground on which the green is perched. Keep the drive away from the dunes on the final hole if there is to be any chance of finding the green with the second shot, a ledge just below the clubhouse terrace, as agreeable a spot as any to assuage the thirst after the toils of the last few hours.

The Grafton Morrish Trophy is played here annually between teams of Old Boys from the public schools.

SANDRINGHAM

The main road from King's Lynn to Hunstanton passes the turn to Sandringham, where the Queen and other members of the Royal Family traditionally spend Christmas. It is a Victorian house, purchased by Edward, Prince of Wales, in 1861. Here King George V died in 1936, and it was at Sandringham that King George VI was born, also dying here in 1952. The house and gardens are open to the public, and the Royal Church is of particular interest because of the number of royal benefactions to its fabric such as the nave roof given by King George V, and the organ, the last gift of King Edward VII.

Hunstanton's 7th. A bench high on the dunes to the left of this green is a good place from which to watch play here and on the parallel par-5 9th.

Royal West Norfolk

Royal West Norfolk Golf Club, Brancaster, Norfolk
PE31 8AX (1892)
TEL: *(01485) 210223* **FAX:** *(01485) 210087*
LOCATION: *Off A149 Norfolk coast road, at Brancaster*
turn into Beach Road and cross marsh
COURSE: *18 holes, 6428yd/5878m, par 71, SSS 71*
TYPE OF COURSE: *Traditional links*
DESIGNERS: *Horace Hutchinson and Holcombe Ingleby*
GREEN FEES: *££££*
FACILITIES: *Pro shop, clubhouse*
VISITORS: *Welcome with handicap certificate, but during*
August must be a member's guest. No four-ball play in
summer

A strong feeling of blissful isolation from the real world prevails as the journey is made along the causeway, across the saltmarshes to the clubhouse. When the tide is especially full you may be stranded on an island, left to play golf ad libitum until the waters have subsided and, reluctantly, you return to everyday life.

The sleepered bunkers are forbidding, the rough at times wicked, the greens firm and true, yet you know in your heart that this is

Royal West Norfolk's 9th. Even trickier than clearing the enormous, sleepered bunker from long range may be trying to stop the ball on this lightning-fast green.

how golf was meant to be played. As early as the 3rd the effect of the sleepered bunker is felt. Push the drive to the right and you are in the salt marsh. Play safely to the left and it is a desperate business to clear the woodwork in front of the raised green. Similarly uncompromising bunkers protect the short 4th.

With its fairway an island amongst the marshes, the 8th is a brilliant short par 5. The more marsh you carry with your drive, the less work you have to do on the second shot across another watery arm. The penalty for over-ambition is appalling. There is also a long carry over the marsh on the 9th if the green is to be attacked, for it lies beyond a huge sleepered bunker, another great hole. The inward nine is apparently much shorter, but the card cannot reflect the wind, rough, bunkers and subtle undulations of the greens which make these holes just as exacting a golfing test.

Sheringham

Sheringham Golf Club, Sheringham, Norfolk NR26
8HG (1891)
TEL: *(01263) 823488* **FAX:** *(01263) 825189*
LOCATION: *On A149 at west end of Sheringham*
COURSE: *18 holes, 6495yd/5939m, par 70, SSS 71*
TYPE OF COURSE: *Seaside/clifftop*
DESIGNER: *Tom Dunn*
GREEN FEES: *£££*
FACILITIES: *Pro shop, clubhouse*
VISITORS: *Welcome weekdays with handicap certificate*

L aid out over 100 years ago on perfect downland, Sheringham is linked particularly with the English Ladies' Championship, which it has hosted three times. In 1920 the 18-year-old, Joyce Wethered, took the title at her first attempt, the beginning of an illustrious golfing career.

The strength and variety of Sheringham's par 4s is noteworthy, and at the 3rd a remarkable sequence of clifftop holes begins. They mount a hill from which the seascapes

are magnificent. From the gun-platform 5th tee the drive is exhilarating, the fairway far below clinging to the cliff edge. The long approach is equally uplifting, across a depression to a brilliantly sited green. A slice at the par-3 6th may tumble down the cliffs to the beach. Moving inland, on the 9th gorse becomes a consistent threat, and from the 15th the holes run alongside the North Norfolk Railway, its steam-hauled trains contributing a nostalgic touch.

9 *Royal Cromer*

Royal Cromer Golf Club, Overstrand Road, Cromer, Norfolk NR27 0JH (1888)
TEL *and* **FAX:** *(01263) 512884*
LOCATION: *East of Cromer, turn left off main Norwich road*
COURSE: *18 holes 6508yd/5951m, par 72, SSS 72*
TYPE OF COURSE: *Parkland, seaside and clifftop*
DESIGNERS: *J.H. Taylor, Harry Colt*
GREEN FEES: *£££*
FACILITIES: *Pro shop, clubhouse*
VISITORS: *Welcome with handicap certificate*

A four-ball leaves the green of Sheringham's short 11th, with the lovely sweep of the 5th running along the clifftops in the background.

A very old club, granted royal patronage even before it opened in 1888, Cromer is a congenial mixture of parkland and clifftop golf. In 1905 it hosted the Ladies' British Open Championship and a series of international matches. Amongst the strong American team were Margaret and Harriot Curtis, the success of the tournaments prompting them to present a cup which is now the greatest trophy in ladies' international amateur golf.

A number of very full-length par 4s contribute to a strong outward half, especially the 6th, played alongside the sea, and the 7th to an elevated green. However, it will be the holes from the 13th which will endure in the memory, high on cliffs by the lighthouse. That 13th is a fine par 3 across a gully, the 14th skirts the cliff edge to a green by the lighthouse, while the 15th drive is exciting, down into a narrow valley.

 *Aldeburgh*

Aldeburgh Golf Club, Saxmundham Road, Aldeburgh,
Suffolk IP15 5PE (1884)
TEL: *(01728) 452890* **FAX:** *(01728) 452937*
LOCATION: *West edge of town on A1094*
COURSES: *18 holes, 6330yd/5788m, par 69, SSS
71; River: 9 holes, 2114yd/1933m, SSS 64*
TYPE OF COURSE: *Heathland with much gorse*
DESIGNERS: *John Thompson, Willie Fernie, J.H. Taylor*
GREEN FEES: *£££*
FACILITIES: *Pro shop, caddies, buggy and club hire,
clubhouse*
VISITORS: *Welcome with handicap certificate*

N arrow strips of bunker-strewn turf
thread a perilous route through a
fearsome mass of gorse, wondrously golden to
the eye but impenetrable to the golfer. Peter
Alliss asks the question, 'Could this be the
hardest place in Britain to play to your
handicap?' The answer lies in the length of its
par 4s, seven of them over 420yd/384m long.
Bernard Darwin once wrote, 'Altogether fours
turn into fives in the most surprising manner
and should you have a misunderstanding with
the gorse they turn into sixes.' Many of the

*The 5th at Aldeburgh, a typicaly testing par 4. With a
gorse-lined fairway, deep bunkers and an angled green
this is no place for the wayward.*

bunkers are sleeper-faced, that on the short
4th a villainous monster half encircling the
green. It is part of a glorious sequence of holes
sweeping up and down hill, the handsome 3rd
curving left through the gorse, the 5th
obligingly downhill, but no less demanding,
and the 6th climbing remorselessly. At least it
ensures that the view from the 7th tee is
particularly rewarding.

The prospect from the 10th and 11th tees
can be alarming, the fairways perhaps even
narrower than before and punctuated with
gloriously old-fashioned cross-bunkers. On
the 14th all musical golfers tug the forelock as
they pass the gates of The Red House,
composer Benjamin Britten's home, now an
important library. The pressure is maintained
to the end with the 15th and 17th excellent
short holes, and the 16th and 18th especially
demanding two-shotters.

Britten and Aldeburgh

History will very likely assign Benjamin Britten the palm as the most significant British composer of the immediate post-war era. At the outbreak of the Second World War Britten was living in America. A chance reading of an article about the Aldeburgh poet George Crabbe persuaded him to come home despite his pacifist beliefs. On his return he began work on an opera, *Peter Grimes*, which immediately established him as the most outstanding English dramatic composer since Henry Purcell in the 17th century. *Grimes* sets an adaptation of *The Borough* by Crabbe, clearly based on life in Aldeburgh in the early 19th century. Crabbe had already painted a far from romanticized picture of the poverty of rural existence and the barren landscape of this part of Suffolk in *The Village* of 1783. It was almost inevitable that Britten should subsequently make his home in Aldeburgh and in 1948, with the help of his English Opera Group, he launched the first Aldeburgh Festival, which continues as one of the most important annual events in the international artistic calendar.

 ## Woodbridge

Woodbridge Golf Club, Bromeswell Heath, Woodbridge, Suffolk IP12 2PF (1893)
TEL: *(01394) 382038* **FAX:** *(01394) 382392*
LOCATION: *2 miles/3km east of Woodbridge on A1152 to Orford*
COURSES: *18 holes, 6299yd/5760m, par 70, SSS 70; Forest: 9 holes, 6382yd/5836m, par 70, SSS 70*
TYPE OF COURSE: *Heathland*
DESIGNER: *F.W. Hawtree (Forest)*
GREEN FEES: *£££*
FACILITIES: *Pro shop, clubhouse*
VISITORS: *Weekdays only with handicap certificate*

'Yee've as gude turf for gowf here as yee'l find in a' Scotland' – the verdict of the first professional at Woodbridge, David Howie. Nowadays there are 27 holes of delightful and beautifully conditioned heathland golf with abundant gorse and heather to punish the errant. The 9-hole Forest Course is a good test in its own right, including the longest hole on either circuit, the 553yd/506m 4th.

The main course is not overly long, yet it tests all departments equally. With its approach across a pond, the 329yd/301m 2nd tries everyone's accuracy, and the 4th is cleverly angled and bunkered. Curving through the gorse, the 5th is a very fine hole playing over a depression to the green. The 10th and 16th are substantial par 4s, but the trickiest may well prove to be the 17th, with a drive to an angled fairway and approach over a gully to the raised green.

Woodbridge's short 7th, Sutton Hoo, on which putts break from right to left on a shallow green.

 Felixstowe Ferry

Felixstowe Ferry Golf Club, Ferry Road, Felixstowe,
Suffolk IP4 9RY (1880)
TEL: *(01394) 283060* **FAX:** *(01394) 273679*
LOCATION: *North-east of Felixstowe, turn left at beach*
COURSES: *18 holes, 6308yd/5768m, par 72, SSS*
70; 9 holes, 2986yd/2730m, par 35
TYPE OF COURSE: *Seaside links*
DESIGNER: *Henry Cotton*
GREEN FEES: *££*
FACILITIES: *Pro shop, clubhouse*
VISITORS: *Welcome with handicap certificate*

Brush up on your Bernard Darwin before playing, as it was here that he began to play golf in 1884. But if you want to frighten yourself silly read the classic M.R. James ghost story 'Oh, Whistle, and I'll Come to You, My Lad'. James had Felixstowe in mind when he wrote it. During both World Wars the course disappeared under the weight of military machinery, so what is played today is relatively modern, laid out by Henry Cotton, though you would be forgiven for thinking it had always been like this.

The first holes demand solid hitting, genuine links golf from the outset. Then from the 4th to the 12th play moves slightly inland with ditches frequently affecting events. The prevailing wind makes the water to the left of the par-5 10th a real danger. From the 13th to the 15th, a sequence of fine holes marks the return to the shore. Strength will be required on the long par-3 16th to carry a cross-bunker and then again on the substantial par-4 17th, arguably the best hole on the course.

 Thetford

Thetford Golf Club, Brandon Road, Thetford, Norfolk
IP24 3NE (1912)
TEL: *(01842) 752258* **FAX:** *(01842) 766212*
LOCATION: *West of Thetford on B1107 to Brandon*
COURSE: *18 holes, 6879yd/6290m, par 72, SSS 73*
TYPE OF COURSE: *Forest/heathland*
DESIGNERS: *C.H. Mayo, Donald Steel*
GREEN FEES: *£££*
FACILITIES: *Pro shop, clubhouse*
VISITORS: *Welcome weekdays with handicap certificate*

Thetford was once the ecclesiastical centre of East Anglia, and Thomas Paine, author of *The Rights of Man*, was born here. Today it is an attractive market town, with a lovely golf course, the rolling fairways cut through deep forest, the turf quick-draining on the Breckland gravel. In 1988 five new holes were constructed to give greater length and better balance.

A 200yd/183m par 3 is no easy start, and the 5th is a fine heathland hole, strongly bunkered. In the forest you could be at Sunningdale. The 421yd/385m 9th is Stroke Index 1, but every hole makes you think, particularly the 380yd/347m 5th, an undulating dog-leg seriously bunkered. The 12th is only a drive and pitch, yet a depression on the right of the drive and several bunkers around the green prevent complacency. Well positioned bunkers make the 14th a tough proposition for all golfers. And the last hole is serious, a long par 4, uphill, curving, and unfailingly beautiful.

Felixstowe's 17th, overlooked by the Martello tower, a reminder of
the vulnerability of this coast to invasion.

Royal Worlington and Newmarket

Royal Worlington and Newmarket Golf Club, Golf Links Road, Worlington, Bury St Edmunds, Suffolk IP28 8SD (1893)
TEL: (01638) 712216 **FAX:** (01638) 717787
LOCATION: 6 miles/10km north-east of Newmarket off A11, signposted to Worlington
COURSE: 9 holes, 6210yd/5670m, par 70, SSS 70
TYPE OF COURSE: Links-like
DESIGNERS: Tom Dunn, Captain A.M. Ross
GREEN FEES: ££££
FACILITIES: Pro shop, clubhouse
VISITORS: Welcome with letter of introduction or handicap certificate weekdays only

Often said to be the best 9-hole course in the world, and likened to a Greek tragedy by many a budding Cambridge Blue, Mildenhall (as it is popularly called) is utterly unique. It is just the same today as it was in 1949 when J. A. Floyd went round in an astonishing 28 shots, and hardly any different from the course Captain A. M. Ross and Tom Dunn laid out in the 1890s. A narrow belt of sandy soil supports links-like turf with excellent drainage giving some of the best

Royal Worlington's 3rd, a par 4 of only 361yd/330m yet providing food for thought on both the drive and pitch, everything depending on the angle of approach.

winter golf in the country. The greens can be a rude awakening for those brought up on heavily watered holding surfaces. Mildenhall is as exacting a test of the pitch-and-run as can be found, the greens brilliantly protected by little ridges and swales and likely to repel all but the most confident of shots.

A short par 5, the 1st provides a gentle introduction. In contrast the par-3 2nd, 224yd/205m long, has been described as 'like pitching onto a policeman's helmet'. The 3rd is a short par 4, but even after a good drive the pitch must be perfectly weighted given the dip before the green and attendant bunkers.

It is the approach over a ridge which makes the 4th hole very tricky to judge, while the 5th is one of the greatest short holes in English golf, bunkerless, but potentially devastating if you miss on either side. The 6th and 8th are superb two-shotters, great examinations of long-iron play, and the last hole is a Cape hole par excellence.

15 Gog Magog

The Gog Magog Golf Club, Shelford Bottom,
Cambridge CB2 4AB (1901)
TEL: *(01223) 247626* **FAX:** *(01223) 414990*
LOCATION: *South-east of Cambridge on A1307*
COURSES: *Old: 18 holes, 6398yd/5850m, par 70,*
SSS 70; Wandlebury:18 holes, 6754yd/6176m, par
72, SSS 73
TYPE OF COURSE: *Hilly, well-drained downland/*
parkland
DESIGNER: *Hawtree (Wandlebury)*
GREEN FEES: *£££*
FACILITIES: *Pro shop, trolley and club hire, clubhouse*
VISITORS: *Welcome weekdays with letter of introduction*
or handicap certificate, member's guests only at weekends

Gog Magog's 17th, a short hole, but one on which it is
difficult to stop the ball on a cunningly downsloping green,
the wind rarely being of assistance.

The giants, Gog and Magog, chose the only hilly ground for miles around on which to live in legend. Those hills now play host to 36 holes of golf giving splendid views of the city of Cambridge and beyond over the flat expanses of the Fens. In winter the winds hurtle in unheated and unbroken on their journey from the Urals which any Cambridge golfer will tell you is the next high ground directly to the east. Winter golf is an important aspect of University golf, and here they are fortunate that the ground is so well drained.

Stiff climbing and a hedge determine events on the first two holes, mid-length par 4s, but the Old Course is gentler thereafter. The par-5 7th is almost a seaside hole transported inland. Perhaps the most individual hole is the 11th, plentifully bunkered, with its green in an amphitheatre of humps and bumps. The 446yd/408m 18th runs obligingly downhill to a plateau green.

OTHER COURSES TO VISIT IN EASTERN ENGLAND

Cambridgeshire	Frinton	Belton Woods	Gorleston
Brampton Park	Orsett	Blankney	Great Yarmouth and
Peterborough Milton	Romford	Elsham	Caister
Thorpe Wood	Stock Brook Manor	Forest Pines	King's Lynn
Essex	Stoke-by-Nayland	Gainsborough	Royal Norwich
Abridge	Theydon Bois	Lincoln	**Suffolk**
Channels	Thorndon Park	North Shore	Brett Vale
Chelmsford	Three Rivers	Stoke Rochford	Bury St Edmunds
Chigwell	West Essex	**Norfolk**	Ipswich
Essex G & CC	**Lincolnshire**	Barnham Broom Hotel	Rushmere
Five Lakes Hotel	Belton Park	Eaton	Thorpeness

REGIONAL DIRECTORY

Where to Stay

Lincolnshire **Winteringham Fields** (01724 733096) near Scunthorpe is a 16th-century country house hotel with a fabulous restaurant.

Hertfordshire If you want to play golf at **Hanbury Manor** (01920 48/722) you will have to stay there.

Norfolk Who could resist sleeping at Great Snoring? The **Old Rectory** (01328 820597) dates back to 1500. **Morston Hall** (01263 741041) near Holt is a small, gastronomically distinguished hotel.

Suffolk **Theberton Grange** (01263 768909) near Leiston, and the **Old Rectory** (01728 746524) at Campsea Ashe near Woodbridge, attract for their comfort and distinctive cooking.

Cambridge **Chiswick House** (01763 260242), at Meldreth, is a peaceful farmhouse almost 700 years old.

Where to Eat

Lincolnshire **Magpies** (01507 527004) in Horncastle and **Harry's Place** (01476 561780) in Great Gonerby are reputed for their cooking, and the **Epworth Tap** (01427 873333) also for its wines.

Norfolk Wine lovers should dine at **Adlard's** (01603 633522) in Norwich , and the cooking is recommended at **Fishes'** (01328 738588) in Burnham Market , **Yetman's** (01263 713320) in Holt, **Rococo** (01553 771483) in King's Lynn, and **Strattons** (01760 723845) in Swaffham.

Suffolk The jewel in Suffolk's vinous crown is **The Crown** (01502 722275) at Southwold. In Aldeburgh, **Lighthouse** (01728 453377) and **Regatta** (01728 450211) gain high ratings for their skillet skills, as do **The Captain's Table** in Woodbridge (01394 383145) and **Theobalds** (01359 231707) in Ixworth.

Essex The cellars at **Le Talbooth** (01206 323150) in Dedham and the **White Hart** (01787 237250) in Great Yeldham are in the championship league. There is much praise for the food at **Dicken's** (01371 850723) at Wethersfield.

Cambridge **Midsummer House** (01223 369299) and **22 Chesterton Road** (01223 351880) are worthy of attention, as are the **Three Horseshoes** (01954 210221) at Madingley, **Sycamore House** (01223 843396) at Little Shelford and the **Pink Geranium** (01763 260215) at Melbourne.

What to See (see also pages 95 to 97)

Norfolk The religious life of Norfolk was enhanced in 1061 when Lady Richeld, having seen a vision, built a small shelter over a statue of the Virgin and Child which soon became one of the most important places of pilgrimage in England, **Walsingham**. The priory subsequently founded here did not survive the Reformation but the churches of almost every town and village in the county are notable, most of them distinguished by their characteristic flint walls. **Walpole St Peter** ('Queen of the Marshes'), **Cromer**, several churches in **King's Lynn**, **Loddon**, **Pulham St Mary**, **Salle**, curious **Little Snoring**, and **Wymondham** are but a few of the many. The remains of **Castle Rising** overlook the fine woodland King's Lynn golf course. **Castle Acre Priory** and the vestiges of its once important Norman castle reward a visit. **Blickling Hall** and **Holkham Hall** are the county's best-known mansions, and others such as **East Barsham** attract the lover of fine architecture. Sailing on the **Broads**, bird-watching at **Cley**, riding behind a steam engine on the **North Norfolk Railway**, exploring prehistory in **Grime's Graves**, or eating lobster and crab at a pub along the coast road, are a few of the worthier distractions.

Suffolk In Suffolk the little towns of **Southwold**, **Eye** and **Framlingham**, **Hengrave Hall**, **Ickworth House**, **Stoke-by-Nayland** village, and **Woolpit**'s renowned church deserve discovery. **Sudbury**, **Hadleigh**, **Boxford**, and **Kersey**, perhaps the prettiest of all Suffolk villages, were at the centre of a thriving cloth trade. **Newmarket** is world-famous as one of the centres of English horse racing.

Essex The village green at **Finchinfield**, the imposing towers of **Layer Marney**'s gatehouse, the charming houses and huge church at **Thaxted**, **Paycocke's House** near Coggeshall, and the extraordinary Saxon wooden church at **Greensted-juxta-Ongar** are rewarding, as is fidelity in marriage: the **Dunmow Flitch** (a side of bacon) is traditionally presented to any couple who can prove that they have never regretted their marriage 'for a year and a day'.

Cambridge is England's most handsome university town, but its colleges are working places of scholarship and admission to many is restricted. If there is time for only one visit it should be to the **Chapel of King's College**, its interior breathtakingly beautiful and generally open to the public when services are not taking place. **Ely Cathedral** towers above the low country of the Fens, an impressive building, not least for its unique octagonal lantern tower, the mighty West Tower, and outstanding wooden ceiling. The west façade of **Peterborough Cathedral** is one of the most dramatic in medieval architecture.

Chapter 5

The North-West

If, today, the principal English cultural, political and economic divide is North–South, the deepest-rooted has always been that between Lancashire and Yorkshire. Its differences have endured since the Wars of the Roses in the 15th century. The hills of the Pennines, the 'backbone of England', form a convenient and practical dividing line. Quite where they begin is open to debate, but for our golfing convenience the North-West begins in their foothills in the Peak National Park in Derbyshire.

Cheshire

On flatter ground, in neighbouring Cheshire, the great city, historically, was Chester, the Roman Deva, founded in the 1st century AD. In a sense the Romans are still here, because they left us their road layout, with the four main streets in the

Left: The 16th at Hillside, showing the expansive dunes, a wildlife haven shared with neighbouring Royal Birkdale. Above: Little Moreton Hall in Cheshire.

shape of a cross, and other treasures such as the Hypocaust. By the late Saxon era Chester had grown into a place of some consequence, even running to its own mint. Around the middle of the 10th century, a church was founded which in time became the cathedral. A good deal of medieval and Tudor Chester has survived, most strikingly the double-decked, half-timbered, wooden shopping arcades, The Rows, and the reasonably complete city walls. Chester encapsulates a great deal of British history, social and political.

Cheshire has long been an affluent county and many of its parish churches reflect this, especially those in the south-west. Perhaps the prettiest ecclesiastical setting, though, is Great Budworth, in the middle of the county, a handsome village much used today for film location work. Of the many black-and-white country houses, Little Moreton Hall is one of the finest examples in all England, and Gawsworth Hall, near Macclesfield, boasts

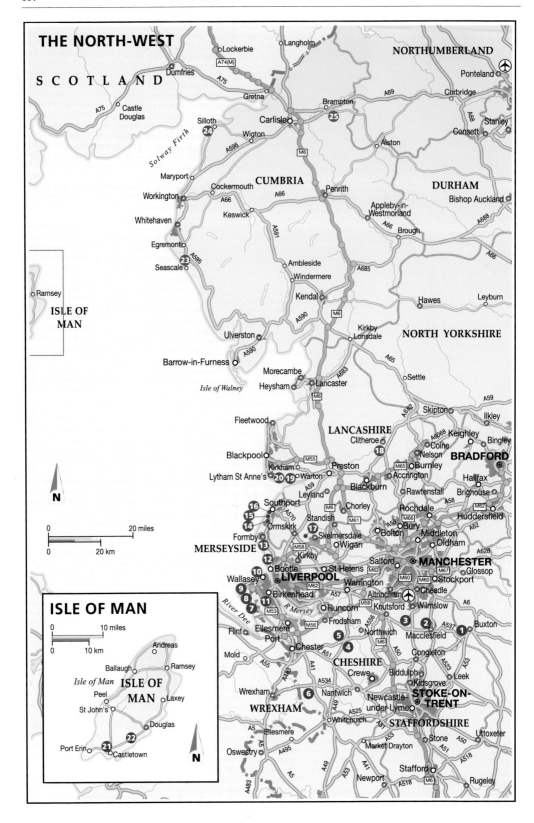

KEY TO MAP

1. Cavendish	14. Southport and
2. Prestbury	Ainsdale
3. Wilmslow	15. Hillside
4. Sandiway	16. Royal Birkdale
5. Delamere Forest	17. Ormskirk
6. Carden Park	18. Clitheroe
7. Heswall	19. Fairhaven
8. Caldy	20. Royal Lytham and
9. Royal Liverpool	St Annes
10. Wallasey	21. Castletown
11. Wirral Ladies'	22. Mount Murray
12. West Lancashire	23. Seascale
13. Formby	24. Silloth-on-Solway
	25. Brampton

links with Elisabeth Fitton, arguably the 'Dark Lady' of Shakespeare's sonnets. A later jewel is found in Legh Road, Knutsford, which contains a run of remarkable Art Nouveau houses rivalled only by the Gaudi creations in Barcelona.

Lancashire

The lasting bequests of the industrial revolution are most apparent in the big Lancashire cities, Liverpool and Manchester. Liverpool's wealth stemmed from its development as a seaport with regular traffic to all parts of the globe. Its civic and commercial buildings continue to impress, though they are the Anglican and Roman Catholic cathedrals which dominate the skyline at either end of the appropriately named Hope Street. Worldwide interest in the Grand National steeplechase held at Aintree exceeds even that for the footballing exploits of Liverpool and Everton.

Liverpool and Manchester were linked by the world's first great railway, opened in 1830. Its Manchester terminal still

exists, now part of the excellent museums of science, technology and aviation. Manchester boasts little of architectural interest, but its significance as a cosmopolitan and increasingly prosperous international city is matched only by the global renown of the Manchester United football club. Wigan and St Helens continue to flourish in the world of Rugby League despite wholescale changes within the sport, but the many industrial towns need not detain us as we head for the golfing shrines of the Lancashire coast. If we play at Royal Lytham we may have to come to terms with Blackpool, the nearest big town, which continues to thrive on its holiday trade despite the dreariness of its buildings (its Tower excepted) and the inconvenience of a tide which goes out so far that aspirant bathers may have a 20-minute hike across the mud to find enough sea in which to float. Inland, passing Pendle Hill, near Clitheroe, with its sinister witchcraft connections, little roads lead to the pretty, unspoiled hill country of the Forest of Bowland. Lancaster retains its historic castle and other significant buildings, and bird watchers flock to the shores of nearby Morecambe Bay.

The Lake District

England's highest mountains and largest lakes combine in splendour in the Lake District, at the north end of which stands Carlisle, a once strategically vital border city, with a number of surviving ancient buildings, not least a small but fascinating cathedral. Nearby are the several extraordinarily preserved sections of the Roman imperial defence, Hadrian's Wall, a treasure shared equally with the North-East, and to this day symbolically keeping England and Scotland apart.

① *Cavendish*

Cavendish Golf Club, Gadley Lane, Buxton,
Derbyshire SK17 6XD (1925)
TEL and **FAX:** (01298) 23494
LOCATION: *West of town centre, take A53 towards
Leek and Macclesfield, club signposted on right*
COURSE: *18 holes, 5721yd/5231m, par 68, SSS 68*
TYPE OF COURSE: *Moorland*
DESIGNER: *Alister Mackenzie*
GREEN FEES: *££*
FACILITIES: *Pro shop, clubhouse*
VISITORS: *Welcome with handicap certificate*

Buxton is one of England's loveliest spa
towns, and Cavendish is one of two
sporting courses there. It is the work of Alister
Mackenzie. Add to this glorious views of the
surrounding Peak District, good value green
fees, and the friendliness of the members, and
a game here really is the perfect prelude to a
rare opera – Buxton hosts one of the liveliest
opera festivals each July.

*Cavendish's 16th, a testing par 4 with out-of-bounds left
and a downhill approach to a cleverly defended green.
The scenery is hard to beat.*

Going out, the 5th is tough, an uphill par 4
with a stream to the right of the drive and a
green which is out of reach to all but the
strongest of men. The 9th is a mischievous
downhill par 3, recently restored to its
original Mackenzie design. The 10th and 11th
are excellent long par 4s, with forced carries
over gullies. Only 116yd/106m long, the
15th is a teaser, while the roller-coaster 18th
is a stern finish.

② *Prestbury*

Prestbury Golf Club, Macclesfield Road, Prestbury,
Macclesfield, Cheshire SK10 4BJ (1920)
TEL: (01625) 829388 **FAX:** (01625) 828241
LOCATION: *South of village on right of Macclesfield
road – well signed*
COURSE: *18 holes, 6359yd/5815m, par 71, SSS 71*
TYPE OF COURSE: *Hilly, wooded parkland*
DESIGNER: *Harry Colt*
GREEN FEES: *£££*
FACILITIES: *Pro shop, clubhouse*
VISITORS: *Welcome weekdays with handicap certificate*

Hidden away behind the affluent village,
Prestbury is a very charming course
built in 1920 by Harry Colt. He took
considerable advantage of the hills and valleys
of this rolling site. So, a great many greens are
either situated on hill tops or protected by the
sort of slopes which repel all but the most
truly struck shot. The 1st green is perched
almost on a cone, a difficult target from afar,
while on the 2nd the problem is preventing
the ball from shooting through the back of
the green. A very long par 4, the 9th involves
a demanding drive downhill towards bunkers
followed by a stiff climb up an ever-
narrowing fairway to a triple-tiered hilltop
green. The guile of Colt is perhaps best
demonstrated on the fine 16th, a par 4
curving uphill, needing perfect line on the
drive and sure control of the approach. This
hole needs no bunker.

At only 146yd/133m, the 9th is the shortest hole at Wilmslow. It needs little more than a wedge but it is still easy to three-putt this sloping green.

3 *Wilmslow*

The Wilmslow Golf Club, Great Warford, Mobberley, nr Knutsford, Cheshire WA16 7AY (1889)
TEL: (01565) 872148 **FAX:** (01565) 872172
LOCATION: *Off B5085 Wilmslow–Knutsford road, follow sign for David Lewis Centre*
COURSE: *18 holes, 6607yd/6041m, par 72, SSS 72*
TYPE OF COURSE: *Parkland*
DESIGNERS: *Sandy Herd, James Braid, Tom Simpson, George Duncan, Fred Hawtree, C.K. Cotton, Frank Pennink, Charles Lawrie, Dave Thomas*
GREEN FEES: *££££*
FACILITIES: *Pro shop, trolley and club hire, clubhouse*
VISITORS: *Welcome with handicap certificate (not Wednesdays)*

Wilmslow is one of the best conditioned courses in the region, even in winter. In the 1980s the Martini International and Greater Manchester Open – European Tour events – were held here and it has been a regular host to the first qualifying round of the Open Championship. Mostly it is easy walking on gentle ground, but there are several lively crossings of a river valley, not least on the opening drive, and the short 14th and 17th are full carries across the ravine at its deepest.

Several holes favour the longer hitter who can take bunkers out of play, the 3rd and 8th, for instance, and good positional play is required to open up the green on the many dog-leg par 4s, such as the 2nd, 4th, 12th and 16th. The closing par 5 rewards those prepared to risk a long second shot downhill to a green on the riverbank.

4 *Sandiway*

Sandiway Golf Club, Chester Road, Sandiway, Northwich, Cheshire CW8 2DJ (1921)
TEL: (01606) 883247 **FAX:** (01606) 888548
LOCATION: *A556 Northwich–Chester road at Sandiway (turn left just before round tower)*
COURSE: *18 holes, 6435yd/5884m, par 70, SSS 72*
TYPE OF COURSE: *Parkland with touches of heathland*
DESIGNER: *Ted Ray, Harry Colt*
GREEN FEES: *£££*
FACILITIES: *Pro shop, trolley hire, clubhouse*
VISITORS: *Welcome with handicap certificate*

A measure of Sandiway's quality is the respect in which it is held by the best players, amateur and professional. There is a compulsion to place the drive precisely, hills and woods thwarting the wayward. The approaches to many greens are narrowed by bunkers or mounds, and subtle borrows enliven the putting surfaces, which can be very fast in summer.

Ted Ray laid out Sandiway in beautiful countryside just after winning the US Open in 1920. He was renowned for his long hitting and there are several holes which reflect this, especially the three lengthy par 4s on the back nine. The 10th is a brute, 467yd/427m, uphill, curving to the left. At 446yd/408m, the 12th is marginally less daunting, though the green is cunningly sited. On the 14th the drive must be hit long over an out-of-bounds field to bring the hilltop green in range of two shots. The 17th is a superb short par 4 over a valley (see page 7).

The 16th on Carden Park's Nicklaus Course is a short par 3, but the slightest pull will sink in the lake, and the putting surface is heavily contoured.

5 *Delamere Forest*

Delamere Forest Golf Club, Station Road, Delamere, Northwich, Cheshire CW8 2JE (1910)
TEL: *(01606) 883264* **FAX:** *(01606) 883800*
LOCATION: *Between Northwich and Chester, from A556 take B5152, at Delamere Station turn right – signposted to golf*
COURSE: *18 holes, 6328yd/5786m, par 69, SSS 70*
TYPE OF COURSE: *Heathland*
DESIGNER: *Herbert Fowler*
GREEN FEES: *£££*
FACILITIES: *Pro shop, clubhouse*
VISITORS: *Welcome (two-ball play only at weekends)*

Delamere enjoys a glorious heathland setting, giving a real sense of escape from the mundane, not only on the course itself, especially on a clear day, but also in the traditional formality of the clubhouse. It retains the old-fashioned bogey system of rating holes, and, with six of the outward nine being over 400yd/366m long, a bogey of 36 is just that little bit more realistic than a par of 34 for 3269yd/2989m.

A Herbert Fowler layout of 1910, the natural contours are used to great effect, making the opening five holes notably exacting, but it is the drive at the 8th which is particularly demanding, across a chasm to an angled, bunkered fairway. The 14th is probably the most enchanting hole, the approach being played from the crest of a hill down to a green in the bottom of a wooded valley.

6 *Carden Park*

Carden Park Hotel, Golf Resort and Spa, Broxton, Chester, Cheshire CH3 9DQ (1993)
TEL: *(01829) 731600* **FAX:** *(01829) 731636*
WEBSITE: *www.carden-park.co.uk*
LOCATION: *10 miles/16km south of Chester on A534 Nantwich–Wrexham road*
COURSES: *Nicklaus: 18 holes, 7045yd/6442m, par 72, SSS 73; Cheshire: 18 holes, 6824yd/6240m, par 72, SSS 73*
TYPE OF COURSE: *Meadowland/parkland*
DESIGNERS: *Jack and Steve Nicklaus (Nicklaus Course), Alan Higgins (Cheshire Course)*
GREEN FEES: *£££££ (Nicklaus Course, includes buggy), ££££ (Cheshire Course)*
FACILITIES: *Pro shop, buggy and club hire, golf academy, range, clubhouse, extensive conference, hotel and leisure facilities*
VISITORS: *Welcome*

Carden, in a very beautiful part of Cheshire, once entertained the royalty of Europe. Now two quite different golf courses challenge visitors to this opulent leisure resort. The Nicklaus Course is the first to be designed jointly by Jack and his son, Steve, and is described by them as a 'thinking man's course'. Despite the contemporary style of architecture, they have been at great pains to preserve the pastoral nature of the land and to conserve the indigenous flora and fauna.

Two holes, the 6th and 17th, involve skirmishes with lakes, both inviting you to chance your arm for the best approach to the green. Most of the challenges are strategic rather than utterly penal, so there are two split fairways, on the 7th and 15th, on which the right-hand route is safer from the tee, but the much more demanding left-hand route sets up a far simpler approach to the green.

 Heswall

Heswall Golf Club, Cottage Lane, Gayton, Heswall, Wirral L60 8PB (1902)
TEL and FAX: (0151) 342 1237
LOCATION: From A540 Chester–Hoylake road turn left at roundabout with A551, follow signs
COURSE: 18 holes, 6492yd/5936m, par 72, SSS 72
TYPE OF COURSE: Estuarine parkland
DESIGNERS: Jack Morris, Frank Pennink
GREEN FEES: £££
FACILITIES: Pro shop, clubhouse
VISITORS: Welcome with handicap certificate

Like its near neighbour, Caldy, Heswall enjoys all the advantages of delightful views across the course to the salt marshes of the Dee Estuary and, beyond, to the hills of Flint and Denbigh. And it was over these salt marshes in 1926 that Pilot Officer Pentland, practising aerobatics, lost control of his plane, leapt out of the cockpit, and entered the history books as the first RAF man to save his life using a parachute.

Heswall is laid out on either side of a long-defunct railway, the six holes on the far side running down to the water's edge. Only the

Caldy's 3rd green and 4th tee, with golfers embarking on one of the prettiest stretches of seaside golf in England, where the Dee Estuary meets the Irish Sea.

par-5 5th actually skirts the shore, but there are plenty of ditches and ponds lurking on each of these holes, of which the strong par-4 14th is probably the pick. The inland holes are more undulating, the downhill par-4 3rd particularly attractive, its green behind a pond.

Caldy

Caldy Golf Club, Links Hey Road, Caldy, Wirral L48 1NB (1907)
TEL: (0151) 625 5660 FAX: (0151) 625 7394
LOCATION: Off A540 Chester–Hoylake road, left B5140 Caldy Road, left into Croft Drive East, left into Links Hey Road
COURSE: 18 holes, 6675yd/6104m, par 72, SSS 73
TYPE OF COURSE: Seaside links, downland and parkland
DESIGNERS: Jack Morris, Donald Steel
GREEN FEES: ££££
FACILITIES: Pro shop, buggy hire, clubhouse
VISITORS: Welcome with handicap certificate

Caldy is triply blessed, for its 18 holes encompass seaside, downland and parkland golf, all in an attractive location overlooking the Dee Estuary. The variety of styles and the variation in the length of its individual holes add greatly to its enjoyment. It is a mere stone's throw from Royal Liverpool and yet the two could hardly be more different.

The 3rd, a challenging dog-leg down to the beach for the ordinary player, can be driven on the direct line by the mighty but, as it involves an enormous carry over rough ground and a pond, the margin for error is slight. Following the line of the shore, the next three holes culminate in an exacting approach shot over a ditch to reach the 6th green. Inland, the 1st is an invigorating opener, while the 16th green is protected by bunkers and an ancient 'rubbing stone', both on downland. The parkland holes are more undulating, the 11th a double dog-leg par 5, and the 12th, a substantial par 4, one of the hardest holes on the course.

9 Royal Liverpool

Royal Liverpool Golf Club, Meols Drive, Hoylake,
Wirral L47 4AL (1869)
TEL: (0151) 632 3101/2 **FAX:** (0151) 632 6737
WEBSITE: www.royal-liverpool-golf.com
LOCATION: A540 Wirral coast road between West
Kirby and Hoylake
COURSES: Championship: 18 holes, 7128yd/6518m,
par 72, SSS 76; Long: 6847yd/6261m, par 72,
SSS74
TYPE OF COURSE: Links
DESIGNER: Jack Morris
GREEN FEES: ££££
FACILITIES: Pro shop, caddies, trolley and club hire,
clubhouse, golf museum and library
VISITORS: Welcome with handicap certificate or letter of
introduction

ROYAL LIVERPOOL
LONG COURSE

HOLE	YD	M	PAR	HOLE	YD	M	PAR
1	429	392	4	10	412	377	4
2	374	342	4	11	200	183	3
3	505	462	5	12	393	359	4
4	184	168	3	13	159	145	3
5	424	388	4	14	521	477	5
6	383	350	4	15	459	420	4
7	198	181	3	16	533	487	5
8	491	449	5	17	393	359	4
9	392	359	4	18	397	363	4
OUT	3380	3091	36	IN	3467	3170	36

6847YD • 6261M • PAR 72

Harold Hilton, Sandy Herd, Arnaud Massy, J.H. Taylor, Walter Hagen, Bobby Jones, A. H. Padgham, Fred Daly, Peter Thomson, and Roberto de Vicenzo: the roll call of Open Champions at 'Hoylake', a list to rival any. There might have been more but the demands on hotel accommodation, road and rail access, and sheer space have prevented a return since 1967 when Vicenzo disposed of the challenge of the mighty Nicklaus, then at the height of his youthful powers. Founded in

Championships in the years before the First World War. Many ladies' championships have been played at Hoylake, perhaps the proudest moment in recent years being when the ladies of Great Britain and Ireland regained the Curtis Cup in a thrilling contest in 1992.

First impressions of Hoylake deceive, for the view from the clubhouse suggests a place of unremitting flatness. It only requires the 1st hole to put everything into perspective, a wicked par 4 on which it is all too easy to go out-of-bounds on both the drive and the second shot.

Evil as a 1st

1869 it is one of the oldest clubs in England. The very first Amateur Championship was played here in 1885. Two of the greatest amateurs of all time were members, John Ball and Harold Hilton. Both won the Open Championship and between them they won 12 Amateur

hole, it is positively venomous as the deciding hole in a tied match. The short 7th, Dowie, was once one of the most capricious holes in golf, with a notorious out-of-bounds cop to the left, and nowhere to drop short. After much soul searching, in 1994 the cop was removed, three bunkers were set into the mounds introduced either side, and a wet area short of the green was re-established to provide a water hazard and greater visual impact. At nearly 200yd/183m, it is still not easy, but it is a lot fairer.

The rolling 8th temporarily troubled Bobby Jones in his all-conquering rounds of 1930. Here he ran up an 8, but all was redeemed on the 9th and the rest is magnificent history. This is the most attractive part of the course, and the 10th and 12th are superb par 4s, both played to greens up on the

The 17th at Royal Liverpool, its green treacherously close to the out-of-bounds fence. In the background can be seen the distinctive towers and turrets of Hoylake's clubhouse.

dunes overlooking the Dee Estuary, Hilbre Island and the North Wales Coast.

Back on flatter ground, once the home of the Liverpool Hunt Club Race Course, the run in needs stamina. The par-5 16th brings another cop into contention, this mound enclosing the (out-of-bounds) practice ground. Vicenzo defied it courageously in the last round in 1967 by hitting his second shot out over the cop to find the green. Even at this stage, success is not guaranteed, for it is all too possible to shoot through the 17th green onto the road behind, while the bunkering on the 18th has been increased further to tighten up a fine finishing hole.

10 *Wallasey*

Wallasey Golf Club, Bayswater Road, Wallasey,
Wirral L45 8LA (1891)
TEL: *(0151) 639 3630* **FAX:** *(0151) 638 8988*
LOCATION: *Wallasey, M53 Jct 1, follow signs towards
New Brighton*
COURSE: *18 holes, 6607yd/6041m, par 72, SSS 73*
TYPE OF COURSE: *Links*
DESIGNER: *Tom Morris*
GREEN FEES: *££££*
FACILITIES: *Pro shop, caddies, clubhouse*
VISITORS: *Welcome with handicap certificate*

*Wallasey's 18th, where the green is the only comparatively
flat ground on this archetypal, undulating links hole.*

Wallasey was the home club of Dr Frank
Stableford, inventor of that popular
competition format. It was also where Bobby
Jones qualified for the Open Championship in
1930, en route to his Grand Slam. But it is
the course which distinguishes Wallasey. How
much of Tom Morris's original layout of 1891
survives is not known. He must have rejoiced
at the sight of the billowing sand dunes, the
1st bumping over them, the 2nd winding
through them, and the 3rd climbing onto
them. From the 4th tee the view is
magnificent: the entire Welsh coastline from
Anglesey to Flint, and the Lancashire coast as
far as Morecambe. The finish is outstanding,
the 16th a long par 3 to a ledge green, the
17th very long, needing a first-rate drive to
open up the green, while the 18th, all humps
and hollows, is a real links speciality.

11 *Wirral Ladies'*

The Wirral Ladies' Golf Club, 93 Bidston Road,
Birkenhead, Merseyside CH43 6TS (1894)
TEL: *(0151) 652 1255* **FAX:** *(0151) 653 4323*
LOCATION: *Claughton. M53 Jct 3 take A552
Woodchurch Road towards Birkenhead, left at lights into
Storeton Road, Ingestre Road, right at Talbot Road,
becomes Bidston Road, club on left*
COURSE: *18 holes, 4966yd/4541m, par 70, LGU
SSS 70*
TYPE OF COURSE: *Parkland/heathland*
DESIGNER: *Harold Hilton (but much altered)*
GREEN FEES: *££*
FACILITIES: *Pro shop, clubhouse*
VISITORS: *Welcome with handicap certficate*

*The clubhouse of Wirral Ladies' Golf Club overlooking
the final green, a typically well-defended short par 4.*

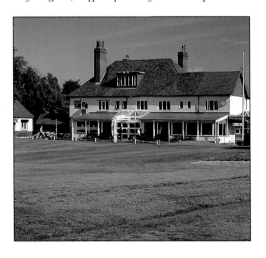

Three ladies' clubs thrive in England, at
Sunningdale, Formby and Birkenhead,
the first two rather like condensed versions of
their masculine counterparts. However, Wirral
Ladies' stands on its own. It was formed in the
1890s when a group of wives of Royal
Liverpool members found themselves unable to
play at Hoylake and persuaded their husbands

to build them a course of their own, though the present layout is post-war. The fairways are narrow with heather and gorse to punish the wayward. The rough can be punitive, much of it left to grow wild, a refuge for the rare Marsh Gentian. The greens make this a fascinating test of golf, deviously contoured, many raised up, and none bigger than a pocket handkerchief, demanding perfect placement on the fairway followed by a sure touch on the approach. Male golfers are welcomed and their game is ingeniously examined.

 **12** *West Lancashire*

The West Lancashire Golf Club, Hall Road West, Blundellsands, Liverpool L23 8SZ (1873)
TEL: *(0151) 924 1076* **FAX:** *(0151) 931 4448*
WEBSITE: *www.merseyworld.com/wlgc/*
LOCATION: *From A565 Liverpool–Southport road, follow signs to club at north end of Crosby*
COURSE: *18 holes, 6768yd/6189m, par 72, SSS 73*
TYPE OF COURSE: *Links*
DESIGNER: *C.K. Cotton*
GREEN FEES: *£££*
FACILITIES: *Pro shop, club hire, clubhouse*
VISITORS: *Welcome with handicap certificate*

Oldest of the famous Lancashire links courses, West Lancashire occupies the southernmost dunes, a place of larks, geese, plovers and oystercatchers. The record books celebrate a day in 1972 when the assistant professional, Peter Parkinson, holed in one at the 357yd/326m par-4 7th. Stand on the tee, drink in the lovely views from the Welsh hills to Blackpool Tower, allow for the wind, observe the four bunkers lying in wait for drives of many strengths, not to mention hillocks and hummocks, nor the fact that the green is little bigger than a pimple in a raging sea, and you begin to understand the nature of that preposterous stroke. A fine stretch of dunes holes begins at the short 12th, with excellent views from the elevated 13th tee – both of the coast and the golfing hazards awaiting. The 440yd/402m 14th is a tough dog-leg, its green under a wooded hill.

West Lancs' short 3rd. The par 3s at West Lancs are not long but each is ingeniously bunkered and several are angled across the line of the approach.

Formby

Formby Golf Club, Golf Road, Formby, Liverpool L37 1LQ (1884)
TEL: *(01704) 872164/874273* **FAX:** *(01704) 833028*
LOCATION: *Off A565 Southport–Liverpool road adjacent to Freshfields station*
COURSES: *18 holes, 6993yd/6394m, par 72, SSS74; Formby Ladies': 18 holes, 5426yd/4962m, par 71, SSS 71*
TYPE OF COURSE: *Links*
DESIGNERS: *Willie Park, Harry Colt, Frank Pennink, Donald Steel*
GREEN FEES: *££££*
FACILITIES: *Pro shop, caddies, bar and restaurant*
VISITORS: *Welcome with handicap certificate (max. 24)*

Running over undulating sandy ground, enclosed in a nature warren, the pines a haven for red squirrels, Formby has always been an outstandingly handsome place. But, when coastal erosion forced the abandonment of several holes, the new ones created out of the forest only served to increase the charm and loveliness of the course. It is no surprise that Formby has hosted all the great

The 8th at Formby, a short par 5 at 493yd/451m, bunkerless at that, but one of the strongest and most attractive holes on this magnificent course.

championships in the amateur calendar, not least when José Maria Olazabal defeated Colin Montgomerie to win the 1984 Amateur Championship. A century earlier the 25 founding members paid a guinea a year to play their nine completely natural holes, and '3d a moderate go' to consume the club's whisky.

Starting alongside the railway, a slice is disastrous though heather is the principal hazard on these opening holes. The 6th is uncompromising, with a testing second shot played blind over a series of ridges to a secretive green. The 7th fairway lurches from side to side as it climbs through trees to its vigorously sloping green. Pines and an angled plateau fairway give a distinctive aspect to the 8th, which is continued as the fairway corkscrews through the trees, rising to a brilliantly placed green.

Back on the original, pre-erosion, course, the 11th is a fine par 4 to an elevated green, and the 12th appeals with its rolling fairway and rigorous second shot across mounds. The drive to the 15th, up towards a crest, is followed by a challenging approach over, and between, lesser dunes.

Southport and Ainsdale

Southport and Ainsdale Golf Club, Bradshaws Lane, Ainsdale, Southport, Merseyside PR8 3LG (1907)
TEL: *(01704) 578000* **FAX:** *(01704) 570896*
LOCATION: *At Ainsdale, 3 miles/5km south of Southport, off A565*
COURSE: *18 holes 6612yd/6046m, par 72, SSS 73*
TYPE OF COURSE: *Inland links*
DESIGNER: *James Braid*
GREEN FEES: *£££*
FACILITIES: *Pro shop, caddies, club hire, clubhouse*
VISITORS: *Welcome with handicap certificate, restricted at weekends*

The Ryder Cup has twice been held at Southport and Ainsdale, Great Britain & Ireland winning in 1933, the outcome being decided by the last putt on the final green.

The Americans won convincingly in 1937 Southport and Ainsdale lies just over the railway line from Hillside, and it has much the same feel about it. The dunes are not as high as those on Hillside's back nine, but it is genuine links golf despite the proximity of housing on two sides. Much of James Braid's 1923 design survives, and the fine 3rd is named after him. A well-bunkered 200yd/183m par 3 is a difficult start, and the par-5 2nd is handsome as it climbs into the dunes. The most famous hole is the par-5 16th, Gumbleys. Alongside the railway, this is an exciting hole, the second shot, even today, a stiff carry over a sand hill.

Hillside

Hillside Golf Club, Hastings Road, Hillside, Southport, Lancs PR8 2LU (1909)
TEL: *(01704) 567169* **FAX:** *(01704) 563192*
LOCATION: *2 miles/3km south of Southport, A565 Hillside railway station, follow sign*
COURSE: *18 holes, 6850yd/6264m, par 72, SSS 74*
TYPE OF COURSE: *Links*
DESIGNER: *Fred Hawtree*
GREEN FEES: *££££*
FACILITIES: *Pro shop, caddies, buggy and club hire, bar and restaurant*
VISITORS: *Welcome with handicap certificate*

Hillside can be said to look down on Royal Birkdale. That is no reflection on the esteem in which these neighbouring clubs hold each other but, rather, that Hillside's back nine passes through mountainous dunes, a number of its tees giving quite marvellous views, not only down onto Birkdale but also, far beyond, up and down the coast from Blackpool to Colwyn Bay. In fact these holes are relatively new, dating from 1967 when a patch of more modest golfing land was sold for housing development. Fred Hawtree, a member of the family firm which has kept Royal Birkdale at the forefront of golf, designed this part and

Possibly the most arresting view in English links golf, that from the 17th tee at Hillside. A footpath is all that separates Hillside from Royal Birkdale at this point.

there are many, Jack Nicklaus included, who rate this as one of the finest nine-hole stretches in the country. Since the alterations it has staged the PGA Championship (Tony Jacklin's last significant victory as a tour player), the Amateur Championship, and the British Ladies' Open Amateur Championship, placing Hillside firmly in the company of the highest.

That back nine could overshadow what comes before, yet scoring is no easier right from the start with a difficult drive alongside the railway. The well-bunkered, short 10th begins the journey into the dunes, pines adding to the beauty. The climb to the 11th is worth every puff on the way with the first of the spectacular coastal views afforded from its tee. Another stunningly located tee awaits on the long par-5 17th, high above Birkdale yet again, and with the fairway far below.

16 *Royal Birkdale*

The Royal Birkdale Golf Club, Waterloo Road,
Birkdale, Southport, Merseyside PR8 2LX (1889)
TEL: (01704) 567920 **FAX:** (01704) 562327
LOCATION: On A565 1½ miles/2.5km south of
Southport
COURSES: 18 holes, Open Championship: 7018yd/
6417m, par 70; Medal: 6690yd/6117m, par 72,
SSS 73
TYPE OF COURSE: Links
DESIGNERS: George Lowe, J.H. Taylor, F.G.
Hawtree, F.W. Hawtree, and Martin Hawtree
GREEN FEES: £££££
FACILITIES: Pro shop, caddies, trolley and club hire,
clubhouse
VISITORS: Welcome with letter of introduction and/or
handicap certificate

ROYAL BIRKDALE
OPEN CHAMPIONSHIP COURSE

HOLE	YD	M	PAR	HOLE	YD	M	PAR
1	449	410	4	10	403	369	4
2	421	385	4	11	408	373	4
3	407	372	4	12	183	167	3
4	203	186	3	13	498	455	4
5	344	314	4	14	198	181	3
6	480	439	4	15	544	498	5
7	177	162	3	16	416	380	4
8	457	418	4	17	547	500	5
9	411	376	4	18	472	432	4
OUT	3349	3062	34	IN	3669	3355	36

7018YD • 6417M • PAR 70

Royal Birkdale may have joined the Open rota relatively late (in 1954) but it has cemented its place for a number of reasons, not only the undoubted quality of the challenge it sets. For one thing, it is a great spectator course, the fairways for the most part running along the bottoms of the valleys between the dunes. A second reason for Birkdale's eminence is its fairness. The professionals recognize it as the course with the fewest capricious bounces and the least element of chance.

and – recently – completely rebuilding the greens (brilliantly, under the direction of Martin Hawtree). Other changes have included the grubbing out of the trees and bushes which were encroaching on the fairways, not only spoiling the drainage and maintenance of the fairways and threatening wildlife, but also altering the nature of the golfing challenge away from that of pure links. But in one important aspect

Practice Ground

Cottage ■

Starter's Hut

The third reason is the club itself and its forward-looking attitude, with no hint of complacency. Since the days of Arnold Palmer and Peter Thomson Royal Birkdale has not been afraid to alter the course, to change holes substantially, adding the lovely short 12th, in effect replacing the old 17th,

the club does look to the past – wildlife conservation.

The 1st is as demanding a start as is found on any Open course, a double dog-leg with out-of-bounds right and a hill on the left. In 1976 Seve Ballesteros announced his arrival in Open golf by driving clean over the hill!

The 2nd green nestles amidst the characteristic dunes which are such a feature of Royal Birkdale. Usually played into the prevailing wind, this is one of the hardest holes for the handicap golfer, the bunkering particularly punishing.

Setting a pattern which applies on many holes, the 2nd green is raised up between the dunes, with tight bunkering and any number of difficult borrows. The professionals play the 6th as a monster par 4 but even as we play it, as a par 5 of the same length, it is a tough proposition with a big hill on the right around which the fairway bends. The green is long, narrow and rolling and set on high ground. Two of the strongest holes are the long par-4 8th and 13th, plentifully bunkered, particularly around their raised greens, while the green on the shorter 11th gives opportunity for some very difficult pin positions.

There is a very different feel to the closing stretch, from the 15th. This is the first of only two par 5s on the Open course, a hole

changed quite dramatically between the 1991 and 1998 Opens. The trees and scrub were removed and the green reshaped to give it greater protection. There are bunkers on the left to catch the weak drive, eight bunkers set in the middle of the fairway which must be cleared with the second shot (not at all easy for the ordinary player into the prevailing wind), a mound on the right and two further bunkers to be avoided on the approach to the green.

Whether or not you are allowed to play from it, you should at least have a look from the Championship tee on the 18th. Imagine standing there, driver in hand, clinging to a slight lead in the greatest golfing event in the world! The carry is formidable, over an impenetrable tumbling wasteland, the out-of-bounds fence close on the right and a narrow strip of angled fairway to aim at. The green, just below the striking, white, nautically-styled 1930s clubhouse, is another gem, broadening out at the back behind three bunkers in close attendance.

THE HAWTREE FAMILY

Since 1912 three generations of Hawtrees have carried on the work of this family firm of course architects, making it the longest continuous practice of its kind. Frederick G. Hawtree began on his own, but in 1922 teamed up with the great Open champion, J.H. Taylor. Their crowning glory was to remodel Birkdale. His son, Frederick W., worked further afield, even in the United States. His La Marache course at Waterloo was a regular European Tour stop, when it hosted the Belgian Open. He, too, made considerable alterations at Birkdale, though many would cite his revisions to neighbouring Hillside as his noblest creation. In turn his son, Martin, entered the practice, which he now runs from a base in Oxfordshire. While their many high-profile courses gain most attention, the family's skill at working on low budgets and on restricted sites has been no less admirable.

17 Ormskirk

Ormskirk Golf Club, Cranes Lane, Lathom, Ormskirk, Lancs L40 5UJ (1899)
TEL and FAX: (01695) 572227
LOCATION: 2 miles/3km east of Ormskirk, off A577 Ormskirk–Skelmersdale road at Hulton Castle pub. Right at next junction
COURSE: 18 holes, 6480yd/5925m, par 70, SSS 71
TYPE OF COURSE: Parkland
DESIGNER: Harold Hilton
GREEN FEES: £££
FACILITIES: Pro shop, clubhouse
VISITORS: Welcome with handicap certificate or letter of introduction

As a perfect foil for the rigours of the Lancashire links courses, Ormskirk, only a short distance inland, offers a retreat of seclusion and peace. Having celebrated its centenary in 1999, Ormskirk is a regular host to regional qualifying for the Open Championship. The original very charming woodland holes were laid out by the great Hoylake amateur Harold Hilton and these are now the back nine. The rest are more open, though shielded from the outside world by woodlands.

A pond is in driving range on the 464yd/424m 3rd. Two long par 4s come together at the 7th and 8th, before play heads towards the woods. The dog-leg 11th is a particularly appealing hole with the pitch plunging through the trees, down to a tiny raised green in front of a stream. The 12th and 14th are attractive short holes in their woodland settings, and the 15th and 16th equally handsome par 4s.

18 Clitheroe

Clitheroe Golf Club, Whalley Road, Clitheroe, Lancs BB7 1PP (1891)
TEL and FAX: (01200) 422292
LOCATION: 2 miles/3km south of Clitheroe near junction of A59 and A671
COURSE: 18 holes, 6326yd/5784m, par 71, SSS 71
TYPE OF COURSE: Parkland
DESIGNER: James Braid
GREEN FEES: £££
FACILITIES: Pro shop, clubhouse
VISITORS: Welcome weekdays

Holding the English Ladies' Intermediate Championship at Clitheroe in 1995 alerted many to its golfing and scenic charms. Deep in the countryside, and enjoying delightful views of the Bowland Fells and Pendle Hill, Clitheroe is well past its centenary, though the present course is mostly the work of James Braid in the 1930s.

There is a pleasing variety to the length of the holes so, after the stern par-4 3rd, there is a mischievous little dog-leg par 4. The fine uphill par-3 8th reveals a lovely panorama of Bowland. On the back nine there is greater length but it is two of the shorter holes which have particular charm. The 16th is only

The 8th is one of four well-varied short holes at Clitheroe, a course on which the scenery makes a significant contribution to its enjoyment.

317yd/290m but the drive is semi-blind and a stream cuts across the fairway. With a narrow entrance, and the stream in attendance, this green is not one to miss. That stream also crosses in front of the 17th green, on which thoughts of Augusta's 12th would not be inappropriate.

19 *Fairhaven*

Fairhaven Golf Club, Lytham Hall Park, Ansdell, Lytham St Annes, Lancs FY8 4JU (1895)
TEL: *(01253) 736741* **FAX:** *(01253) 731461*
LOCATION: *Off A584 Lytham–Blackpool road, take B5261, club next to rugby ground*
COURSES: *18 holes, 6883yd/6294m, par 74, SSS 73*
TYPE OF COURSE: *Parkland*
DESIGNER: *J.A. Steer, James Braid*
GREEN FEES: *£££*
FACILITIES: *Pro shop, club house*
VISITORS: *Welcome with handicap certificate*

Only a stone's throw from Royal Lytham, Fairhaven could hardly be more dissimilar. Fairhaven is parkland, albeit on quick-draining sandy soil, and in late spring is pretty with rhododendrons in full bloom. It is long, at almost 6900yd/6309m, but the par of 74 includes six par 5s. Fairhaven was laid out in the early 1920s by a local golfer, J.A. Steer, advised by James Braid, counteracting the flatness of the land with bunkers, 365 of them, one for every day of the year! Only a third of them survive, plenty enough for the modern game.

The 4th is reckoned to be the hardest hole, a 451yd/412m par 4 that seems to play even longer. The par 5s, however, are not over-facing and offer birdie hopes to the aspirants who come here for final qualifying every time the Open is played next door. With their many bunkers the par 3s are all good value, particularly the 161yd/147m 17th surrounded by sand and with out-of-bounds just through the back.

Every green at Fairhaven is tightly bunkered. A par 4 of only 362yd/331m, the 9th is played to the shallowest green of the round.

20 Royal Lytham and St Annes

Royal Lytham and St Annes Golf Club, Links Gate, Lytham St Annes, Lancashire FY8 3LQ (1886)
TEL: *(01253) 724206* **FAX:** *(01253) 780946*
LOCATION: *Between Lytham and St Annes, one block in from A584*
COURSE: *Open Championship: 18 holes, 6892yd/ 6302m, par 71; Medal: 18 holes, 6685yd/6113m, par 71, SSS 74*
TYPE OF COURSE: *Inland links*
DESIGNERS: *George Lowe, Harry Colt, Tom Simpson, C.K. Cotton, Colin Maclaine*
GREEN FEES: *£££££*
FACILITIES: *Pro shop, caddies, club hire, clubhouse*
VISITORS: *Welcome midweek with handicap certificate*

ROYAL LYTHAM AND ST ANNES
OPEN CHAMPIONSHIP COURSE

HOLE	YD	M	PAR	HOLE	YD	M	PAR
1	206	188	3	10	334	305	4
2	437	400	4	11	542	496	5
3	457	418	4	12	198	181	3
4	393	359	4	13	342	313	4
5	212	194	3	14	445	407	4
6	490	448	5	15	463	423	4
7	553	506	5	16	357	326	4
8	418	382	4	17	467	427	4
9	164	150	3	18	414	379	4
OUT	3330	3045	35	IN	3562	3257	36

6892YD • 6302M • PAR 71

It goes without saying that all Open Championship courses are complete examinations, thoroughly testing every department of the game, and in this respect Royal Lytham has been described as the diploma paper. Yet Lytham has on occasions also conjured up a distinct sense of theatre. Its first Open, in 1926, almost did not happen because of the General Strike. The great amateur, Bobby Jones, only entered at the very last minute. The field included Walter Hagen and Tommy Armour, Jim Barnes and Al Watrous, and the American press came in force. Charges for

all carry over savage rough to the 17th green. A plaque, erected in the bunker, is there to remind us of the wonder of it.

Royal Lytham was also the setting for the revival in fortunes for British golf when Tony Jacklin held his rhythm and nerve over the fearsome finishing stretch to take the 1969 title by two shots. But for exciting spectacle nothing can compare with the extraordinary recovery powers of the 22-year-old Severiano Ballesteros whose driving had taken him to sand and scrub, footpaths, tracks and even the car park. That gained him the 1979 championship. In 1988 his golf was more orthodox, though no less brilliant.

This is a plain links, out of sight of the sea, bounded by a railway, but it probes relentlessly. Unusually

Dormy House

admission were made for the first time and Jones, returning from lunch without his player's pass, found himself paying his entrance fee alongside the spectators who would soon be cheering his victory. It took a spectacular shot to achieve it, a 175yd/160m bunker shot,

it begins with a short hole, 206yd/188m as the professionals play it to a green attended by nine bunkers. With the railway threatening on several holes caution is required going out, yet a good score is built here for the finish from the 14th is wicked. In 1988 this proved

the most difficult hole on the course. Most players would instinctively give that accolade to the 15th, with its troublesome drive to a rising, angled fairway, and the approach hard to judge for length. 'God, it's a hard hole,' was Jack Nicklaus's opinion when he played it in the 1974 Open.

Some twenty bunkers govern proceedings on the notorious 17th, the green only in view to those who have driven long and right. Many have arrived on the 18th tee with a chance of victory subsequently to perish in the bunkers which make this drive so formidable. In 1926, with Bobby Jones already in with a score of 291, Walter Hagen drove needing a 2 to tie. He avoided the bunkers, thereupon sending his caddie forward to remove the flag. His second shot was almost perfect, dead on line, and might just have pitched straight in. It did not, and Jones became Open Champion for the first time. 'I had to fight every hole of the way. There was never an easy round for me over that sunny wind-swept course.'

The flatness of Lytham's closing hole is deceptive. The foreground bunkers must be cleared with the drive, no easy task in a wind, if there is to be any chance of threading the approach through the necklace of bunkers surrounding the green.

LYTHAM AND THE AMERICANS

After Bobby Jones won Lytham's first Open Championship in 1926 it was a further 70 years before Tom Lehman became the next American to lift the Claret Jug there. Despite this apparent lack of empathy, Lytham was in fact a very happy hunting ground for Americans, particularly during the Second World War. One of the biggest American Air Force bases in Britain was nearby at Warton and the club in its generosity opened its doors freely to active servicemen, even lending them clubs if need be. One who came in 1944, playing an exhibition match in uniform to raise funds for the Red Cross, was Bobby Jones himself.

The Open Championship in England

When the Open Championship was first played in Scotland in 1860 no links course, not even Royal North Devon, existed in England, and only a links was recognized as the real thing by the Scots. Tom Morris and Willie Park, Scottish professionals, dominated the early events, but in 1890 an English amateur, John Ball of Royal Liverpool, came to Prestwick and walked off with the Claret Jug. Four years later it was felt that the quality of English golf courses had progressed sufficiently that the Championship might be held outside Scotland for the first time, J.H. Taylor winning the first of his five titles at Royal St George's.

Royal Liverpool was added to the rota in 1897 and the club's other distinguished amateur, Harold Hilton, took the trophy. Between them these two clubs had hosted no fewer than 15 Opens by the outbreak of the Second World War. The Championship had also come south twice to Royal Cinque Ports at Deal, but by the time of its second Open, in 1920, the event was developing at a pace. Overseas players came in increasing numbers and huge crowds were attracted. Only a few courses could cope.

The Americans dominated the Open in the 1920s and early 30s, Walter Hagen winning on English soil at Sandwich (twice) and Hoylake, and Bobby Jones at Lytham and Hoylake, only the third amateur to win the trophy and very probably the last. Jones's triumph at Hoylake in 1930 came as part of his astonishing Grand Slam, taking the Amateur and Open Championships of both the USA and Britain in the same year. Another American to win in England in this period was the diminutive Gene Sarazen, whose victory happened at Sandwich, but not at Royal St George's, rather at adjoining Prince's. That was in 1932. It was next door at Royal St George's two years later that Henry Cotton at last broke the sequence of American victories with a doggedly determined performance.

After the Second World War there was no question of returning to Prince's which had been used as a battle training ground and had been utterly obliterated. Hoylake, though, was still in good shape, and Fred Daly became the only Irishman to win the Open when he took the 1947 title there. Remarkably, Royal St George's had remained more or less intact and the South African, Bobby Locke, gained the first of his four Opens there in 1949. But the little roads in and around Sandwich could no longer cope with the demands of an Open, and the Championship disappeared from the South of England for over thirty years.

Lytham was still very much in the frame, but another English venue was required, and in 1954 Birkdale (not yet Royal) held its first Open, won by the Australian, Peter Thomson. Happily in 1981 a new road meant that Royal St George's could be restored to the rota, but, sadly, by then the pressures of space had removed Hoylake, probably for ever. It would seem that the extraordinary room required to accommodate all the equipment of the world's media, tented villages, and many thousands of spectators precludes, for the moment at least, the possibility of any other English course becoming an Open Championship venue. Regretfully, the Open has never been played in Wales.

21 Castletown

Castletown Golf Links Hotel, Fort Island, Derbyhaven,
Isle of Man IM9 1UA (1892)
TEL: *(01624) 822201* **FAX:** *(01624) 824633*
LOCATION: *South-east of Castletown near airport*
COURSE: *18 holes, 6711yd/6137m, par 72, SSS 72*
TYPE OF COURSE: *Links*
DESIGNER: *Mackenzie Ross*
GREEN FEES: *££*
FACILITIES: *Pro shop, trolley, buggy and club hire, full*
hotel facilities
VISITORS: *Welcome*

Mackenzie Ross rebuilt the Castletown links just after the Second World War, at much the same time as he restored the Ailsa course at Turnberry. On a rocky promontory in the south-west corner of the Isle of Man, with unrivalled views of the sea, Castletown is nowadays a hotel course, conveniently close to the airport. The first maritime encounter comes on the 5th, a long par 4 with a tricky green. And now we are on hallowed ground, the very spot on which the first Derby was run (it was later to be moved to Epsom), Castletown being the Earl of Derby's residence. The 7th is named Racecourse to commemorate the event.

The most spectacular part of the course is the finish from the short 16th over the cliffs below which the waves crash onto the shore. The 17th is the star hole with its big carry over the sea and almost as thrilling is the 18th, the approach this time being over the rocks.

22 Mount Murray

Mount Murray Hotel and Country Club, Santon, Isle
of Man IM4 2HT (1994)
TEL: *(01624) 661111* **FAX:** *(01624) 611116*
WEB SITE: *www.mountmurray.com*
LOCATION: *Santon on Castletown–Douglas road*
COURSE: *18 holes, 6715yd/6140m, par 73, SSS 73*
TYPE OF COURSE: *Meadowland/moorland*
DESIGNER: *Bingley Sports Turf Research*
GREEN FEES: *£*
FACILITIES: *Pro shop, range, sports within hotel complex*
VISITORS: *Welcome with handicap certificate*

For many years Castletown was the only genuinely long course on the Isle of Man, the other six old layouts being full of charm, but on the short side. With the opening of Mount Murray the island gained a second course on a larger scale. Here you quickly discover the golfing problems posed by Manx hedges. Gorse bushes, streams and ponds, and hilly ground complete the picture.

Going out there are high marks for the views over the island from the short 6th. The 8th, second of a pair of long par 5s, is beset with gorse and the 9th rates highly with its Manx hedging and a difficult bunker right of the green. The 435yd/398m 11th is tough, particularly when the wind is up, and you are invited to gamble on the dog-leg of the 14th. Views are again splendid on the 16th, while the home hole is a par 5 on which those who seek to get home in two must make a long carry over a pond.

The proximity of the sea causes concern for golfers of all abilities as they drive at Castletown's 17th, the pivotal hole in a glorious closing trio.

OTHER COURSES TO VISIT IN THE NORTH WEST

Cheshire	Stockport	Chesterfield	Fleetwood
Crewe	Tytherington	Kedlestone Park	Formby Hall
Dunham Forest	Warrington	Sickleholme	Haydock Park
Knutsford	**Cumbria**	**Isle of Man**	Hesketh
Mere	Appleby	Douglas	Lancaster
Mottram Hall	Carlisle	Rowany	Lytham Green Drive
Portal/Portal Premier	Furness	**Lancashire**	Manchester
Prenton	Penrith	Ashton under Lyne	North Manchester
Ringway	Windermere	Blackpool North Shore	Pleasington
Romiley	**Derbyshire**	Bolton Old Links	St Anne's Old Links
Shrigley Hall	Buxton and High Peak	Dean Wood	Wilpshire

23 *Seascale*

*Seascale Golf Club, The Banks, Seascale, Cumbria
CA20 1QL (1893)*
TEL and **FAX:** *(019467) 28202*
LOCATION: *Cumbrian coast, turn right at Seascale
seafront*
COURSE: *18 holes, 6416yd/5867m, par 71, SSS 71*
TYPE OF COURSE: *Undulating links*
DESIGNERS: *Willie Campbell, George Lowe*
GREEN FEES: *££*
FACILITIES: *Pro shop, club hire, clubhouse*
VISITORS: *Welcome*

Beyond the tourist attractions of the Lake
District, Seascale keeps company with
the Sellafield nuclear giant, yet it is a first-
rate links test. The first eight holes occupy
high ground, seriously exposed to the wind.
Of these the 3rd is a mischievous par 4,
driving down to a corner protected by an
out-of-bounds stone wall before turning
right, the next stretch of wall, a bank of
dunes and cross-bunkers providing more
than adequate hazards for the lengthy second
shot. On the 9th the descent is made, an
attractive hole teeing off by an ancient stone
circle and dropping in stages to a green
beside a stream. The hardest hole must be
the par-4 16th, 473yd/434m into the
prevailing wind, climbing over bumpy

ground, with a great pit to the right of the
green and a bunker occupying the only bit
of level ground anywhere near the entrance.
The drive at the 17th is made spectacularly
uphill.

24 *Silloth-on-Solway*

*Silloth-on-Solway Golf Club, Silloth, Carlisle Cumbria
CA5 4BL (1892)*
TEL: *(016973) 31304* **FAX:** *(016973) 31782*
WEBSITE: *www.sillothgolfclub.co.uk*
LOCATION: *to follow*
COURSE: *18 holes, 6616yd/6050m, par 72, SSS 73*
TYPE OF COURSE: *Links*
DESIGNERS: *David Grant, Willie Park, Alister
Mackenzie*
GREEN FEES: *££*
FACILITIES: *Pro shop, club hire, clubhouse*
VISITORS: *Welcome with handicap certificate*

One of the great links courses, remote
Silloth has hosted many important
Ladies' championships including the British
Strokeplay, British Amateur, and English
Amateur. Undulating fairways running
through wild dunes, serious rough, gorse
bushes, cunningly shaped greens, and
omnipresent wind characterize it. Bunkering
is sparing, and while length is not always at a
premium, accuracy most certainly is.

Along the shore, the 5th gives glorious views across the Solway Firth to the hills of Galloway, and the 7th involves that traditional seaside difficulty, a long approach shot blind over a ridge. A new championship tee has further strengthened the par-5 13th, already a great hole. Usually playing into the wind, with the second shot climbing over a ridge, it feels much longer than the card indicates. The green is perched on high ground, a devilish target on which the wind can affect even the shortest of putts. Amongst the gorse the short 16th is both attractive and testing, and the drive at the 17th is no place to top the ball.

 Brampton

Brampton Golf Club, Brampton, Cumbria CA8 1HN
TEL: *(016977) 2255 (1907)*
LOCATION: *1 mile/1.6km south of Brampton on B6413 to Castle Carrock*
COURSE: *18 holes, 6407yd/5859m, par 72, SSS 71*
TYPE OF COURSE: *Moorland*
DESIGNER: *James Braid*
GREEN FEES: *££*
FACILITIES: *Pro shop, clubhouse*
VISITORS: *Welcome*

In the far north of England, almost on Hadrian's Wall, on rolling upland and in invigorating fresh air, Brampton enjoys stunning views from the Lakeland Fells past the Solway Firth to the hills of Galloway, and, nearer at hand, to views over the forested valleys and sheep pastures of Northumbria. The clear waters of Talkin Tarn complete an enchanting picture.

Six holes are on gentle ground close to the comfortable modern clubhouse. The rest are distinctly hilly. Of the flatter holes the 3rd, alongside the main Carlisle–Newcastle railway, is admirable. On the higher ground the 11th is a very long par 4 on which the adventurous hit their second shots out over trees and rough country to find the distant green far below. Good distance is also required on the uphill 13th, alongside Talkin Tarn, but it is the variety of holes and their individual characters in an incomparable setting which makes Brampton so appealing.

The par-5 5th is typical of many of Silloth's holes, running in the valley between the dunes, clad in grasping rough grasses and utterly unforgiving to the wayward shot.

REGIONAL DIRECTORY

Where to Stay

With several cities and many large industrial towns concentrated in the south of the region there is an abundance of perfectly functional hotels geared mainly for the business visitor. But for the visitor wishing to complement the exceptional golf available with accommodation of a similar standing it is necessary to journey into the more scenic parts, such as the hills of the *Peak District*. Here **Callow Hall** (01335 343403) and **Stanshope Hall** (01335 310278) at Ashbourne, Croft Country House (01629 -640278) near Bakewell, **Fischer's Baslow Hall** (01246 583259) at Baslow, and **Wind in the Willows** (01457-868001) at Glossop provide true style and genuine country living. *Cheshire* **Nunsmere Hall** (01606 889100) at Sandiway, **Broxton Hall** (01829 782321) near Chester, and **White House Manor** (01625 829376) at Prestbury are very convenient for the selected courses, and at the **Belle Epoque** (01565 633060) in Knutsford rooms with a difference are available at what is principally an ornate Art Nouveau restaurant. **Carden Park Hotel** (01829 731000) offers extensive leisure facilities in addition to its two golf courses, and **De Vere Mottram Hall** (01625 828135) and **Shrigley Hall** (01625 575757) both run to their own seriously challenging golf courses. *Lancashire* A new and testing 18-hole golf course attracts at the **Marriott Manchester Hotel** (0161 975 2000) which has the advantage of being close to the motorway network, giving easy access to the featured courses on the Lancashire coast and in Yorkshire. Male visitors to Royal Lytham might enjoy staying at the on-course **Dormy House** (01253 724206). Also near Lytham is **Mains Hall** (01253 885130) at Poulton-le-Fylde, a house built by monks in the 16th century. *Isle of Man* The logical places for a golfer to stay are at the **Castletown Golf Links Hotel** (01624 822201) or **Mount Murray Hotel** (01624 661111), whose courses are featured within. *Lake District* It would appear that at least half the best restaurateurs and hoteliers in the country have been attracted to the Lake District. It simply abounds with lodgings and dining rooms of distinction. There is not space to list a fraction of them, but those which combine stately living with cooking of the highest order include: **Uplands** (015395 36248) at Cartmel, **Michael's Nook** (015394 35496) at Grasmere, the famous **Sharrow Bay** (017684 86301) at Ullswater, and **Holbeck Ghyll** (01539 432375) and **Miller Howe** (015394 42536) at Windermere. **Farlam Hall** (016977 46234) at Brampton, and **Hornby Hall** (01768 891114) near Penrith offer peaceful seclusion away from other tourists, and the **Black Swan** at Ravenstonedale (01539 623204) is a real English country inn with traditional values.

Where to Eat

Most of the country hotels and inns listed above are no less renowned for the excellence of their cuisine. *Derbyshire* **Darleys** (01332 364987) in Derby is highly rated for its culinary imagination. *Cheshire* **Bank Square** (01625 539754) in Wilmslow is currently highest ranked of the many cafés which abound in this part of East Cheshire, while in the Wirral a meal at **Beadles** (0151 653 9010) might fittingly follow a round at Hoylake or Wallasey. *Manchester* **Juniper** (0161 929 4008) in Altrincham, **Moss Nook** (0161 437 4778) near the airport, and **Rhodes and Co** (0161 868 1900) in Trafford Park have attracted positive notices from the critics, while in the city centre the French Restaurant in the **Crowne Plaza Midland Hotel** (0161 233 3333) and **Simply Heathcotes** (0161 835 3536) currently get the highest ranking, but Manchester's Chinatown is vibrant and extensive, and of a good many very high quality Chinese restaurants the **Yang Sing** (0161 236 2200) is exceptional. A little way north of Manchester is quaintly named Ramsbottom where the **Village Restaurant** (01706 825070) is much more than that, and a wine buff's paradise. *Central Lancashire* is well served with high-class restaurants, with **Auctioneer** (01200 427153) at Clitheroe, **Cromwellian** (01772 685680) at Kirkham, and **Paul Heathcote's** (01772 784969) at Longridge in the first division, currently headed by **Northcote Manor** (01254 240555) at Langho. *Lake District* Here the restaurants are as profuse and distinguished as its hotels. To those already mentioned should be added **Porthole Eating House** (01539 442793) at Bowness-on-Windermere which is celebrated for its wine list, as is **White Moss House** (015394 35295) at Rydal Water.

What to See

Beginning in *Derbyshire*, the Duke of Devonshire's home at **Chatsworth** is one of England's great country houses with, incidentally, one of Europe's most spectacular fountains. In total contrast are the subterranean attractions of the caverns open to the public around **Castleton**, or the splendid museums attached to the many world-renowned porcelain factories in and around the towns of **The Potteries**. Just north of The Potteries, in *Cheshire* past **Little Moreton Hall** (see page 113), is the village of **Astbury** with its charming church set above a triangular green which is a joy at daffodil time. **Tatton Hall**, **Arley Hall**, **Dunham Massey**,

The BBC Philharmonic with their Principal Conductor, Yan Pascal Tortelier, at Manchester's Bridgewater Hall, a world-class orchestra in a magnificent concert hall.

Capesthorne Hall, and **Lyme Park** each warrant visits, often staging special events from vintage-car rallies to doll's-house fairs. Cheshire's industrial heritage is well represented in the **Silk Heritage Museum** in Macclesfield (where the last few remaining examples of famous Macclesfield silk may be purchased until stocks run out, the factory having recently closed for good). As an example of modern academic enterprise the **Jodrell Bank Radio Telescope** is still at the forefront of scientific discovery, yet also open to the public, a fascinating visit. The wealth acquired by the soap-manufacturing Leverhulme family is reflected in the splendid art gallery at **Port Sunlight** on the Wirral. Passing through the Mersey Tunnel into *Liverpool*, the **Walker** and **Tate** art galleries are outstanding, the latter in the regenerated dockland area which also houses a fine maritime museum. The Royal Liverpool Philharmonic Orchestra is one of the oldest established in the country.

Sports enthusiasts are well catered for with many prominent **football** clubs in the region, though tickets for **Manchester United** games are very hard to come by, and those without tickets may have to make do with the (highly enjoyable) tour of the ground on days when no match takes place. One of the great test and county **cricket** grounds is just down the road, also called **Old Trafford**. **Rugby League** remains very popular in the bigger Lancashire towns (and over the Pennines in Yorkshire), and **racing** takes place throughout the region at **Aintree, Chester, Haydock Park, Cartmel** and **Carlisle**.

Culturally *Manchester* leads the way with its superb new concert hall, the Bridgewater Hall, where the **Hallé and BBC Philharmonic Orchestras** provide a lavish season of serious music, and the **Royal Exchange Theatre** has a high reputation for its productions. In the adjoining city of Salford **The Lowry** on the Quays is both a permanent home for Salford's enormous collection of Lowry pictures and a state-of-the-art lyric theatre.

The poets, Coleridge, Southey, Wordsworth and De Quincey, were perhaps the earliest to bring a literary cachet to the Lakes, **Dove Cottage** and the **Wordsworth Museum** (Grasmere) reflecting that heritage. Later, **Beatrix Potter** wrote many of her stories at **Hilltop**, near Sawrey, Hawkshead, which is open to the public.

Nowadays the *Lake District* is exceptionally well geared for tourists – it has to be, otherwise it would smother in the fumes of the thousands of vehicles which crowd its tiny roads. The continued industrial significance of the region can be seen in such diverse attractions as the **Cumberland Pencil Museum** (Keswick), **Windermere Steamboat Museum**, and **Sellafield Visitor Centre**. Climbing and fell-walking, boating, and riding are as popular as ever. The pretty village of **Hawkshead** is today pedestrianized. Away from the central Lakes there are delights not to be missed such as the village of **Cartmel** with its squat Priory and narrow streets, and in the Pennines **Dent** (crafts and antiques) and **Appleby** (old county town of Westmoreland) are the gateways to splendid uplands, including the wide expanses of moorland alongside **Hadrian's Wall**. The spectacular clifftop sites at **Steel Rigg** and **Housesteads** are complemented by the extensive **Vindolanda** and smaller gems such as the atmospheric **Temple of Mithras**.

Chapter 6

The North-East

From the North West we have chosen to enter the North East by following Hadrian's Wall, the Romans' most visible legacy, built to keep the Picts and Scots out of their territory. The wall and its various adjuncts, such as the camp at Corstopitum (Corbridge), give a fascinating insight into the workings of an unparalleled empire, influential even here at its very edge where so few of its people can ever have been anywhere near its centre, Rome. Inevitably, it was one of the earlier parts of Britain to be abandoned and the Angles and Saxons were frequent marauders.

Hexham Abbey, in which Roman stones with pagan images can be found doing novel duty in the finest Anglo-Saxon crypt in England. From Holy Island Christianity spread to Durham where, from the Norman Conquest on, the Prince Bishops controlled this part of medieval Britain as a kingdom, with their own parliament, coinage, tax-raising powers, and laws. To this day Durham's magnificent Norman cathedral remains one of Europe's most impressive architectural treasures, spectacularly sited on its clifftop alongside the castle.

The Coming of Christianity

Another invader was Christianity which came to Northern England via Holy Island. There are marvellous conjunctions of these several cultures in such jewels as

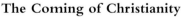

Left: The 6th at Fulford, for many years a significant European Tour venue. Above: Hadrian's Wall, which once marked the northern limit of the Roman Empire.

Yorkshire

Yorkshire fared less well, for a family feud had brought the Norsemen on an invasion, instigated by Tostig, banished brother of Harold, King of England. Harold defeated them. However, while Harold was in Yorkshire, William of Normandy invaded Sussex. Harold rushed south and was immediately crushed. The north did not take kindly to the Norman invasion and

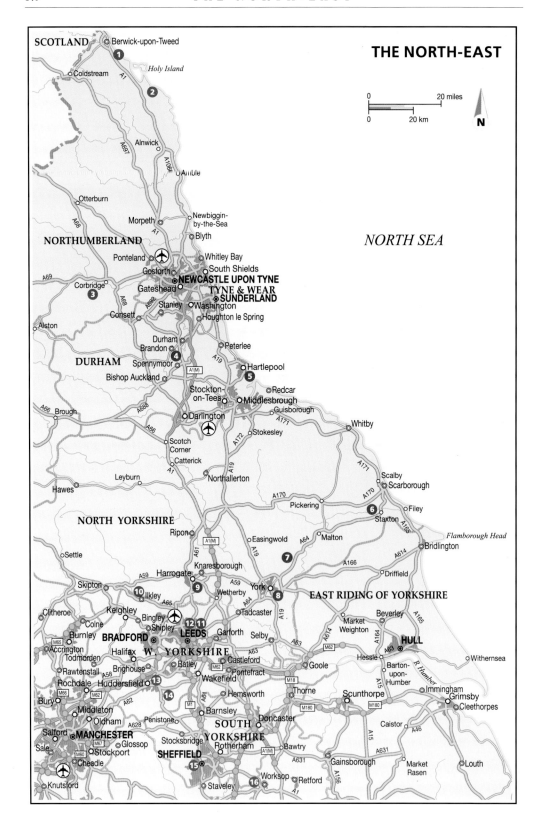

THE NORTH-EAST

SCOTLAND

NORTH SEA

NORTHUMBERLAND

DURHAM

TYNE & WEAR

NORTH YORKSHIRE

EAST RIDING OF YORKSHIRE

W. YORKSHIRE

SOUTH YORKSHIRE

0   20 miles
0   20 km

N

KEY TO MAP

1. Berwick-upon-Tweed
2. Bamburgh Castle
3. Slaley Hall
4. Brancepeth Castle
5. Seaton Carew
6. Ganton
7. York
8. Fulford
9. Pannal
10. Ilkley
11. Alwoodley
12. Moortown
13. Huddersfield
14. Woodsome Hall
15. Hallamshire
16. Lindrick

several times rebelled. William's ferocious purge by fire and sword left the region almost uninhabited. In the rebuilding which followed, the most important buildings were the monasteries, and Yorkshire's allocation was generous. Fountains, Rievaulx, Byland and Jervaulx are unsurpassed in their ruin, while Whitby links us with the abandonment of Celtic rites and the adoption of Rome, that is until King Henry VIII's marital difficulties turned England into a protestant state. York Minster, the largest gothic church in England, and Beverley Minster survive as working places of worship, York Minster in the centre of one of the great medieval 'walled-cities of Europe, Beverley Minster as one of two magnificent churches in a handsome small market town.

In golf Yorkshire has won the English County Championship many more times than any other county, which is hardly surprising when it is realised that it occupies one-eighth of the area of England, making it by some margin the largest. All three north-eastern counties share an interest in the Pennines, the mountains and moors which form the backbone of England, and each has a splendid variety of countryside giving golf of all kinds – links, parkland,

heathland, moorland, and so on. Strangely, despite its considerable coastline, Yorkshire has only one true links course, the Cleveland at Redcar, a thoroughly good test of golf which shares with its illustrious neighbour over the water, Seaton Carew, a somewhat industrial skyline. Whether amongst the sheep farms of the Yorkshire Dales, the uninhabited expanses of the North York Moors, or the rugged cliffs of its coastline, Yorkshire is a handsome county, but perhaps nowhere more than in the pretty villages of the Howardian hills north and east of the city of York. York's diverse industrial heritage is reflected in the superb collection of the National Railway Museum and Rowntree's chocolate factory.

Northumberland and Durham

In an industrial sense Northumberland and Durham are inseparable, both driven initially by coal. Ships were built to transport it away, and the first steam turbine was invented here. Railways were introduced to get the coal to the ports. Then in 1825 the Stockton and Darlington Railway became the first passenger-carrying railway in the world. The great engineer and railwayman George Stephenson was born in Wylam in the Tyne Valley.

Amongst many brilliant north-eastern inventions were the first dynamo, first self-righting lifeboat, and first friction matches. Yet within a few minutes of the industrial cities one can be in the wildest country, the Durham grouse moors, the Keilder Forest and Cheviot Hills, or the timeless towns and villages such as Alnwick, Barnard Castle, Blanchland, Brinkburn, Gainford, Hexham, Roscastle, Staindrop (and nearby Raby Castle), Warkworth, and Whittingham.

Berwick-upon-Tweed

Berwick-upon-Tweed (Goswick) Golf Club, Beal,
Berwick-upon-Tweed, Northumberland TD15 2RW
(1890)
TEL *and* **FAX:** *(01289) 387256*
LOCATION: *5 miles/8km south of Berwick-upon-*
Tweed, follow signs off A1
COURSE: *18 holes, 6452yd/5900m, par 72, SSS 71*
TYPE OF COURSE: *Links*
DESIGNERS: *James Braid, Frank Pennink, Donald Steel*
GREEN FEES: *££*
FACILITIES: *Pro shop, trolley and buggy hire, range,*
clubhouse
VISITORS: *Welcome with handicap certificate*

Well over 100 years old, Berwick's links occupy a wonderfully remote location close to Lindisfarne, the birthplace of English Christianity. There is an ancient feel to the golf, too, with several short par 4s full of character, and many cunning greens adding spice. Constant movement in the ground, however gentle, calls for crisp striking from the fairway. With many holes running alongside (or occasionally into) the dunes there are sufficient natural hazards and, thus, relatively few bunkers.

TODAY'S ARCHITECTS

Most golfers are still challenged by the best designs of Colt and Mackenzie almost a century after they were created. Who knows if the designs of today's architects wil continue to test the best golfers until the year 2100? The most likely candidates must include: **Peter Alliss**, once Europe's top player, now respected TV commentator; his partner in the design of The Belfry, **Dave Thomas**, twice second in the Open; **John Jacobs**, fine player, Ryder Cup captain, distinguished teacher; **Donald Steel**, golfing polymath, amateur international, author, past broadsheet correspondent; **Neil Coles**, consistently competitive on the European Tour and now as a senior, champion of stadium courses; **Martin Hawtree** (see page 128); and six-times Major winner, **Nick Faldo**.

Of the early holes, the curving par-4 3rd and par-5 6th, on which out-of-bounds threatens, receive much praise. Those who value the anachronisms of traditional links golf will enjoy holes such as the 12th on which the approach to the green is blind over a ridge. Only 150yd/137m long, the 15th is a tricky drop shot over bunkers to a sunken green, its tee blessed with lovely views to sea.

 ## *Bamburgh Castle*

Bamburgh Castle Golf Club, 40 The Wynding,
Bamburgh, Northumberland NE69 7DE (1904)
TEL: *(01668) 214378*
LOCATION: *In Bamburgh by sea shore*
COURSE: *18 holes, 5621yd/5140m, par 68, SSS 67*
TYPE OF COURSE: *Seaside/heathland*
DESIGNER: *George Rochester*
GREEN FEES: *££*
FACILITIES: *Clubhouse*
VISITORS: *Welcome with handicap certificate*

Visually Bamburgh is in the first division. The ancient castle is one of the finest in England, and from the 15th tee Ross, Dunstanburgh, Haggerstone and Lindisfarne castles are also visible. This stretch of coast near the Farne Islands is particularly attractive. Though relatively short, with six par 3s and several diminutive par 4s, there is great charm to the course, abundant heather and gorse complementing the seascape, the views on every hole unsurpassed.

Starting with a couple of short holes by the shore the course gradually winds its way inland, the hardest hole being the 6th, an uphill 224yd/205m par 3. If you miss the green of the short 8th punishment can be severe amongst the rocks. There is plenty of length and challenge in the par-5 3rd, whereas the two-shot 16th and 17th can be driven by good players. But principally you play Bamburgh for its unique atmosphere.

Slaley Hall

De Vere Slaley Hall Golf and Country Club,
Hexham, nr Newcastle upon Tyne, Northumberland
NE47 0BY (1988)
TEL: (01434) 673350 **FAX:** (01434) 673152
LOCATION: South-east of Hexham. Take B6306
towards Blanchland, follow signs in Slaley village
COURSES: Hunting: 18 holes, 7088yd/6481m, par
72, SSS 74; Priestman: 18 holes, 7010yd/6410m,
par 72, SSS 74
TYPE OF COURSE: Hilly parkland/moorland
DESIGNERS: Dave Thomas
GREEN FEES: £££production£
FACILITIES: Pro shop, range, club and buggy hire,
extensive leisure, conference and hotel facilities
VISITORS: Welcome (hotel and members' guests only at
weekend)

Set in beautiful hill country, both courses are long and challenging, the newer Priestman Course set on high ground with magnificent views. The Hunting Course is the one used for European Tour events, some greens full of subtle borrows, others rolling quite severely. The front nine runs through

The 9th, possibly the finest hole at Slaley Hall, a demanding uphill par 4 of 453yd/414m, with trees and rhododendrons narrowing the fairway as it climbs.

pine forest beguilingly, while the back nine explores higher, more open ground. As you struggle to defeat nature and the architect, reflect on Colin Montgomerie who set a course record 65: he covered these inward holes in only 30 strokes!

A new green adds to the beauties of the 3rd, one of the best holes on the course, a dog-leg demanding a perfectly lined tee shot. Pools on the 5th, an all-or-nothing carry across a lake on the 6th, a tight drive at the 7th, and the downhill corkscrew of the 8th contribute greatly to a memorable outward nine, but the 9th, by a whisker, is the outstanding hole. The par 4s of the back nine are slightly shorter, but the 18th is a 463yd/423m brute on which a stream limits the length of the downhill drive. Not only for its beauty is Slaley known as the Augusta of the North.

Brancepeth Castle

Brancepeth Castle Golf Club, Brancepeth Village,
Durham DH7 8EA (1924)
TEL: *(0191) 378 0075* **FAX:** *(0191) 378 3835*
LOCATION: *4 miles/6.5km south-west of Durham on
A690 to Crook, turn left in Brancepeth immediately
before castle gates*
COURSE: *18 holes, 6415yd/5866m, par 70, SSS 71*
TYPE OF COURSE: *Parkland*
DESIGNER: *Harry Colt*
GREEN FEES: *££*
FACILITIES: *Pro shop, clubhouse*
VISITORS: *Welcome with handicap certificate*

Golf at Brancepeth is incomparable, the course laid out in the 1920s around the castle and village church. The eye is led to the Durham uplands once roamed by the wild boar which gave the village its name (Braun's Path). A number of ravines cross the land in dramatic fashion, entering play on no fewer than eight holes. This is the last place on which to develop a tendency to topping! Otherwise this is parkland of an aristocratic kind, with a clubhouse to match.

The 9th at Brancepeth is magnificent, 214yd/196m of carry across a wooded valley to a green perched on the side of a hill beneath the castle.

The first big carry is required at the 2nd, across an abyss to a ledge target. Then it is out into the country strongly with two very substantial par 4s to contend with, a long par 3, and a 550yd/503m par 5. It is at the 8th that the next ravine is encountered, a 339yd/310m Cape hole running towards a drunken green lurking behind bunkers.

Like Ballybunion and Cypress Point, Brancepeth boasts back-to-back par 3s, both corkers. The 9th is quite outstanding. Again over 200yd/183m long, the 10th returns over the chasm, and then there is a drive from the 11th over another vertigo-inducing void. Holes of comparative respite follow, but the last drive, across a deep valley, is uncompromising. If successful, it is followed by a gentle pitch to a green beside the village church.

Seaton Carew

Seaton Carew Golf Club, Tees Road, Seaton Carew, Hartlepool, Durham TS25 1DE (1874)
TEL: *(01429) 266249* **FAX:** *(01429) 261473*
LOCATION: *2 miles/3km south of Hartlepool on A178 coast road*
COURSES: *(22 holes) Old: 18 holes, 6613yd/6047m, par 72, SSS 72; Brabazon: 18 holes, 6855yd/6268m, par 73, SSS 73*
TYPE OF COURSE: *Links*
DESIGNERS: *Dr McCuaig, Alister Mackenzie, Frank Pennink*
GREEN FEES: *££*
FACILITIES: *Pro shop, caddies, club, trolley and buggy hire, clubhouse*
VISITORS: *Welcome with handicap certificate*

One of the oldest courses in England, Seaton Carew was founded by a Scotsman, Dr McCuaig. He was distressed to find that the locals were so uncivilized that they did not play golf! He bequeathed to us, admittedly upgraded by Alister Mackenzie, a superb links test, its industrial surroundings notwithstanding. In 1974 four extra holes were constructed and, by combining these with fourteen from the Old Course, the Brabazon championship layout is formed.

A spine of dunes gives character to many holes, including the short 3rd, the only surviving McCuaig hole. On Lagoon you must flirt with marshy ground if you want to see the flag. The direct route, over sandy hummocks, is more of a gamble. Here the Brabazon strikes out for the beach, Gare a fine medium-length par 4. Chapel Open, following, is a terrific driving hole, out over dense buckthorn to an angled fairway. Buckthorn is a feature from here on and it is utterly impenetrable. The finish from the 14th is common to both courses, strong holes all of them. The great hole, though, is the 17th, Snag. The pear-shaped green is set on the dunes, rising in stages past bunkers, a very challenging target.

Gare, one of the newer holes, is played as the 10th hole on Seaton Carew's Brabazon Course. It climbs gently through the dunes and buckthorn.

 *Ganton*

Ganton Golf Club. Station Road, Ganton,
Scarborough, Yorkshire YO12 4PA (1891)
TEL: (01944) 710329 **FAX:** (01944) 710922
LOCATION: On A64 York–Scarborough road
COURSE: 18 holes, 6884yd/6295m, par 71, SSS 74
TYPE OF COURSE: Heathland
DESIGNERS: Tom Dunn, Harry Vardon, James Braid,
Harry Colt, C.K. Cotton
GREEN FEES: ££££££
FACILITIES: Pro shop, caddies, trolley hire, clubhouse
VISITORS: Welcome with handicap certificate

GANTON

HOLE	YD	M	PAR	HOLE	YD	M	PAR
1	373	341	4	10	168	154	3
2	445	407	4	11	417	381	4
3	334	305	4	12	363	332	4
4	406	371	4	13	524	479	5
5	157	144	3	14	282	258	4
6	470	430	4	15	461	421	4
7	435	398	4	16	448	410	4
8	414	378	4	17	249	228	3
9	504	461	5	18	434	397	4
OUT	3538	3235	36	IN	3346	3060	35

6884YD • 6295M • PAR 71

Gary Player once said that Ganton is the only inland course worthy of holding the Open Championship. Professionals have rarely tested themselves here under tournament conditions, one of the few occasions being the 1949 Ryder Cup. Food was still rationed in Britain at this time, so the Americans, under Ben Hogan's captaincy, brought with them 600 steaks, 12 roasting ribs, a dozen hams and 12 boxes of bacon! It gave them the strength to come back from a disastrous foursomes to sneak a 7–5 victory.

Ganton is unique in that it is the only inland course to have hosted the Amateur Championship, which it has done three times. The Curtis Cup in 2000 and Walker Cup in 2003 confirm its excellence as a venue for matchplay at international level.

The first thing you see, as you drive down the lane to the club, is what Patric Dickinson described as a 'superintendent of a cross-bunker' over which you must drive on the 16th. A little further on your eye is caught by a 'sandpit of vast dimensions' threatening the tee shots on the 17th and 18th. These holes are part of a great finish, but there is a feast of outstanding golf preceding them. Savage rough and inhospitable gorse punish profligate golf. Some of the deepest and most prolific bunkers to be found in Britain await the careless.

The start is made back and forth across rising ground calling for straight driving from the outset and the 3rd is cleverly bunkered.

Harry Colt is credited with creating the 4th, a delightful par 4 with the approach played across a shallow valley to

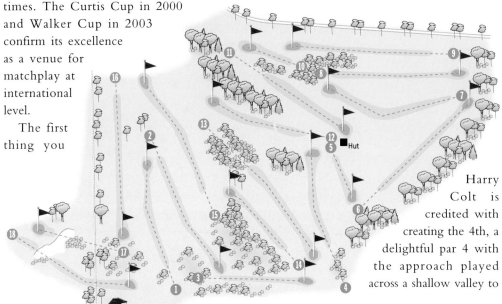

Ganton's 6th green, viewed from the 7th tee. The 6th is a muscular par 4, seriously bunkered, the green framed by trees. Members play it as a par 5.

a tricky green. The 5th green is almost totally surrounded by sand, and the 6th takes play to the farthest corner of the course.

There is little length in the par 5s, but the 9th is narrow enough to encourage caution. Following a very individual short hole, the 11th strikes out again for the central heath, the fairway interrupted by wicked cross-bunkers. The 12th is the one hole on which trees are significant, a right-hand dog-leg on which you are invited to drive out over them if you are strong enough.

A mere 282yd/258m long, the 14th is tempting, but there is no room for error, and the 15th is a strong two-shotter. Shortly we are confronted by that monster bunker on the 16th. In truth, it is not an enormous carry and the greater difficulty is positioning the drive to give a clear shot to the raised green. The famous 17th is the very devil of a hole with a

quarry to be carried, bunkers both sides of the landing area, and the green elusive beyond. A classic Cape hole remains on which it is easy to get blocked out by the firs on the left. And, as you review your score in the comfort of the clubhouse, put it all in perspective by thinking of Michael Bonallack's 61 here (albeit under matchplay conditions) in the first round of the final of the English Amateur in 1968. Out in 32, back in 29!

CAPE HOLES

Cape holes appeal to the vanity of the golfer. They involve a drive out over an uncompromising obstacle – trees, deep rough or water – rewarding those who hit furthest with a simpler second shot. However, because the drive is to an angled fairway, the longer the drive the less margin for error there is, and the greater the inherent risk. The best examples deceive the eye, encouraging over-optimism – usually disastrously.

York's 5th, a mid-length par 4 very typical of the attractiveness of the course. Trees frame many holes without unduly interfering with play.

York

York Golf Club, Lords Moor Lane, Strensall, York YO32 5XF (1890)
TEL: *(01904) 491840* **FAX:** *(01904) 491852*
LOCATION: *Strensall village, 4 miles/6.5km north-east of York (village signposted from York ring road, A1237)*
COURSE: *18 holes, 6301yd/5762m, par 70, SSS 70*
TYPE OF COURSE: *Wooded moorland/heathland*
DESIGNERS: *J.H. Taylor, C.K. Cotton*
GREEN FEES: *£££*
FACILITIES: *Pro shop, clubhouse*
VISITORS: *Welcome*

York, one of the oldest Yorkshire clubs, moved to this common-land site amidst the army ranges in 1904. Parts of the course enjoy the good drainage of sand and gravel deposits, while sedges and rushes, orchids, marsh gentians and willows characterize the rest. J.H. Taylor's layout is hardly changed to this day and could be said to have one of everything except a really long par 3.

Down an avenue of trees, the par-4 1st is lengthy, and the 2nd is a tricky shot over a hedge to a well-defended green. The substantial 6th is governed by a stream crossing the fairway, while the 7th and 8th are both affected by the same pond. The short 11th is played from a remote tee deep in the woods and the par-4 14th involves a cross-bunker which in theory affects neither drive nor pitch, but its very presence is often enough to induce a sloppy second shot.

Fulford

Fulford Golf Club, Heslington Lane, York YO1 5DY (1906)
TEL: *(01904) 413579* **FAX:** *(01904) 416918*
LOCATION: *South of York city centre. Leave A64 onto A19 towards city centre and Fulford, right at traffic lights for Heslington and University. Club is on right*
COURSE: *18 holes, 6775yd/6195m, par 72, SSS 72*
TYPE OF COURSE: *Parkland/heathland*
DESIGNER: *Alister Mackenzie*
GREEN FEES: *£££*
FACILITIES: *Pro shop, trolley and buggy hire, clubhouse*
VISITORS: *Welcome with handicap certificate – weekends often restricted*

The names of Lee Trevino, Tony Jacklin, Greg Norman and Tom Weiskopf adorn the honours boards, for it was here in the 1970s and 1980s that the cream of world golf contested the Benson and Hedges International. They appreciated the fairness and immaculate preparation of the course, though scoring was therefore low.

Alister Mackenzie designed the original course, later split by the York by-pass. Now it is a succession of strong parkland holes taking play to the A64 bridge and the old Fulford. No putt is conceded on the par-3 10th. The 13th and 15th are demanding par 4s with a ditch on the left, while the 17th is celebrated in history as the hole from which Bernhard Langer played a remarkable recovery shot from the branches of a tree into which he had climbed. For the majority of us the 18th, bending to the right, is a subtle par 5, for the tournament professional an eagle opportunity.

9 *Pannal*

Pannal Golf Club, Follifoot Road, Pannal, Harrogate, Yorks HG3 1ES (1906)
TEL: *(01423) 872628* **FAX:** *(01423) 871641*
LOCATION: *South of Harrogate on A61 at Pannal*
COURSE: *18 holes, 6622yd/6055m, par 72, SSS 72*
TYPE OF COURSE: *Moorland/parkland*
DESIGNER: *Sandy Herd*
GREEN FEES: *££££*
FACILITIES: *Pro shop, trolley hire, clubhouse*
VISITORS: *Welcome with handicap certificate*

In 1975 Nick Faldo won the British Youths' Championship here, and in 1985 Neil Coles took the PGA Seniors' Championship. Also hosting the Ladies' British Amateur of 1991, Pannal is noted for its situation and its greenkeeping. It benefits from a combination of wooded, gorse-lined and open holes, the latter giving views to Turner's famous viaduct, Harrogate, and the North Yorks Moors beyond.

The opening is serious, two sturdy par 4s of which the 2nd climbs as it swings left to a ledge green. Another ledge green awaits on the 5th before a stiff climb brings you to the 6th tee and Stroke 1. The 12th, Secretary's Wood, involves a drive out of a chute of

Ilkley's 16th. The river holes may be more famous, but the long par 4s of the back nine are one of Ilkley's great strengths.

trees. With a narrow entrance to the green between bunkers a straight approach is essential. Over the next few fairways, running back and forth on high ground, the vistas are expansive and impressive. Despite the views, the 17th demands full concentration with the green almost 200yd/183m away, perched on the side of a steep hill. The 18th is kinder, descending encouragingly towards that first refreshing pint.

10 *Ilkley*

Ilkley Golf Club, Myddleton, Ilkley, Yorkshire LS29 0BE (1890)
TEL: *(01943) 600214* **FAX:** *(01843) 816130*
LOCATION: *North-west of Ilkley. At traffic lights in town centre take road downhill over river bridge. Turn left having crossed river, clubhouse about 1 mile/1.6km on right*
COURSE: *18 holes 6262yd/5726m, par 69, SSS 70*
TYPE OF COURSE: *Parkland*
DESIGNERS: *Harry Colt, Alister Mackenzie*
GREEN FEES: *£££*
FACILITIES: *Pro shop, trolley and club hire, clubhouse*
VISITORS: *Welcome*

Set in the valley of the River Wharfe, with Ilkley Moor on one side and a wooded hill on the other, Ilkley Golf Club enjoys a prime location. Its greens are renowned for being exceptionally true. Their quality is often attributed to their proximity to the river.

The first seven holes are laid out along the river bank. Part of a remarkable sequence, the 2nd is played to an island in the river, the 3rd along it (both are short holes), and the par-5 4th is then played from the island back onto terra firma, a superb test of resolve. On the back nine there are five par 4s over 400yd/366m in length, and with its elevated tee and adjoining trees the 16th is particularly attractive. Tom Vardon was one of the club's early professionals, and his famous brother Harry is said to have earned his first professional prize here.

11 Alwoodley

*The Alwoodley Golf Club, Wigton Lane, Leeds,
Yorkshire LS17 8SA (1908)*
TEL: *(0113) 268 1680* **FAX:** *(0113)293 9458*
WEBSITE: *www.alwoodley.co.uk*
LOCATION: *North Leeds, A61 towrds Harrogate, cross
ring road, then right at lights into Wigton Lane. Club on
left*
COURSE: *18 holes, 6785yd/6204m, par 71, SSS 73*
TYPE OF COURSE: *Heathland*
DESIGNERS: *Harry Colt, Alister Mackenzie*
GREEN FEES: *££££*
FACILITIES: *Pro shop, caddies, trolley and club hire,
clubhouse*
VISITORS: *Welcome*

All students of golf architecture should
visit Alwoodley as it was here that Alister
Mackenzie made his earliest essay in the art of
design, the first of a noble and influential line.
And it should be played by everyone who
appreciates the finer things in golf, for this is
not only a distinguished course with a
magnificent clubhouse but also one of the best
conditioned in the land. Over the last decade
the club has restored the course as close as
possible to Mackenzie's plans. It is an object
lesson for all Chairmen of the Green.

Heather and gorse are the principal natural
defences, trees for the most part giving
seclusion rather than affecting strategy.
Bunkers are used economically but tellingly,
and, interestingly, there are none of those
vulgar, exaggerated, two-level greens which
have come to be called 'Mackenzie greens'.

A par 5 with only one bunker, the 3rd is
much celebrated, the real difficulty being the
sunken green which runs away into a hollow.
The toughest outward hole is the 6th, and the
approach to the 8th over heather-encrusted
bunkers teases. Quite possibly Alwoodley's
10th was Mackenzie's prototype for the 13th at
Augusta National, a short par 5, first climbing
and bending sharply left, then sweeping
downhill over a bunker and ditch to a target
green. From the 13th the finish is frequently
into the wind, a succession of lengthy par 4s,
and a substantial par 3, the 14th. A new tee has
stretched the 18th to a daunting 470yd/430m.

*Alwoodley's 11th, a slightly later hole, which
Mackenzie introduced to reproduce the characteristics of
his par-3 Gibraltar, recently opened to great acclaim at
neighbouring Moortown.*

12 Moortown

Moortown Golf Club, Harrogate Road, Leeds, Yorkshire
LS17 7DB (1909)
TEL: *(0113) 268 6521* **FAX:** *(0113) 268 0986*
LOCATION: *North Leeds, on A61 just by garage on left (signposted)*
COURSE: *18 holes, c.7000yd/6400m, par 72, SSS 74 (course under alteration at time of writing)*
TYPE OF COURSE: *Moorland/woodland*
DESIGNER: *Alister Mackenzie*
GREEN FEES: *££££*
FACILITIES: *Clubhouse, club and trolley hire, pro shop*
VISITORS: *Welcome with handicap certificate*

Moortown's standing was high from the moment Alister Mackenzie, then secretary at neighbouring Alwoodley, laid out the course in the first decade of the 20th century. Uniquely for that time, Mackenzie designed and constructed the greens. Up to then, greens had simply been natural areas where the grass had been mown a little shorter. The par-3 Gibraltar gained immediate fame as one of the first entirely artificial holes (constructed at the cost of £85) and people came from far and wide just to view this novelty. The cream of American professional golf also came in 1929 for the first Ryder Cup

Moortown's 9th, a strong par 4 curving and sweeping downhill to a green amongst the birches, a golfing oasis within minutes of Leeds city centre.

to be held on British soil and, against expectations, lost. It is recorded that the cheering of the crowd of 10,000 during play was every bit as loud as that at football matches and partisan behaviour was apparently no different from that in the most recent encounters.

The course has undergone many changes over the years and the recently constructed 6th and 7th amongst the trees are impressive. Gibraltar is now played as the 10th. The long par-5 12th, its fairway interrupted by a heathery ridge, and the 13th, climbing back in parallel, are muscular challenges. As you cross the stream on the difficult 16th think of Sam King who had the planks removed in order to play his shot from its waters during a tournament which he eventually won. Playing Moortown today it is salutary to realize that when it was built workmen had to be roped together to avoid drowning in the stagnant pools which then proliferated.

Dr Alister Mackenzie (1870–1934)

Mackenzie was one of the most influential golf course architects of the 20th century. He was not as prolific as his contemporaries Donald Ross, Harry Colt or James Braid, but his flair and creative individuality set him apart. Once the Cypress Point Club in California had opened to considerable critical acclaim in 1928, his designs became the models for others to emulate. That Bobby Jones should choose Mackenzie as his collaborator on the development of Augusta National gives an indication of the esteem in which he was held.

Mackenzie was born in Yorkshire of Scottish parents. After Cambridge he set up in medical practice, becoming a surgeon with the forces fighting in the Boer War. There he was impressed by the ability of the Boer soldiers to remain hidden in what was otherwise a totally treeless landscape. He returned to civilian life, but in 1907 Mackenzie provided overnight accommodation for Harry Colt who had come to Leeds to work on the new course at Alwoodley. Mackenzie showed him some of his designs and models. Colt was so impressed that he invited Mackenzie to join with him in the design. Medicine became a dwindling interest as, first, he became Secretary of Alwoodley, and, then, began to practice golf design full time.

During the First World War he joined the Royal Engineers, brilliantly adapting his observations in the Boer War to become an expert in camouflage. Marshall Foch reckoned that he reduced casualties in that bloody conflict by a third. With the coming of peace Mackenzie took up golf design once again, often in collaboration with others, travelling to the USA, Australia, Argentina and New Zealand. His work at Royal Melbourne, New South Wales, Pasatiempo, Valley Club of Montecito, and Crystal Downs is still acknowledged alongside Cypress Point and Augusta in most listings of the world's top courses.

13 Huddersfield

Huddersfield Golf Club, Fixby Hall, Lightridge Road, Huddersfield, Yorkshire HD2 2EP (1891)
TEL: *(01484) 420110* **FAX:** *(01484) 424623*
LOCATION: *M62 Jct 24, at roundabout take Brighouse road. At traffic lights turn right (back under the motorway), turn right into Lightridge Road*
COURSE: *18 holes, 6447yd/5895m, par 71, SSS 71*
TYPE OF COURSE: *Moorland*
DESIGNER: *Herbert Fowler*
GREEN FEES: *£££*
FACILITIES: *Pro shop, clubhouse*
VISITORS: *Welcome with handicap certificate*

In a northern suburb, very close to the M62, is Fixby Park. Here Huddersfield Golf Club has been established, in remarkable seclusion, for over a century. Moorland turf, beautifully drained, provides an ideal base for golf, the only vestiges of urbanity being the views from the higher ground over the town below, almost as if it were an architect's model.

The front nine are gentle in comparison with what is to come, yet you will be at full stretch on the 5th, a short uphill par 5, curving right past an out-of-bounds wood, cross-bunkers threatening many second shots. A towering drive, uphill and across the slope, is called for on the 10th, with all manner of evil awaiting over the ha-ha on the right. Long drives are advantageous, especially on the 12th, with its vigorously sloping fairway, and a big carry across a valley is required on the 215yd/197m 13th. On the 487yd/445m 18th you might almost drive the green if you find the ideal line over the marker post.

Woodsome Hall

Woodsome Hall Golf Club, Woodsome Hall, Fenay
Bridge, Huddersfield, Yorkshire HD8 0LQ (1922)
TEL: (01484) 602739 **FAX:** (01484) 608260
LOCATION: 6 miles/10km south-east of Huddersfield
on A629 towards Penistone
COURSE: 18 holes, 6096yd/5574m, par 70, SSS 69
TYPE OF COURSE: Hilly parkland
DESIGNERS: W. Button, James Braid
GREEN FEES: ££
FACILITIES: Pro shop, clubhouse
VISITORS: Welcome with handicap certificate, jacket and
tie in clubhouse

The scene is set for quality golf by the
16th-century Grade 1 listed mansion
which forms the clubhouse. Laid out in 1922
by Mr W. Button, the professional, with James
Braid's advice, Woodsome enjoys a woodland
setting with rolling fairways. Greens are small
by modern standards and well guarded by
bunkers.

There is something special about making the
opening drive from the lawn of the mansion.
Other star holes on the outward nine include
the 8th and 9th, the 8th a 455yd/416m par 4
curving to the out-of-bounds on the right, but
leaning to the left.
Playing safely puts the
green out of range.
The 9th is a genuine
par 5 for all but the
mighty, this time
winding gradually to
the left, once more
against the slope.
Water in front of the
green makes this a
difficult approach.
There is less distance
but more hill climbing
on the back nine, the
steep ascents of the
12th and 14th offset by
the plummeting short
par-4 17th.

Hallamshire

Hallamshire Golf Club, Sandygate, Sheffield S10 4LA
(1897)
TEL: (0114) 230 1007 **FAX:** (0114) 230 2153
LOCATION: 2 miles/3km west of Sheffield city centre,
take A57 towards Glossop, turn left at Crosspool pub,
club on right
COURSE: 18 holes, 6359yd/5815m, par 71, SSS 71
TYPE OF COURSE: Moorland/parkland
DESIGNER: Unknown
GREEN FEES: £££
FACILITIES: Pro shop, clubhouse
VISITORS: Welcome with handicap certificate

Hallamshire's clifftop site offers extensive
views into the Peak District. Add
excellent drainage, crisp moorland turf, and a
ravine and the scene is set. At 1000ft/305m
above sea level the wind will always be a
major ingredient, and with only 98 acres/40
hectares available fairways are narrow and no
place for the wayward.

The start is fearsome into the wind, a
strenuous par 4 with out-of-bounds the length
of the hole on the right. The pitch to the 7th
green, perched above a stream, needs skill, and
the next drive, uphill over the ravine, needs
muscle. Coming home
there is greater length,
though the wind is at
your back. While the
10th and 11th bound
across the ravine
excitingly, the 13th
captures the fancy,
only 345yd/315m
long, but utterly
uncompromising. The
distinguished players,
Percy Alliss, Mary
Everard and Alison
Nicholas learned their
golf here, carrying the
club's name with great
credit within the
international game

*Hallamshire's 6th, an attractive par 3 played
downhill over a ravine to a well-bunkered green, with
the Pennine moors as a noble backdrop.*

16 *Lindrick*

Lindrick Golf Club, Lindrick, Worksop, Notts S81 8BH (1891)
TEL: *(01909) 475282* **FAX:** *(01909) 488685*
LOCATION: *On A57 4 miles/6.5km west of Worksop*
COURSE: *18 holes, 6606yd/6041m, par 71, SSS 72*
TYPE OF COURSE: *Heathland*
DESIGNERS: *include Tom Dunn, Willie Park, Herbert Fowler*
GREEN FEES: *££££*
FACILITIES: *Pro shop, clubhouse*
VISITORS: *Welcome with handicap certificate Monday, Wednesday to Friday, Sunday afternoon by arrangement*

The record books show Lindrick to have hosted a glittering array of top amateur and professional events. British golfers will always associate it with the 1957 Ryder Cup, captained by Dai Rees, the first home victory for 24 years. Lindrick only begins to reveal itself after several rounds, for it is a place of subtleties rather than bold statements. On this close-knit turf golf is a pleasure even in winter and the greens have a reputation for truth which makes putting a delight. Birches and gorse abound, but do not generally intimidate. So the golfer is lulled into a false sense of security: even Greg Norman, at the height of his powers, fell foul of this, running up a 14 at the 17th!

The 2nd is not long, but swings late up and to the left to a heavily bunkered green beside the main road. Described by Bernard Darwin as the 'worst hole on the course . . . yet it should never be altered', the 4th has not been altered. The green lies low down behind a bank of rough and just in front of a stream. It is a historic spot, where the boundaries of Yorkshire, Nottinghamshire and Derbyshire meet – in times past, it was the ideal place to hold clandestine bare-fist and cock fights, escape easily being made into an adjoining county. The 13th is superb, the downhill drive forced to the right by a pair of fairway bunkers. Then it is all carry up to the hilltop green with bunkers each side of the entrance.

The 15th is an excellent bunkerless hole on which the approach is made downhill through a series of humps and hollows to a sunken green, charmingly old-fashioned. A quarry to the left of the 16th green devours the slightest pull. Lindrick's finish is unusual, a long, well-bunkered par 3 with a deceptively sloping green.

OTHER COURSES TO VISIT IN THE NORTH-EAST

Durham	Dunstanburgh Castle	Easingwold	Sitwell Park
Barnard Castle	Hexham	Harrogate	**Yorkshire, West**
Beamish Park	Magdalene Fields	Oakdale	Bingley St Ives
Bishop Auckland	Matfen Hall	Rudding Park	Dewsbury District
Castle Eden and	Northumberland	Scarborough North Cliff	Halifax
Peterlee	Whitley Bay	Scarborough South Cliff	Headingley
Hartlepool	**Yorkshire, East**	Selby	Leeds
South Moor	Beverley and East	**Yorkshire, South**	Meltham
The Wynyard	Riding	Abbeydale	Moor Allerton
Northumberland	Hornsea	Doncaster	Otley
Alnmouth	Hull	Dore and Totley	Sand Moor
Arcott Hall	**Yorkshire, North**	Renishaw Park	Scarcroft
City of Newcastle	Cleveland	Rotherham	Temple Newsam

REGIONAL DIRECTORY

Where to Stay
Northumberland The **De Vere Slaley Hall Hotel** (01434 673350) overlooks its fine courses. Also near Hexham is 14th-century **Langley Castle** (01434 688888). Rooms in the **Lord Crewe Arms** (01434 675251) in the pretty village of Blanchland are reputed to be haunted.
Durham **Lumley Castle** (0191 389 1111) at Chester-le-Street is the real thing, the **Rose and Crown** (01833 650213) at Romaldkirk a good country pub, while **Grove House** (01388 488203) at Hamsterley Forest is a superb guest house in the depths of a forest. **Ramside Hall Hotel** (0191 386 5282) runs to 27 holes of golf.
Yorkshire **De Vere Oulton Hall** (0113 282 1000) near Leeds, **Marriott Hollins Hall** (01274 530053) near Shipley, **Rudding Park Hotel** (01423 871350) near Harrogate, and **Aldwark Manor** (01347 838146) near York are golf hotels. **Amerdale House** (01756 770250) at Arncliffe, **Foresters Arms** (01969 640272) at Carlton-in-Coverdale, and the **Sportsman's Arms** (01423 711306) at Wath-in-Nidderdale boast splendid kitchens. For country-house style, **Dunsley Hall** (01947 893437) near Whitby, **Simonstone Hall** (01969 667255) at Hawes, **Lastingham Grange** (01751 417345) outside York, **Ryedale Country Lodge** (01439 748246) at Nunnington, **Rangers House** (01347 878397) at Sheriff Hutton, and **Sedbusk House** (01969 667571) in Wensleydale offer the right ingredients.

Where to Eat
Northumberland Distinguished eating is to be done at **Horton Grange** (01661 860686) at Seaton Burn, **Fisherman's Lodge** (0191 281 3281) and, especially, **21 Queen Street** (0191 222 0755) both in Newcastle-upon-Tyne. **Manor House Inn** (01207 255268) near Consett offers something rather above the normal run of pub food.
Durham **Bistro 21** (0191 384 4354) in Durham and **Brasserie 21** (0191 567 6594) at Sunderland are praised for their enterprising menus.
Yorkshire **The Box Tree** (01943 608484) at Ilkley is one of the outstanding restaurants in the country. Fine wines abound at the **Angel Inn** (01756 730263) at Hetton, and **Leodis** (0113 242 1010) and **Souz le Nez en Ville** (0113 244 0108), both in Leeds. Other good Leeds restaurants include **Brasserie Fourty Four** (0113 234 3232), **Harvey Nicholls Fourth Floor** (0113 204 8000), **Pool Court** (0113 244 4242) and **Rascasse** (0113 244 6611). **Chadwick's** (01642 788558) at Yarm espouses café style.
Interesting restaurants in the depth of the Yorkshire countryside include **The Devonshire Arms** (01756 710441) at Bolton Abbey (Burlington Restaurant), **Dusty Miller** (01423 780837) and the **Yorke Arms** (01423 755243) near Pateley Bridge, the **General Tarleton** (01423 340284) off the A1 at Ferrensby, the **Star Inn** (01439 770397) at Harome near Helmsley, **Floodlite** (01765 689000) at Masham, the **Black Bull** (01325 377289) near Scotch Corner, **Boar's Head** (01423 771888) at Ripley, and the **Bruce Arms** (01677 470325) at West Tanfield in Wensleydale. Good town and city eating is to be found at **Armstrongs** (01226 240113) in Barnsley, **Hamilton's** (01302 760770) in Doncaster, **Thorpe Grange Manor** (01484 425115) and **The Weavers Shed** (01484 654284) near Huddersfield, the **Drum and Monkey** (01423 502650) at Harrogate, **Rafters** (0114 230 4819) and **Smith's** (0114 266 6096) in Sheffield, and **Melton's** (01904 634341) in York.

What to See (see also pages 139 to 141)
Northumberland The northernmost town in England, Berwick-upon-Tweed is still, it seems, at war with Russia, having been specifically left out of the 1856 peace treaty signifying the end of the Crimean War! Reached by a tidal causeway, **Holy Island** is a must for birdwatchers and pilgrims to **Lindisfarne**. A few miles inland, **Chillingham** is home to a herd of white cattle descended from prehistoric wild oxen. After exploring the Roman sites of **Hadrian's Wall** a drive over the moors from Allendale or Blanchland is rewarding, passing **High Force waterfall**, handsome **Barnard Castle** and visiting the **Bowes Museum** nearby.
Yorkshire The two grandest stately homes are **Harewood House** and **Castle Howard**. Bradford's cultural riches include the large **David Hockney collection** in Saltaire and the excellent **National Museum of Photography, Film and Television**. Asian arts flourish, with the Mela, now the climax of the annual **Bradford Festival**, attracting 100,000 visitors. Genteel **Harrogate**, **Howarth** (of Brontë fame), **Whitby** (inspiration for Bram Stoker's *Dracula*), **Richmond** (gateway to the Dales with a charming Georgian Theatre Royal and imposing Norman castle), the pretty market town of **Helmsley**, **Howden** (with its noble church) are but a handful of worthwhile excursions, while dozens of fascinating villages should not be missed: **Coxwold**, **Crayke**, **Easingwold**, **Great Ayton**, **Hovingham**, **Middleham**, **Sledmere**, to name but a few. Whether steam train rides from **Pickering**, cheese making in **Hawes**, reliving the Second World War at **Eden Camp**, or opera going in **Leeds**, Yorkshire's attractions are diverse indeed. But, above all, leave time to explore the medieval city of **York** itself - a week or two would suffice!

Chapter 7

Wales

The history of Wales is one of a Celtic tradition, little affected by the Romans whose influence was rather more lasting in England. Christianity came in the 3rd century AD, but the country was made up of a number of small kingdoms rarely at peace with each other, and usually in conflict with their neighbours in Mercia (now the English Midlands). In the 8th century the Mercian King, Offa, built his famous earthwork, Offa's Dyke, to contain the Welsh. If found to the east of it a Welshman would, on being caught for a first time, lose his right hand, and, if caught again, lose his life.

A Proud Nation

As with the Roman invasion, the Norman Conquest largely ignored Wales, and it was not until 1276 that King Edward I of England decided to quell Llywelyn ap Gruffud whom he viewed as a rebel and the instigator of too many predatory invasions for comfort. Over the next twenty years a number of military

Left: Tenby's 4th, The Bell, a period-piece, long par 4 at the oldest established club in Wales. Above: Pony trekking on Conwy Mountain in the heart of Snowdonia.

campaigns ensured English supremacy, the enduring legacy of which is a chain of magnificent castles which rank amongst the finest in Christendom. Though many rebelled, not least Owen Glendower in the 14th century, they were crushed, and in the 16th century, through the Acts of Union, English rule was formally established. It has remained in place until, only at the close of the 20th century, a measure of devolution has given Wales its own National Assembly in Cardiff.

The Landscape

For the most part Wales is a hilly country with rapid transport practicable only along its north and south coasts. The quickest way to get from north to south is, perversely, to drive through England, but for those with the time to spare the journey along the winding roads of mid-Wales is rewarding, their traffic light and the scenery rarely less than arresting. While Snowdonia in the north-west offers the highest mountains and craggiest skylines, moving southwards there is magnificent countryside to be found first in the Berwyn and Arenig Mountains, then in the wild, unspoiled, sparsely inhabited upland country of mid-Wales, in turn giving way to the Black

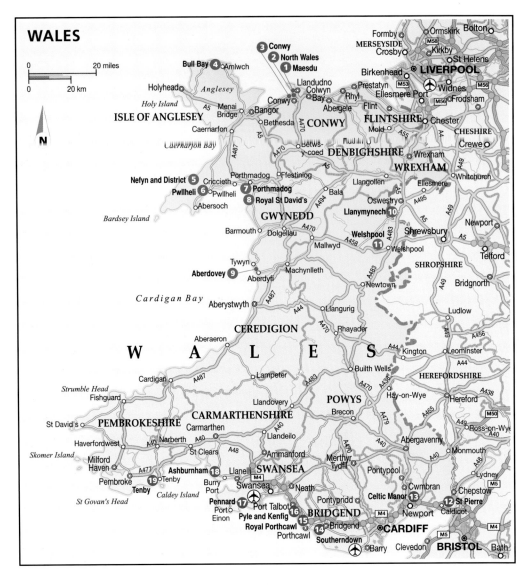

Mountains and Brecon Beacons in the south. There is a total contrast in the south-west where the gentle contours of Pembrokeshire lead to its nickname of 'Little England beyond Wales'. It shares with all of West Wales a superb coastline and fine beaches. Here too is the shrine of Wales's patron saint at St David's, the smallest cathedral city in Britain. It is said that Christianity in Wales spread from this remote spot.

The industrial revolution brought huge change to what had been very much a sheep-farming country. Rich seams of coal in the north-east around Wrexham and, more extensively, in the valleys of South Wales brought work, of an exceedingly hazardous nature, to many. Most mines are now closed, the victims of economic pressures and the switch to alternative energy sources. Culturally these areas have been the strongholds of that peculiarly

Welsh institution famous the world over, the male voice choir. The mining towns of the south have also played host to the great teams of that most intense of Welsh sporting passions, rugby union.

Eight drum towers are distinctive features of Conwy Castle which overlooks the pretty harbour of one of the most attractive of all Welsh towns.

Golf in Wales

Golf in Wales is particularly good value and visitors are warmly welcomed, though the best courses are now so

popular that some even run a booking system all year round. With so many courses located on or near the coast, and served by excellent roads, thousands of English golfers have discovered that, whereas their clay-based parkland courses may be waterlogged or frostbound for much of the winter, an hour's car journey takes them to a picturesque links course on which winter play is little different from that in summer, well drained on sandy soil and with no hint of the dreaded matting tees or temporary greens which often afflict winter golf inland.

The golf courses selected for this chapter merely scratch the surface of Welsh golf. An excellent guide, *Golf Wales*, is published annually by the Wales Tourist Board. It is also available from tourist information centres throughout Wales and gives information about hotel golfing packages, discount cards, and open competitions.

THE WELSH LANGUAGE

With the anglicization of Wales in the 16th century the Welsh language came under threat. Though it continued as a literary medium, Welsh began to dwindle as industry, particularly coal mining, grew in the 19th century, principally in the north-east and the valleys of South Wales, the language preserved mainly in the remoter parts of the west. Happily, since the Second World War, Welsh has been revived and is now the first language of many, not least the members of a number of golf clubs in the north-west.

Maesdu

Llandudno (Maesdu) Golf Club, Hospital Road,
Llandudno, Conwy LL30 1HU (1915)
TEL: *(01492) 876450* **FAX:** *(01492) 871570*
LOCATION: *South-west of Llandudno on A546 to*
Deganwy
COURSE: *18 holes, 6545yd/5985m, par 72, SSS 72*
TYPE OF COURSE: *Seaside parkland/links*
DESIGNERS: *Harry Colt, Tom Jones*
GREEN FEES: *££*
FACILITIES: *Pro shop, buggy hire, clubhouse*
VISITORS: *Welcome with handicap certificate*

In the 1950s and 1960s Maesdu hosted
many professional tournaments, with
Henry Cotton, Peter Alliss and Harry
Bradshaw amongst the winners. One of golf's
great ambassadors, Tom Jones, extended and
improved on Colt's original design. Jones
was professional here from 1915 until his
death in 1967 and Captain and Chairman of
the PGA.

Maesdu combines parkland and links
characteristics, its fairways giving gorgeous

The par-4 16th is one of the strongest holes at Maesdu.
From every hole the views along the North Wales coast
are captivating.

views along the North Wales coast. Ditches
and ponds frequently complicate play. A
lovely stretch from the 9th to 11th runs
alongside the railway. The 13th can be
treacherous, first climbing a hill then curling
down through gorse to a sunken green. The
parallel 14th is a beauty, out over the crest of
a hill before bounding down to the green. For
many the toughest hole is the 16th, uphill
with water on the right, the green very hard
to find beyond bunkers and a ditch.

North Wales

Llandudno (North Wales) Golf Club, 72 Bryniau Road,
West Shore, Llandudno, Conwy LL30 2DZ (1894)
TEL *and* **FAX:** *(01492) 875325*
LOCATION: *West of Llandudno at West Shore*
COURSE: *18 holes, 6247yd/5712m, par 71, SSS 71*
TYPE OF COURSE: *Links*
DESIGNERS: *T.D. Cummins, Harold Hilton*
GREEN FEES: *££*
FACILITIES: *Pro shop, buggy and club hire, clubhouse*
VISITORS: *Welcome with handicap certificate*

North Wales has a number of blind shots,
traditional features of seaside golf, and
distance on the card is fairly irrelevant, the
strength and direction of the wind being of
greater importance. Only two of the par 4s
are over 400yd/366m long, yet North Wales
– a good course for matchplay – is a regular
host to championships, the Welsh Amateur
Team event coming here in 1995, for
instance.

The only par 3 going out, the 4th, is a
testing 200-yarder to a two-level green with
the railway close on the left. The railway also
threatens the 8th, with its blind drive to a
narrow fairway, all humps and bumps, and a
two-tier green awaiting at the far end of the
course. Three gloriously old-fashioned short
holes grace the back nine, the 16th named
OL – reportedly what you say when you fail
to find the sunken green!

 Conwy

Conwy (Caernarvonshire) Golf Club, Morfa, Conwy,
Gwynedd LL32 8ER (1890)
TEL: *(01492) 593400* **FAX:** *(01492) 593363*
LOCATION: *Off A55 North Wales coast road
signposted at west end of Conwy tunnel*
COURSE: *18 holes, 6936yd/6342m, par 72, SSS 74*
TYPE OF COURSE: *Links*
DESIGNER: *Not known*
GREEN FEES: *££*
FACILITIES: *Pro shop, buggy, trolley, club hire,
restaurant and bar*
VISITORS: *Welcome with handicap certificate, restricted
weekends*

One of the oldest clubs in Wales,
idyllically situated at the foot of the
mountains where the Conwy Estuary meets
the sea, this is a long, hard links of
international championship status. It can be
very punishing, especially in a wind, and the
finish is ferocious for all but the straightest

*Conwy's 15th, a short hole on which it is all too easy to
underclub, the tee being sheltered from the wind amongst
the gorse bushes.*

hitter. The deep banks of gorse lining the
fairways can be merciless, especially on the last
three holes, of which the 17th is a notorious
card-wrecker. But Conwy is flat, and walking
is easy.

D-Day's Mulberry Harbour was built just
behind the short 2nd, a recently remodelled
hole. One of several long par 4s, the 7th is
particularly attractive, playing to a secretive green
beside the shore. The first trial by gorse comes
on the 11th drive, a substantial carry into the
wind from the back, the green hard to find, low
down between bunkers. The putting surfaces are
superb, and there is no warmer welcome for
visitors than from the professional, Peter Lees,
one of the real characters of Welsh golf.

④ *Bull Bay*

Bull Bay Golf Club, Bull Bay Road, Amlwch, Isle of
Anglesey LL68 9RY (1913)
TEL: (01407) 830213 **FAX:** (01407) 832612
LOCATION: On A5025 1 mile/1.6km west of Amlwch
COURSE: 18 holes, 6217yd/5685m, par 70, SSS 70
TYPE OF COURSE: Seaside rocky heathland
DESIGNER: Herbert Fowler
GREEN FEES. £
FACILITIES: Pro shop, clubhouse
VISITORS: Welcome with handicap certificate

On a rocky outcrop on the Anglesey coast, Bull Bay's defences are natural. In such terrain little artifice was needed by Herbert Fowler to make it an exacting test of approach work. A good number of greens sit on top of hillocks, many of them domed. Bunkering is minimal, the lie of the land being far more penal, and gorse abounds.

The opening holes climb a hill calling for stout hitting, while the 220yd/201m 3rd is brutal without wind assistance, a very full carry over a ravine. Even a par 4 as short as the 290yd/265m 6th needs strength, the drive having to climb to a plateau fairway, the pitch to the green semi-blind. The 7th is tough with trouble just off the fairway and a full second shot is required in order to mount the rise to the green. Up behind is the 10th, a rewarding par 3 if you manage to find the sloping green from the tee, but wicked if you slide away down the hill. Appropriately, two long par 4s close the round on this rugged course, the most northerly in Wales.

⑤ *Nefyn and District*

Nefyn and District Golf Club, Morfa Nefyn, Pwllheli,
Gwynedd LL53 6DA (1907)
TEL: (01758) 720102 (pro) **FAX:** (01758) 720476
LOCATION: On Lleyn Peninsula 2 miles/3km west of
Nefyn, off B4417
COURSES: (26 holes) Old: 18 holes, 6342yd/5799m,
par 71, SSS 71; New: 18 holes, 6548yd/5987m, par
71, SSS 71
TYPE OF COURSE: Seaside/clifftop
DESIGNERS: J.H. Taylor, James Braid
GREEN FEES: ££
FACILITIES: Pro shop, buggy, trolley and club hire,
clubhouse
VISITORS: Welcome

No course in Wales can quite equal the spectacular situation of Nefyn's 26 holes. Twenty-six? The final eight holes, the most famous, of the original course run out and back on a narrow peninsula above the beachside hamlet of Porthdinllaen. In summer, with tourists taking the track down the middle of the course on their way to the Ty Coch Inn, these holes can be hazardous. A recent landslip, too, has emphasized the wisdom of providing relief holes for emergency use.

The first 10 holes are common to both courses, sweeping down to the cliff edge, running along it from the 2nd. On the original 12th thirsty golfers will descend to Ty Coch, literally on the beach. The short 14th plunges downhill to the water's edge, the twin peaks of the Lleyn Peninsula beyond. There, with seals playing beneath, is the 15th tee (see cover). On a fair day it is magical.

The 16th at Bull Bay is a mid-length par 3 by the clubhouse, very much at the mercy of the wind.

 Pwllheli

*Pwllheli Golf Club, Golf Road, Pwllheli, Gwynedd
LL53 5PS (1900)*
TEL *and* FAX: *(01758) 701644*
LOCATION: *1 mile/1.6km south-west of Pwllheli*
COURSE: *18 holes, 6091yd/5570m, par 69, SSS 69*
TYPE OF COURSE: *Parkland/links*
DESIGNERS: *James Braid, club members*
GREEN FEES: *££*
FACILITIES: *Pro shop, clubhouse*
VISITORS: *Welcome*

Pwllheli is a combination of parkland and dramatic links. The wind is rarely absent and can be very punishing, compensating for any apparent lack of length – there are no par 5s.

After an inland start the course toughens up at the 8th, the first of the links holes. Gorse bushes abound, and the bunkering is more prolific, with tees built on the sea wall giving expansive views over Tremadog Bay. Many drives are angled with substantial carries over inhospitable ground and the threat of gorse ever-present. Grassy ridges punctuate the 9th short of the green, and the 10th is a charming short hole in front of a white cottage. The 13th to 15th add water to their defences, fine dog-legs each of them. The last of the traditional holes, the 16th, is a favourite of many, with a rolling fairway threading an avenue of gorse to an undulating green.

In 1909, David Lloyd-George was made an honorary member of the club and given freedom of all club facilities – with the exception of its whisky!

 Porthmadog

*Porthmadog Golf Club, Morfa Bychan, Porthmadog
Gwynedd LL49 9UU (1905)*
TEL: *(01766) 512037* FAX: *(01766) 514638*
LOCATION: *2 miles/3km south of Porthmadog*
COURSE: *18 holes, 6330yd/5788m, par 70, SSS 71*
TYPE OF COURSE: *Mainly links*
DESIGNER: *James Braid*
GREEN FEES: *££*
FACILITIES: *Pro shop, clubhouse*
VISITORS: *Welcome*

You play Porthmadog for its back nine, wonderfully old-fashioned links golf. So it is at the 10th that the romantic golfer's heart beats faster, a well-bunkered par 4 with out-of-bounds, gorse, and a narrow entrance to the green. The 11th is a fearsome par 3 of 221yd/202m with out-of-bounds on the left, the green overlooking the beach. The views grow ever more magnificent as the glorious 12th unfolds, the drive played parallel to the beach to a low fairway. The approach is uphill to a ledge green amidst the sandy dunes, a delightful spot.

A punchbowl green awaits on the 13th, another substantial par 3, played from a high tee giving majestic views across the bay to Snowdon and Harlech. However, the 14th may well prove to be the hardest hole of the round, with a blind drive over a sandy waste followed by a shot that must be threaded through tight bunkers to find the green.

The parallel 15th is a favourite of many with a billowing fairway and hillside green.

*The view up the estuary towards the mountains of Snowdonia
which rewards golfers reaching Porthmadog's 12th green.*

🏌 *Royal St David's*

Royal St David's Golf Club, Harlech, Gwynedd LL46 2UB (1894)

TEL: *(01766) 780361* **FAX:** *(01766) 781110*

LOCATION: *Harlech on A496*

COURSE: *18 holes, 6571yd/6008m, par 69, SSS 73*

TYPE OF COURSE: *Links*

DESIGNERS: *W.H. More, H. Finch-Hatton, Harry Colt, Charles Lawrie*

GREEN FEES: *££££*

FACILITIES: *Pro shop, buggy, trolley and club hire, clubhouse*

VISITORS: *Welcome with handicap certificate*

ROYAL ST DAVID'S

HOLE	YD	M	PAR	HOLE	YD	M	PAR
1	443	405	4	10	453	414	4
2	376	344	4	11	153	140	3
3	468	428	4	12	436	399	4
4	188	172	3	13	450	411	4
5	378	346	4	14	222	203	3
6	403	368	4	15	432	395	4
7	494	451	5	16	354	324	4
8	517	473	5	17	428	391	4
9	175	160	3	18	201	184	3
OUT	3442	3148	36	IN	3129	2861	33

6571YD • 6009M • PAR 69

One day, in the 1890s, William Henry More, standing on his balcony overlooking the wild dunes between him and the sea, saw a man doing something peculiar. That man introduced himself as Harold Finch-Hatton, recently returned from Australia. He had brought with him a boomerang. A few days later Mr More observed Finch-Hatton up to new tricks. 'Capital place for a golf links,' said he, 'Let's lay one out.'

Despite knowing nothing about golf, More entered into the project wholeheartedly and became the club's first secretary when it opened in 1894. He held the post for more than 40 years and earned the description by Arthur Croome of being the eighth of the seven wonders of the world. More presided over the growth of the club until it became the premier club in North Wales. It acquired Royal status in 1909 and was honoured that Edward, Prince of Wales, accepted the captaincy in 1934. One of Harlech's favourite anecdotes is that of David Lloyd-George who was accosted for not paying his green fee – he was at that time Chancellor of the Exchequer.

With Snowdon behind, clearly visible in good weather, Harlech Castle is an imposing backdrop for the course, stern and sturdy, as the golf will be. Some have said it is the hardest par-69 course in the world. Oddly enough it only penetrates the dunes proper from the 14th, much of the course, like Hoylake, being remarkably flat. Here the wind, rough grass and gorse, and

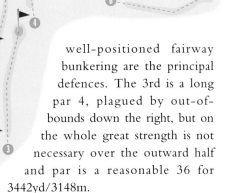

well-positioned fairway bunkering are the principal defences. The 3rd is a long par 4, plagued by out-of-bounds down the right, but on the whole great strength is not necessary over the outward half and par is a reasonable 36 for 3442yd/3148m.

The greens at Royal St David's tend to be long, but narrow, and their condition is invariably superb. The rough is deep and penal.

Thereafter length really is required. Of the six par 4s coming in only one is shorter than 428yd/391m, and much depends on the direction of the wind on the day. The 222yd/203m 14th was once a totally blind hole, played over a large dune with a vast sleepered bunker set in its face and wild briars in the hollows on the far side. Now that there is a sight of the green it is not so unfair, though still a substantial carry.

One of the holes for which Royal St David's is renowned is the 15th, requiring a precise drive over rough ground to an angled fairway. The green is blind, on the far side of ridges, and surrounded by rough-covered hummocks, but a little homework will tell you where the flag is. Despite being only 354yd/324m long, the 16th nevertheless needs a big drive over swelling ground to give a sight of the green, low, beyond bunkers. The 17th is also celebrated, with a decision

needed on whether or not to attempt to carry cross-bunkers short of the green. And to finish, there is another long par 3, this time probably downwind, with the inspiring sight of Harlech Castle directly behind the green.

THE CASTLES OF EDWARD I

Llywelyn ap Gruffud, proud and defiant leader of many a Welsh uprising, was a thorn in the side of King Edward I. When, in 1276, Edward decided to crush Llywelyn he intended that his supremacy should be lasting. He instituted the construction of 10 new castles, coupled with town fortifications and the upgrading of several Welsh castles which had fallen into his hands. Most of these stand on the coast of North Wales and survive sufficiently intact to provide an extraordinary insight into many aspects of life, not just military, in the late 13th century. Flint, Rhuddlan, Conwy, Beaumaris, and Harlech are remarkable in their architectural variety, but the crowning glory – literally, for it is the ceremonial seat of the Prince of Wales – is Caernarfon, very plausibly modelled on the Theodosian Wall of Constantinople.

Aberdovey

Aberdovey Golf Club, Aberdovey, Gwynedd LL35
0RT (1892)
TEL: *(01654) 767210* **FAX:** *(01654) 767027*
LOCATION: *2 miles/3km north-west of Aberdovey on
A493*
COURSE: *18 holes, 6445yd/5893m, par 71, SSS 71*
TYPE OF COURSE: *Links*
DESIGNERS: *James Braid, Herbert Fowler, Harry Colt*
GREEN FEES: *£*
FACILITIES: *Pro shop, buggy hire, clubhouse*
VISITORS: *Welcome with handicap certificate*

One ought to travel to Aberdovey by train both to assimilate its special atmosphere and to recreate the pioneering spirit of Bernard Darwin whose uncle laid out the first course. Aberdovey's greens are some of the truest in the country, though none is easy to hit, for this is a well-defended links. The club's first professional was one J.S. Cooper. His son, Harry 'Lighthorse' Cooper, subsequently had a distinguished playing record as a professional in Canada and the USA, winning the Canadian Open, and finishing second twice and third once in the US Open.

The early holes play through the dunes, the short 5th descending to lower ground, though the golf is equally testing, the flat 10th

Aberdovey's 3rd, Cader, once a notorious blind par 3, now much fairer, the putting surface in a basin stoutly defended by mounds, bunkers and sleepers.

and 11th notably strong par 4s. There are probably as many theories about how to play the 16th as there are members at Aberdovey – a brilliant short par 4 beside the railway to a wicked green. But there are also no fewer than seven par 4s over 400yd/366m.

Llanymynech

Llanymynech Golf Club, Pant, Oswestry, Shropshire
SY10 8LB (1933)
TEL: *(01691) 830542*
LOCATION: *Signposted off the A483 between Pant and
Llanymynech*
COURSE: *18 holes, 6114yd/5591m, par 70, SSS 69*
TYPE OF COURSE: *Mountain*
DESIGNER: *Unknown*
GREEN FEES: *£*
FACILITIES: *Pro shop, clubhouse*
VISITORS: *Welcome*

Golf at Llanymynech is international: on the 4th you drive in Wales and putt out in England, returning to Wales on the 7th tee. The views over the whole of Shropshire and a great deal of mid-Wales are majestic. Ian Woosnam played his early golf here and the names of several members of the family can be found on the club's honours boards.

Some holes run through attractive woodland alongside historic Offa's Dyke, others traverse the mountain top. Of these, the 12th is a good test of nerve, the tee on the edge of a cliff, the drive having to hold a narrow fairway with a big drop into terrible trouble on the left, the long approach to be made over a deflecting ridge, and the green on the edge of the mountain. The 13th drive is exhilarating, over the corner of the hillside to a fairway far below.

 ## *Welshpool*

Welshpool Golf Club, Y Golfa, Welshpool, Powys SY21 9AQ (1929)
TEL: *(01938) 850249*
LOCATION: *4 miles/6.5km west of Welshpool on A458*
COURSE: *18 holes, 5708yd/5219m, par 70, SSS 69*
TYPE OF COURSE: *Mountain*
DESIGNER: *James Braid*
GREEN FEES: *£*
FACILITIES: *Clubhouse (no professional)*
VISITORS: *Welcome*

A strenuous mountain course situated over 1000ft/305m above sea level, Welshpool is something different, and far from easy. It is golf in the raw, primeval you might say. The air could not be fresher, the views are inspirational, and the golfing challenges unique. The 4th, for instance, is a very short par 4, only 297yd/272m long, but the green is perched on top of a conical hill and the approach to it is utterly uncompromising. The outward half ends with a very strong par 4 curving round a hillside.

Several of the shorter par 4s might be driven by the strong, but hardly the 295yd/270m 10th which climbs relentlessly. The 14th – 185yd/169m across a valley and steeply up to an angled ledge green – is one of several fine short holes. Pick of the longer holes must be the 12th and 18th. The 12th calls for a very precise approach downhill to a green beyond which the ground tumbles away alarmingly, while the 18th needs an enormous drive over a wide valley to find an angled fairway on the hillside opposite.

Welshpool's par-3 3rd, expansive mountain views typical of both Welshpool and nearby Llanymynech.

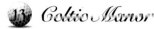 St Pierre

Marriott St Pierre Hotel and Country Club, St Pierre Park, Chepstow, Monmouthshire NP6 6YA (1962)
TEL: *(01291) 625261* **FAX:** *01291 629975*
LOCATION: *2 miles/3km west of Chepstow on A48*
COURSES: *Old: 18 holes, 6818yd/6234m, par 71, SSS 74; Mathern: 18 holes, 5732yd/5241m, par 68, SSS 68*
TYPE OF COURSE: *Parkland*
DESIGNER: *C.K. Cotton*
GREEN FEES: *££££*
FACILITIES: *Pro shop, buggy and club hire, range, clubhouse, full hotel and leisure facilities*
VISITORS: *Welcome with handicap certificate*

Television coverage of the Dunlop Masters, Epson Grand Prix and Solheim Cup has made St Pierre familiar to many armchair golfers. The estate had been a reward to St Pierre de Caen from William the Conqueror. Even the trees have celebrated antiquity, the vast chestnut which so thwarts golfers on the 2nd being at least 400 years old.

Recent alterations have involved a number of new greens, the most remarkable being that on the tough par-4 5th, across a gully and wickedly contoured. From a high tee the 7th drive is stunning but requires precise alignment to open up the green. On the 10th a new

The 5th at St Pierre, with the Severn Bridge in the background, is a tough, recently changed hole with plenty of trouble on the right.

green has been constructed, jutting out into the lake, and both the 15th and 17th run downhill to striking peninsula greens. The par-3 18th, across water and uphill to the green, shows the great merit of a strong short hole to finish.

Celtic Manor

The Celtic Manor Hotel and Country Club, Coldra Woods, Newport, Gwent NP6 2YA (1995)
TEL: *(01633) 413000* **FAX:** *01633 410284*
LOCATION: *M4 Jct 24, A48 towards Newport, golf second on right*
COURSES: *Wentwood Hills: 18 holes, 7403yd/6769m, par 72, SSS 77; Roman Road: 18 holes, 7001yd/6402m, par 70, SSS 74; Coldra Woods: 18 holes, 4094yd/3744m, par 61, SSS 60*
TYPE OF COURSE: *Hilly woodland and river plain with many lakes (Wentwood Hills)*
DESIGNERS: *Robert Trent Jones Snr; Wentwood Hills with Robert Trent Jones Jnr*
GREEN FEES: *££££*
FACILITIES: *Full leisure complex facilities, range, academy, buggy and club hire, luxury clubhouse (buggy advisable – distances considerable)*
VISITORS: *Welcome with handicap certificate*

In 1999 the new Wentwood Hills course opened, designed jointly by Robert Trent Jones Snr and 'Bobbie' (Robert Jnr), combining with the tour-standard Roman Road Course and impressive executive course, both also Jones designs. On the European Tour, Wentwood Hills hosts the Celtic Manor Wales Open.

Architecturally, no recent British course is so emphatic. The grand scale is exemplified by the fact that it occupies 350 acres (142 hectares), enough for three full-length courses, and takes 24 greenkeeper-hours to rake the bunkers before play each day! It is a breathtaking mixture of mountain and Floridian golf, with touches of California for good measure. One of the most spectacular holes is the 613yd/561m 2nd, which pierces a gap in the forest before plunging down the mountainside. The strategic brilliance is

Florida translated to Wales – a view over Celtic Manor's lowland holes, with the 5th, 6th, 7th and 8th alongside the two most prominent lakes.

demonstrated on the 6th. From the tee, a lake and bunkers force you to the right. Only from here do you see the second stretch of water which you now must carry all the way to the green. The 13th climbs remorselessly as it turns through a right-angle over a stream to a hillside green. To say that there are no mundane holes is a gross understatement.

🕤 *Southerndown*

Southerndown Golf Club, Ewenny, Ogmore-by-Sea, Bridgend, Mid Glamorgan CF32 0QP (1906)
TEL: *(01656) 880476* **FAX:** *(01656) 880317*
LOCATION: *3 miles/5km south of Bridgend on B4524, turning (signposted) at Ogmore Castle ruins*
COURSE: *18 holes, 6417yd/5868m, par 70, SSS 72*
TYPE OF COURSE: *Downland*
DESIGNER: *Willie Fernie, Harry Vardon, James Braid, Herbert Fowler, Willie Park, Harry Colt, Donald Steel*
GREEN FEES: *££*
FACILITIES: *Pro shop, buggy, trolley and club hire, clubhouse*
VISITORS: *Welcome with handicap certificate*

Overlooking the Ogmore Estuary and Porthcawl, Southerndown (see page 11) is a course of great natural feel with rippling, crisp downland turf, gorse and bracken everywhere, and sheep for companionship. Very often, on this expansive upland, you find yourself playing to greens almost touching the sky, and nowhere more obviously than the 1st. Henry Cotton said that it was one of the hardest opening holes he had encountered, but the views alone make the climb worthwhile, as they do on the 2nd, heading towards the sea.

The short holes tackle the wind from every quarter, the 220yd/201m 7th being downhill but well bunkered and usually played into the wind. Cross-bunkers are a feature of the par-5 13th, cleared only by the mighty in search of a birdie. The two-shotters to finish are engaging, the 15th with cross-bunkers, the 16th climbing past bunkers set into a mound, the 17th needing a solid second to clear a valley of humps and bumps, and the drive at the last made to a split-level fairway.

15 *Royal Porthcawl*

Royal Porthcawl Golf Club, Rest Bay, Porthcawl, Mid Glamorgan CF36 6UW (1891)
TEL: *(01656) 782251* **FAX:** *(01656) 771687*
LOCATION: *Porthcawl, turn right at seafront*
COURSE: *18 holes, 6691yd/6118m, par 72, SSS 74*
TYPE OF COURSE: *Links*
DESIGNER: *Tom Simpson*
GREEN FEES: *££££*
FACILITIES: *Pro shop, club and trolley hire, clubhouse, Dormy House*
VISITORS: *Welcome weekdays with handicap certificate or letter of introduction*

ROYAL PORTHCAWL

HOLE	YD	M	PAR	HOLE	YD	M	PAR
1	326	298	4	10	337	308	4
2	447	409	4	11	187	171	3
3	420	384	4	12	476	435	5
4	197	180	3	13	443	405	4
5	513	469	5	14	152	139	3
6	394	360	4	15	467	427	4
7	116	106	3	16	434	397	4
8	490	448	5	17	508	465	5
9	371	339	4	18	413	378	4
OUT	3274	2993	36	IN	3417	3125	36

6691YD • 6118M • PAR 72

For many, the abiding memory of Royal Porthcawl will be that famous victory by Great Britain and Ireland over the Americans in the 1995 Walker Cup. The American team contained the young Tiger Woods, already the most feared amateur in the world and soon to be the professional No. 1. That this victory should have happened on Welsh soil was all the more gratifying to the Captain, Clive Brown, himself a Welshman and a distinguished Welsh international in his own right.

Porthcawl has also played host to no fewer than five Amateur Championships, the Home Internationals (men's and ladies'), the Curtis Cup, and occasional professional tournaments – confirmation of the excellence of the

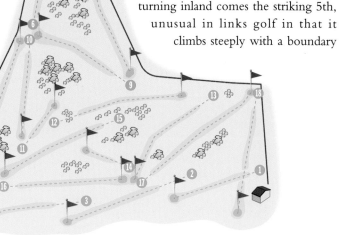

challenge set by this glorious seaside course. It has the distinction of being one of the very few courses on which the sea is visible from some part of every single hole, the majority occupying slightly higher ground, perhaps more heathland in character. Porthcawl is particularly renowned for the quality of its greens. The bad news is that there is not enough space for it ever to host the Open Championship – it is the only Welsh course with the stature do so – but the good news is that it is relatively easy on the pocket.

Skirting the beach, the first three holes set off to the west into the wind, the greens of the solid par 4s, the 2nd and 3rd, perilously close to the shore and slightly raised. After a well-bunkered par 3 turning inland comes the striking 5th, unusual in links golf in that it climbs steeply with a boundary wall encroaching from the left as the hole progresses. Up on the high ground the short 7th is impish, little more than 100yd/91m long but the putting surface is very narrow between mounds and bunkers and there are some devilish borrows. The 9th may be only a mid-length par 4 but it is Stroke Index 1, a glorious hole swinging left and uphill to a small, sloping green, exposed to the full force of the wind and giving magnificent views.

Back on the lower ground, the later par 4s are longer, turning the screw inexorably, the 13th invitingly downhill from the tee but very often played into the wind, many second shots perishing in the bunkers short of the green. Together, the 15th and 16th total 900yd/823m and run in opposite directions to each other and the wind, rugged holes. The 15th green is up beyond a ridge, while the drive at the 16th is governed by whether or not cross-bunkers can be carried. The journey continues gently upward on the par-5 17th, with gorse bushes to catch the wayward shot if a tired swing induces a slice. From its elevated tee, the final

Royal Porthcawl's 4th. Even on a clear summer evening there is a stiff breeze blowing across the line, bringing the deep greenside bunkers very much into play.

TOM SIMPSON (1877–1964)

One of the most colourful characters in golf architecture, Simpson was originally a lawyer and played his golf at Woking, where he was influenced by the pioneering work done there by Stuart Paton and John Low. Abandoning the bar in 1910, Simpson joined Herbert Fowler in a design practice. A wealthy man, habitually dressed in beret and embroidered cloak and chauffeur-driven in his Rolls-Royce, much of his finest work was done in France and Belgium, notably Chantilly, Fontainebleau, Morfontaine, Royal Belgique, Royal Antwerp and Royal GC des Fagnes. In the UK, his masterpieces are Cruden Bay in Scotland and his remodelling of Royal Porthcawl.

hole is good fun, straight down towards the sea, but there is a gully in which many drives perish and an over-exuberant hook can slide out-of-bounds. The green, just above the beach, is not one to overshoot and its slopes and borrows make long putts difficult to gauge.

16 *Pyle and Kenfig*

Pyle and Kenfig Golf Club, Waun-y-Mer, Kenfig, Mid Glamorgan CF33 4PU (1922)
TEL: *(01656) 783093* **FAX:** *(01656) 772822*
LOCATION: *2 miles/3km north-west of Porthcawl*
COURSE: *18 holes, 6688yd/6116m, par 71, SSS 73*
TYPE OF COURSE: *Links*
DESIGNER: *Harry Colt*
GREEN FEES: *£££*
FACILITIES: *Pro shop, buggy and club hire, clubhouse*
VISITORS: *Welcome weekdays with handicap certificate*

To the west of Porthcawl is an extensive wilderness of dunes into which the championship links of Pyle and Kenfig ventures. It does so on the back nine, celebrated holes. But the flatter outward half should not be overlooked, the short 4th and 6th holes, for instance, and the par-5 5th and 9th, all fine holes.

Over the road the landscape becomes almost lunar. The par-5 11th creeps into the sand hills, and the short 12th demands a sure strike to avoid the bunkers. The 13th and 14th are pure joy, medium length dog-leg par-4s swinging through the heart of the dunes, both greens cradled in sand hills. There is no let up on the 15th, a sturdy par 3 across a wasteland of humps and bumps. The strong finish is through bracken and gorse, and though the greens are relatively flat the rough can be savage, the bunkers deep. It is good enough to have hosted the Welsh Amateur Championship twice in the 1990s.

17 *Pennard*

Pennard Golf Club, 2 Southgate Road, Southgate, Swansea, West Glamorgan SA3 2BT (1896)
TEL: *(01792) 233131* **FAX:** *(01792) 234797*
LOCATION: *8 miles/9km south-west of Swansea via A4067 and B4436*
COURSE: *18 holes, 6329yd/5787m, par 71, SSS 71*
TYPE OF COURSE: *Links in the sky*
DESIGNER: *James Braid, C.K. Cotton*
GREEN FEES: *££*
FACILITIES: *Pro shop, club hire, clubhouse*
VISITORS: *Welcome*

Over tumbling linksland at clifftop height, with magical views of the Gower coastline, many Pennard holes are old-fashioned in the best possible sense, utterly natural, making strategic use of this wild site. Pennard's name has been carried worldwide with distinction by its Curtis Cup golfer, Vicki Thomas.

After a tough start through gorse the undulations gradually increase as the cliffs are approached, the lovely 7th bouncing past an old church on its way to a sunken green set romantically beside the ruins of a castle overlooking the sea. Despite the very rugged terrain of the back nine there should be plenty of opportunities to drink in the ravishing views. Those from the 16th green are particularly noble, but the green itself is not an easy one to read. And there are two exacting holes to finish, the par-5 17th climbing and bending past gorse-clad hummocks, the 18th continuing the climb over a ridge.

Pennard's 7th, its shallow green typical of many, presenting a difficult target. The views from much of the course are splendid.

Ashburnham

Ashburnham Golf Club, Cliffe Terrace, Burry Port,
Carmarthenshire SA16 0HN (1894)
TEL and FAX: (01554) 832269
LOCATION: 5 miles/8km west of Llanelli off A484
COURSE: 18 holes, 6936yd/6342m, par 72, SSS 74
TYPE OF COURSE: Links
DESIGNER: J.H. Taylor
GREEN FEES: ££
FACILITIES: Pro shop, trolley and club hire, clubhouse
VISITORS: Welcome with handicap certificate,
restrictions at weekend

Dai Rees, Bernard Gallagher and Sam
Torrance have won professional
tournaments at Ashburnham, seeming to
prove the adage that 'Only good players win
on good courses.' Harry Vardon declared it to
be the course he liked best in all Wales.

The 6th is a fine short hole with a bunkered
mound on the left and a drop to further
bunkers on the right of the ledge green. With
a mound forming the angle of the dog-leg, the
par-5 8th reminds one of the 6th at Birkdale.

Coming in there is great length on both par
5s, and the 15th is a big par 4, with its green
in a quarry. However, two shorter par 4s are
particularly appealing, the 12th with its
curving fairway and
green raised behind
mounds, and the
18th, its approach
climbing steeply
uphill past the
clubhouse to a ledge
green with fine
coastal views over
Carmarthen Bay.
Course maintenance
is an example to
all, Howard Swan
having undertaken
restoration and
revision of the
bunkering.

*Ashburnham's 12th. Two PGA Championships have been
held over Ashburnham's wind-swept links.*

 Tenby

Tenby Golf Club, The Burrows, Tenby, Pembrokeshire
SA70 7NP (1888)
TEL and FAX: (01834) 842978
LOCATION: Tenby, south of town centre, follow signs
for Station and South Beach
COURSE: 18 holes, 6337yd/5795m, par 69, SSS 71
TYPE OF COURSE: Links
DESIGNER: James Braid
GREEN FEES: ££
FACILITIES: Pro shop, club and trolley hire, clubhouse
VISITORS: Welcome with handicap certificate

Befitting the oldest affiliated golf club in
Wales, Tenby's course is a links of
enormous character, due largely to the
splendour of its dunes and glorious seascapes.
Marker posts abound, some blind shots too,
but good play is fairly rewarded. Many
formidable carries are required from the back
tees (no topping here!), especially the opening
drive through a narrow gap in the sand hills.

Of some fame is the 3rd, the green set up
above very rough country, the approach made
through a narrow opening in the dunes.
Greatly admired by Dai Rees, it is now
named after him. The 4th, The Bell, is a
unique hole with a blind drive and blind
second down to a
sloping green in a
hollow. A stirring
par 3 is the 12th,
Y Ddau Gwm, its
Welsh name refer-
ring to the two
valleys which must
be crossed *en route*
to the table-top
green. And there is
an old-fashioned
approach over
humps and bumps
to the 18th green,
character aplenty
to the end.

REGIONAL DIRECTORY

Where to Stay
North and Mid Wales **Bodysgallen Hall** (01492 584466) near Llandudno offers true country-house style, and the small **Tan-y-Foel** (01690 710507) at Capel Garmon near Betws-y-Coed is renowned for its cooking. Further west, the **Porth Tocyn Hotel** (01758 713303) at Abersoch is a splendidly sited country hotel with a distinguished kitchen, and **Maes y Neuadd** (01700 780200) at Talsarnau also offers true gourmet dining. On Anglesey, the **Olde Bull's Head** (01248 810329) at Beaumaris is a 15th-century coaching inn. Aberdovey boasts two interesting small hotels with fine sea views and excellent food, **Plas Penhelig** (01654 767676) and **Penhelig Arms** (01654 767215). The **Lake Country House** at Llangammarch Wells (01591 620202) is reputed for its comfort and cuisine.
South Wales There is much to commend the **St David's Hotel** (029 2045 4045) in Cardiff, particularly its wine list. On The Gower, at Reynoldstown, **Fairyhill** (01792 390139) is both enchanting and vinously distinguished.

Where to Eat
In addition to the restaurants of the hotels listed above a number of Welsh restaurants are noted for their cuisine at the very highest level.
North and Mid Wales **Plas Bodegros** (01758 612363) at Pwllheli has won high praise both for its striking cooking and its (notably Alsatian) wine list, while **The Old Rectory** (01492 580611) at Llansanffraid Glan Conwy offers accommodation as well as glorious views, an imaginative kitchen, and a 'benevolently priced' wine list. Llanwrtyd Wells in Powys boasts **Carlton House** (01591 610248), a small hotel and highly rated restaurant. Also in Powys are the **Red Lion Inn** (01544 350220) at Llanfihangel Nant Melan and **Pavement** (01497 821932) at Hay-on-Wye, the little town which is a magnet for bibliophiles.
South Wales Two fine restaurants stand out, **The Crown** (01600 860254) at Whitebrook, Monmouthshire, and **The Walnut Tree** (01873 852797) at Llandewi Skirrid, which ranks with the finest the province can offer.

What to See
North Wales The North Wales coast is littered with **Edward I's castles** (see page 165). Overlooking the coast, **Holywell** is re-emerging as a place of religious pilgrimage. Whereas **Rhyl** offers all the amusements of a modern seaside town, **Llandudno** maintains a gentility which is no less attractive. It is a good centre for tram or cable-car trips up the Great Orme, sea fishing, walking and pony trekking, the **Welsh Mountain Zoo** at Colwyn Bay, or exploring the famous **Bodnant Gardens**. On the other side of the estuary is **Conwy** with its magnificent castle, fine town walls, picturesque harbour, and the smallest house in Britain.
The mountains of **Snowdonia** offer climbers and walkers excursions of all degrees of difficulty. Snowdon itself is climbed by a steam railway which has been running for over a century. Other renowned narrow-gauge steam railways include Ffestiniog (Porthmadog) and Talyllyn (Tywyn).
Anglesey can be reached by Thomas Telford's beautiful suspension bridge of 1826. **Beaumaris** is a fascinating town, not only for its handsome castle, but also for a remarkable courthouse and gaol.
Moving down the west coast from Bangor, visits to **Caernarfon Castle**, **Portmeirion**, the extraordinary Italianate village created by Clough Williams-Ellis, and **Trawsfynydd Power Station** might be followed by one to **Harlech**, one of the historic towns of Welsh nationalism.
Mid-Wales Those with time on their hands might turn inland from **Aberdovey** to explore one of the quietest parts of the British Isles. **Welshpool** and **Newtown** were once the centres of the Welsh flannel industry, and **Llandrindod Wells** and **Builth Wells** are ideal bases from which to explore the upper **Wye Valley**. **Montgomery** is a charming mix of Elizabethan and Georgian houses nestling under the fragmentary walls of the castle. Heading back north, there are good castles (**Powys** and **Chirk**), famous aqueducts on the **Llangollen canal**, fascinating **Erddig Hall** near Wrexham, and many delights in **Llangollen** from a steam railway to horse-drawn boats, **Plas Newydd** (home of the two 'Ladies of Llangollen'), haunting **Vale Crucis Abbey** and one of the big international arts festivals. From here the little road over the Horseshoe Pass leads to the old towns of **Denbigh** and **Ruthin** and their many fine buildings. Alternatively, heading south past Ross-on-Wye, magnificent **Goodrich Castle**, and the spectacular Wye Valley at **Symonds Yat**, the route to Chepstow takes one past **Tintern Abbey**, in the hills above which Wordsworth's memorable lines were composed.
South Wales The most extensive Roman remains in Wales are to be found at **Caerleon**, close to the Celtic Manor golf courses, and **Caerphilly Castle**, one of the most extensive in Britain, is superb. The sporting, historic and cultural attractions of **Cardiff** are many, while the **Cardiff Bay Centre** and **Swansea Maritime Museum** have breathed new life into idle dockland. The atmospheric coastline of the **Gower Peninsula** makes for a charming detour before our golfing journey ends at **Tenby**, whose medieval walled town makes a good base for exploring the delights of **Pembrokeshire**.

Index

Numbers in **bold** refer to main entries for the 150 selected courses. Numbers in *italic* refer to illustrated courses.